GREEN FIELDS

GREEN FIELDS

A Journal
of
Irish Country Life

BY

STEPHEN RYNNE

LONDON
MACMILLAN & CO
1938

COPYRIGHT

PRINTED IN GREAT BRITAIN
BY R. & R. CLARK, LIMITED, EDINBURGH

TO
MOTHER

CHAPTER I

THERE IT GOES AT LAST, WADDLING DOWN the avenue, straws streeling, black smoke lacing in the reddening beech boughs, and behind it a cortège of tired men shoving bicycles. How pleasant is the emptiness left by a threshing set! For two days the turbulent engine clattered and vibrated in Cloonmore yard, screamed out for coal and bawled for water. For two days the hungry mill roared for fodder, devoured three corn-ricks, spewed out straw, and remained unappeased. Now the train rocks at the avenue bend —big exacting brute—making gruel of the road surface. Now the tail of it drags round the corner out of sight. Let the Recording Angel point his quill; seventy-odd barrels of oats, thirty barrels of barley, and twelve barrels of wheat, the grain produce of Cloonmore farm this season; let him score a heavy line under the entry for here is the nearest a farmer can attain to finality.

The farm is now a pool of peace: the Bloody Assizes are over, the court has risen, the chaff is sentenced to be burnt, the tailings to be thrown to the fowl, the straw is let out on bail, while judgment is reserved on the grain. Mrs. Meehan's frown, occasioned by the stress of providing four successive meals for nineteen men, gives way to her usual look of serenity. Laddie's bristles of indignation are smoothed into his normal shaggy coat. No longer flying dust and sooty smoke in the yard, nor chaff in a whirl, nor an eternal droning, nor the Trojan efforts of a score of men to allay the hunger of a Wooden Horse. Instead of the din and fury, there is now only the ghostly groaning of grain-laden lofts.

The silence would be absolute if Mrs. Meehan had not decided to set the house to rights. Jimmy, apparently, has been nobbled, and can be heard staggering up the kitchen stairs with a burden of chairs which were borrowed from the dining-room for the threshers' dinners. If I were not addicted to the vice of writing out things in secret I would supervise his barging up from the basement. Young Jimmy has clear-cut ideas on what comprises man's work and woman's work, and he is now probably signalising his resentment for having been given a cissy job by crashing the chairs against the balusters, and he is about to prove his manliness by chipping the white paint in the back hall. But I will continue to lie low and trust Mrs. Meehan; I only wish I knew how to handle men so effectively as an elderly woman manages a youth. My callous hands have earned the soothing feel of a pen between fingers; for two days I have been plying a four-grain fork in chaff which began as a heap under the threshing-mill and ended up as a range of mountains spread across the yard.

The threshing is over and the year is a hag. I am too weary to flatter her, chivalry drops from me. The earth is no longer lovely and alluring. She is a painted hussy; rouged, lip-salved, wizened but bold, harassed and drag-heeled but still saucy.

2

Mornings start valiantly and birds sing, but quickly get cold about the shoulders and cease singing. Sunlight has a washed-out appearance. The bees are in the ivy. Wagtails twinkle again about the farmyard and the robin redbreast begins to make bold. Flowers are drooping and the grass is ever wet. Far in the south, the swallows are toasting Old Sol. Soon the whole farm will be tight and cosy, proof against the storms and famine of winter. The threshing is over, the turf is drawn from the bog and clamped, the hayrick is anchored to earth with red rope, and stored apples sweeten the basement air. Soon we shall plough out the potatoes, and pull and pit the mangolds, and then we can put a nightcap on Cloonmore and tuck it up for its long winter sleep.

* * *

Ballycomin Fair is Ballycomin Fair to me because each year when I attend it Pat Mangan is invariably by my side with his marvellous fund of anecdotes, his wisdom and his digs at that which he deems green youthfulness. But he has been in bad health lately, and despite his assurance to his good woman that the change of air would benefit him, she was very reluctant to let him go with me this morning. The upshot of our argument was that Kevin Molloy, her nephew and a clerical student, was told off to come with us. Pat and I exchanged eloquent looks when we heard who our companion was to be. "A lot of use he'll be ketchin' ewes," grumbled Pat.

The sun has paid us a return call. When it peers out from the blue and shaggy clouds, it alights on beech boughs, and for short spells all is violently orange. Ballycomin, high up on a roll of mountains, now in a swirl of autumn-touselled leaves, is quilted with sheep and cattle, creels of pigs, lorries and motor cars, and moving men. Having parked the car, we walked out along the gentle, balmy roads, now lined with sheep, shadows scaling the surrounding walls of mountains, wayside cottage gardens mauve nests of Michaelmas daisies, a sweetness in the air.

At the end of one of the roads (there are five of them leading out from Ballycomin), Pat, for the sheer artistry of it, engages with a sheep-dealer as though he were seriously bent on buying up all the dealer's exhibits. Pat knew his man only slightly, but well enough to know the most suitable weapon in the duel of words. This dealer has the hide of an elephant, so Pat prods him with a bayonet. According to the seller, his flock is as sound as the Bell of Armagh . . . and sure he never sold a wrong ewe in his life! "No," agreed Pat sarcastically, "but maybe you didn't sell wethers instead of ewes to Johnnie Leahy out of Tincurragh the day he was drunk. He was like a lunatic when he found it out." "Is that a fact?" said the dealer eagerly, very interested but not a whit abashed. On he flowed, boasting of his own integrity and the beauties of his ewes. If the Bell of Armagh did not suit him for the purpose of comparison, he used the Rock of Cashel or the Hill of Tara. He assures us he would not sell these particular ewes

4

but for such and such reasons. . . . . "Ah, go on," Pat cuts in, "wouldn't you sell your own mother?" This upsets the dealer and he tells us the number of years his mother is dead. We leave him still pouring out bombast and exaggerations, his voice dipping a little at the end of every sentence, as though tired of his endless lies.

I reminded Pat of the last day we had attended this fair, which happened to be the day the pound fell. He smiled reluctantly. A sheep-seller had asked a price which Pat thought exorbitant. "Well, haven't you great impudence," he exclaimed, "to ask that price now and the pound only worth 15s. 6d.?" "What's that got to do with it?" asked the seller in surprise. "Don't you know England is gone off the Gold Standard and . . . and . . ." Pat had been eager, but at a loss for words. "Go on, Pat," I had mischievously urged, "give it to him. Tell him about the stabilisation of the franc too. . . ." But Pat's notions of international finance were already spent. "Stop that now," he said; "do you want to put me in a blooming hobble?"

At the commencement of a mountain travelling road, we hit on the bunch of ewes which I ultimately bought. They consisted of a score of fairly good ewes, and two others obviously battered and droopy, not so young as they might be. At the end of our bargaining, five shillings are divided and a certain go-between, who sprung up out of nowhere, a lantern-jawed man, finds that "his word is not broken." Specimens are snared by the aid of a crooked walking-stick, and finally the flock is marshalled into a publican's yard. Kevin has meanwhile vanished into thin air. I go to a chemist's to buy a lump of raddle, while Pat Mangan and our commercial opponent take drinks.

When it comes to the final examination and marking of the sheep, Pat is not able for the work of catching them, and as Kevin has made himself scarce, I find I have to go through the whole twenty-two, examining their mouths and udders. I discover a defective udder in one of them and thank Heaven I had had the gumption to feel them all. Then, as I refuse to take the defective ewe, there ensues a to-do, followed by lies (always rills of mountainy lies in sheep-dealing). Then we have to decide on a parking-place for the sheep until I can get home and instruct Lawlor, the lorryman, to collect them, and this causes further debating. We make a slow and none too friendly move for the bank, the matter of the ewe with the defective udder being still in abeyance. We behave decorously within the holy precincts of the bank, but in the outer porch we again set to: finally the ewe with the lump in her "elder" is amicably disposed of, and I consent to take her at a much reduced price.

Better spirits prevail as we lurch through the cattle fair on our way back to the pub premises, where the sheep have temporary quarters. Our man stands us drinks. As the driver of a car on mountain roads, I play for safety, my choice being a bleak, tasteless mineral not unlike a large dull apple such as a Golden Spire. We talk pig prices

6

as compared with the price of bacon in the shops, and butchers' profits which we unanimously agree are outrageous, compared with the prices farmers receive for their stock, thus, I suppose, manifesting the narrow-mindedness of our calling. When we part company, Pat remarks that our host "is a terror for porter," and surely I noticed it as "it comes out in his face." We then made another round of the fair, our ostensible object being to find Kevin, though as a fact we hardly cared (and Pat especially) whether he was at the bottom of the sea.

Pat Mangan is a low-sized man and he talks almost in a whisper, but it is worth bending sideways to catch his most offhanded comment. When he is not giving me a biography of someone, with pedigrees attached, he is droll, or ironic, or he simply makes a critical remark on some fine point in a passing horse, or greyhound. We amble about as though time and ties never were; Pat is of that school of farmers whose notion in going to a fair is to make it a day out.

Again we move amidst the grey-eyed and shaggy Wicklow-Cheviot sheep, Pat pointing out to me subtle distinctions in the hue of their fleeces, which indicate that the sheep were either always on mountain ranges, or had spent a spell on lowland pasture. Then we saunter through the thick of the cattle fair in the main street, watching the bargaining progress from the slapping of palms to the disappearance of the antagonists into a public-house. We meet a sheep-owner known to us because he takes summer grazing near Graigue.

"Ewes were purty dear today, Matty," remarks Pat, who would have been glad of a little inside information. "That's right, Pat, they were surely dear." "All the same, I thought they'd be a shade dearer," pursued Pat. "That's right, Pat, you'd think they'd be dearer now." Then I varied the theme: "I suppose cattle are as bad as ever, Matty?" Matty laughs, showing a glorious flash of small even teeth, and the flutter of long black eyelashes. "Oh, every bit as bad as ever, sir." "No change here today?" I ask, making a final effort with him. "That's right, sir, no change." When we leave him, I say to Pat, "That fellow would agree with archangels and devils if they went about in pairs." Pat answers with a discourse about mountain men, so many of whom are like Matty, gentle, soft-spoken, shy, and above all nervous about getting into disputes. Pat opines that their work of tending ewes and lambs all their lives makes them thus timid.

We find our stray sheep, Kevin. He had poked out the house of a fellow clerical student and had been regaled with tea and soda-bread. Just at the same time we are joined by Bill Liddy of Ballinamona, who insists on standing us a round of drinks. It transpires that Bill is in the same position as myself: he has made a purchase of ewes, he has them in a yard, and he also intends getting Lawlor to fetch them home. As I am anxious to get away, and as Bill shows no such desire, we arrange that I should deliver the message to Lawlor and that Bill should see my ewes safely on the lorry when it arrives. We then agree to put all

8

our ewes together in the same yard where Bill's are now collected. Going down the street to make this change, I hear a man roar at a small boy who is running along the pavement: "Sonny, sonny, do you see that man with the stick? Tell him to come back here." Interested in this none too graphic description of a man, I take note of those who carry sticks, and as far as eye can reach, there is not a man without a stick in Ballycomin. But no doubt the smart boy picked out the right man with the right stick.

In the backyard where the sheep are gathered, a ghastly lousy fellow attaches himself to us for the sake of coppers. He is a type rare enough now within the Pale and non-existent in the rest of Ireland. He twice tells me in most unctuous and soapy tones "to mind my little hand": once when I am marking ewes near a wall, and again when I open a gate. I give him threepence halfpenny and it has not even the effect of making him indignant. "The poor man," says simple Kevin, "maybe he is starved." "Maybe he is—for porter," says Pat drily.

We set off down the mountains, Pat sighing wistfully because he has to leave the fray of Ballycomin Fair so early in the day.

*　　*　　*

The potato-drills are smothered in weeds, of which chickweed is most in evidence, growing in luxuriant bosses of brilliant green, the green of aquatic plants. Kit Healy goes ahead, pulling up the grosser weeds such as sowthistle, sorrel, and nettles, but soon gives up, discouraged by the immensity of the task, and we make no serious effort to clean the drills before ploughing out. The plough sticks repeatedly in the drill, the horses move slowly, and every few yards a stop has to be made to clear the coulter of its weed accumulation. Soon the crop lies revealed and we know the worst or the best. Results are good, thank God, the severed drill displaying an abundance of tubers, and closer inspection shows that these are a good size and free from disease.

The pickers flop down, two to each potato-basket, and the rooting begins. The drills being about one hundred and twenty yards long, the upturned tubers at the very end show up like mere dots in the distance. Beneath our feet they are like white billiard balls, free from stain in the dry soil, hard and healthy to the touch.

We decide on making temporary field-pits in order to give the tubers a chance of sweating, and also to avoid the nuisance of untackling the horses from the plough, a necessary move if we were to draw the potatoes immediately to permanent pits. The sites are roughly prepared by scraping the surface before tipping out the contents of the baskets on to them. Soon the heaps of tubers are rising knee-high: Arran Banners, big, white, and uneven-shaped; Kerr's Pinks, rosy-coloured and round; Shamrocks, deep-red, coarse-skinned, and irregularly shaped; Spry's Abundance, white, large, and round; Golden Wonders, walnut-coloured and tapering; Chieftains, white, spherical, and even.

There is still another variety in our crop, but as we have lost its name and as it is a poor cropper, its identity is of no consequence; it will be fed to pigs, anyhow, not kept for seed.

There is a slight feeling of excitement amongst us as the contents of each drill are revealed. This is the first year I have tried the varieties Spry's Abundance and Golden Wonders. I was nervous about the first-named, as it was a seed purchased locally at a suspiciously low price, and at sowing-time the seed seemed very flaccid as though it had not been properly pitted. But the result is splendid, in fact it is by far the best cropping variety in the field. The Golden Wonders are a bitter disappointment. I scoured the whole district for the seed, and happily, as it turns out now, I could procure only about two stone. The plough reveals a slender little tuber with the complexion of an Egyptian. When these elongated potatoes were turned up, Kit Healy, a wag, exclaimed that they were like something you'd root up in a graveyard, a sally that provoked much laughter.

We make no attempt to keep all these varieties separate. The Banners, Shamrocks, and Kerrs have been grown too long on this farm to permit keeping them for another season's sowing, so they are jumbled together for a common destination in the pig boiler. The pink-and-white tubers in a heaped-up mass are a pleasing sight.

Mick, who follows the plough, halts for a moment beside me. With his legs splayed over the open drill, he turns his head and indicates a clump of potatoes just exposed: "They got their health anyway," he grins, before he "Hep-horses" and continues to keel open the weed-matted drill.

Potato harvesting can be unmixed misery in wet weather, but today we cannot complain. It may be a little raw, with bitter winds rising up and falling away, but the day is an open one, and better still for our toil's sake, the soil is almost dust dry.

When darkness is descending on us, Mick untackles the horses from the plough and goes to the yard for a load of barley straw. We tighten-in the pits and smother them in big heaps of straw for the night.

All-day-long potato picking did not quite wear the edge off my energy. By yard-lamp light, I fixed up the last few hundredweight of homeless Bramleys, reflecting that after this I shall have data enough on apple-storing to last me for a lifetime. Of these same Bramleys, I buried one lot in a barrel of moist sand; I pitted another lot in the secret passage, covering them with wheaten straw and turf mould; I pitted another lot in the garden (main purpose of this experiment, will they be stolen?); I placed a further lot on shelves in a lightsome room; and I stored away one barrelful with each apple wrapped in waxed paper. Finally, tonight, I placed the remainder on the earthen floor of the dark wine-cellar.

I think it will be neck-and-neck between the sand and the waxed paper.

* * *

There are no days so pleasant as those on which I stay at home and do ordinary things. I might have gone to Colonel Hawthorn's auction today at Belsize House; I ought certainly to have gone to Mrs. Maher's funeral, or, if I were the sort of Irishman believed typical by most Englishmen, I should have spent the day merrily at the Ballynash races. I remained at home instead and pottered shamelessly. I asked Jimmy the sort of questions about the poultry which do service as reprimands and are taken by him as such. I dogged John on his yard round, watched the fuel he used for boiling the pig potatoes, watched him mix cow feeds, watched him grease the drays, and, for once in a while, proved to him that I am observant. Mick I leave peacefully ploughing the ground recently vacated by the potatoes.

Joe Tracey is helping at Mangan's threshing (because Pat lent a man to us on our day of trial): all day long, the pant of the engine makes a pulse in Cloonmore, and its smoke wreaths can be seen through the trees.

For me the furthest point east today was the junction of house and yard avenues; the furthest point west was the wood; north, the crab-apple tree at the entrance to the Night Park; and south, that plane-tree hanging its branches over the ha-ha at the back of the house.

One pauses to look at the bronze and golden trees: every beech a Titian, every lime a Norse goddess, elms like sunsets, and oaks like Vandyke's old men. Boastfully a Spanish chestnut holds up her unlocked seed-vessels. The berry clusters of the hollies bite out like rubies from the rich velvet of the foliage. The brownish-green masses of the

13

sycamores seem like tapestry in which one could imagine pictures: horses and huntsmen, or mediæval battles. In the wood, this year's leaves lie with the skeletons of their ancestors.

Yet give me gleaming autumn with its fast, sweet hours, its replete grandeur, its pacific beauty languishing on earth and bending from the sky. Just now the world is like a Dutch kitchen: all bronzes, lustre and pewter. There are calm, gold days making up weeks together, each day rich as the woven costume of a mandarin. Leave me autumn with its threat of winter, and let romantic-minded urban dwellers enjoy the summer to their heart's content.

The last ten minutes of the dinner hour at Cloonmore is the nearest approach we have to a board meeting. The men in the workshop are first joined by Jimmy, who finds Mrs. Meehan's company in the kitchen uninspiring; next comes John, who takes his dinner at home, but always hastens back here for a chat with the others before resuming work; then I come from the house and somewhat, but not altogether, disturb the three men and the boy from their lolling attitudes. Mick will most likely be seated on an upturned butter-box, his pipe crackling, his big red face glowing, his hands stuck in his trousers pockets, six feet of well-fed contentment in repose. Joe Tracey will have made himself comfortable on a folded-up sack placed on an oil drum; he will be puffing a cigarette stump (I have yet to catch him with a full-length one in his mouth) and reading the bits of yesterday's newspaper which

14

enfolded his dinner an hour ago. John Kelly will be sitting somewhere close to the floor, if not actually on the floor. A quiet, saddish man, and humble in debates, John never rushes in where Joe and Mick don't fear to tread, although his years and farming experience are greater than theirs. Jimmy, whatever his position in the workshop may be, will have a leg swinging free throughout the council meeting; one feels that he is all the time restraining himself from breaking out into whistling, or from taking up a tool and banging it on another so as to make a rhythmic but hideous din.

Discussion may range around the fact that two cows have calved within a week and one must be sold, or else the butter production will bound up, while the demands of customers remain static. Mick will champion the retention of the Milltown cow and Joe will advise holding Hogan's Polly; Mick will argue that the Milltown cow is only on her second calf, whereas the Polly is old; that the Milltown will improve greatly; that she will fetch a better price on her third calf if I want to sell her by and by. Joe will insist that the Milltown cow will sell flying; that she has the colour the English buyers want, whereas the Polly would be the better cow to keep; she can fill a tub with milk and she can be fattened off later. John, who after all milks and feeds the cows throughout the year, will remain silent and never take it on himself to put in his spoke unless directly asked. In the case of the two cows under discussion one gathers that he sides with the garrulous Joe and the motion in favour of keeping the Polly is carried.

15

Today, the after-dinner debate raged round the best site for pitting mangolds, and when that is decided, we discuss possible houses in which to erect an engine-driven mill. I am, and have been for a long time, open to buy an oats-crusher, but the problem of housing it is apparently insurmountable. There is no out-office which combines a loft overhead for tipping in the grain, and, at the same time, sufficient length on the ground floor for the belting between the engine and the mill. In this debate, Jimmy is vocal. His father being a lorry driver, he feels that in questions of machinery he is on his own ground. As usual, the council feel they can take no action and the matter is held over.

Not always, however, are we such a happy democratic assembly. Often I poke my head in towards the end of the dinner hour and curtly cut into an animated discussion on last Sunday's match with the announcement, "It's a minute to two." Although there is a yard-bell in Cloonmore, a relic of the Devon régime, it is left to muse idly on its landlord past. Bell-ringing is a foolish business on a smallish farm such as this (rather over one hundred statute acres). I believe that my few men are better left to their sense of decency than coerced into punctuality, which is anyhow not one of their natural traits. On a farm, it is never so much a question of "Is it six o'clock yet?" as "Did you feed the spotted calf?" or "Did you let the sow back to her bonhams?" Six o'clock can wait ten minutes more or less most evenings if one does not use a yard-bell, whereas if one does, it is surprising how sharply and finally the farm is emptied of men at the toll of six.

I made an inspection of the beehives, seeing that all was in order before the bees settled down for their winter sleep. This meant uncovering the frames, removing the empty ones, and pushing up the dummies so as to confine the bees in the smallest possible space for greater warmth. Though I found ample stores of honey on the combs, I nevertheless put a large cake of candy on two sticks placed crosswise on the frames. The bees were very quiet and seemed hardly aware of my intrusion as though they were already sunken in their winter lethargy. Over the sheets I put extra quilts (egg-box felt serves for these) and filled the remaining space under the roof, first with sacking and then with piles of crumpled paper. Having found dampness in one of the hives, I mended the leaking roof by painting it, sticking a sheet of calico on the wet paint, and then painting over the calico at once. I may follow up later with a second coat of paint when this is dry, and that should bring the roof watertight through the winter. I did not think it necessary to peg down the hives, as they stand in a very sheltered position in the walled garden. Every job that has to be done in connection with the bees must needs be done by myself, as the men are unreasonably scared of them and no-one will go within a ten-yard circle of the hives. They won't complain if their work brings them into contact with wild horses and raging bulls, but don't ask them to face up to a bee!

Orion has arisen from his sick-bed and showers

diamonds on a chilly world. The stars fill one with an unnamable consternation, being so large and mute, swinging wreaths of unknown worlds above one's head. Refuge from their searching is found before a turf fire when the day's work is done.

*   *   *

Within the past week, I have sawn branches from oak, ash, sycamore, elm, holly, beech, walnut, apple, London plane, and hawthorn. Of all these trees, the holly dies most like a gallant gentleman. It neither frowns nor smiles but stands erect, a noble to its very topmost leaf; it retains its bough until the very ultimate fibre is disconnected and then the limb falls without a groan or a heave. The oak is brave, holds fast, and does not whine after the operation. The ash is manly, holds firm, and keeps its teeth set until the saw snaps the last thread. But the sycamore is a craven fellow; he shouts before the limb is even half severed, flings his branches to the ground in terror, and, most shameful of all, weeps profusely after the amputation, whole pints of lachrymose sap drip mournfully from the cut surface of large limbs. Elm gets all hot and bothered, cracks on the first incision of the saw, but is tenacious to the last well-cursed strand. The beech churns out sawdust, resists valiantly for a while, then crashes woefully, is no coward, but has a kind of constitutional nervousness. Walnut is not so brave as one would imagine; it seems to know what is afoot, and midway in the operation gives up the contest with

18

a shout of rage. Apple is brawny and stout, bred to stoical resignation, shows no resentment but, on being mutilated, expresses its self-pity by oozing sap like the sycamore and shows a frothy surface where the severance was made. London plane seems terrorised at the approach of the saw; it makes a poor battle and snaps with a loud yell. Hawthorn is the hardest wood next to holly; it blunts the saw and, unlike the holly, fights like a cat in a corner, resisting until the last filament that holds limb to tree is parted. I also cut back elders, but I do not count these as trees; they are only growing garbage.

*　　*　　*

I have begun work on what may turn out to be a rockery without rocks or, at worst, a catmintary (if I may be permitted the coinage). For long I smoked pipes over the proposed site much as the honest Dutch burghers are said to have done when planning the building of New York (or at least according to that scamp, Knickerbocker). I gazed, I ruminated, I expectorated, and I flicked off snapped match-sticks; I thrust my head this way and that, and I even went the length of doubling up and viewing the site through my legs (which method, they say, puts things in their right perspective). But now the business is fairly in hand at last: the site has been excavated, the stones ("borrowed" from a crumbled part of the ha-ha) deposited conveniently near; and soil from the secret passage, soil that is largely leaf-mould, has been wheeled into position. Jimmy does most of the barrowing; he goes off whistling, and when sufficiently far removed from my sobering presence, he breaks out into raucous song. Apart from the fact that such rocks as will appear in the rockery will be only moderate-sized stones and not rocks at all, the finished result is bound to be mean, but then I'm not competing with suburbanites. In place of the "regulation" rockery plants, I intend to use only common or garden plants already growing here in abundance: I shall put in loads of catmint, forget-me-not, Siberian wallflower, London Pride, viola, valerian, and perhaps some specimens too of the native flora, such as stonecrop, or bugle. I may do my bit of fiddling while Rome burns, but the burden of unremunerative farming is too heavy to permit the spending of money on rockery plants. In addition to podging in stones and spreading soil on the new bed, I transplanted from an over-crowded bed about twenty-four cottage tulips (I like them best of all tulips, they are more graceful than the stiff-necked varieties) and as many more Spanish irises.

Dusk descends to scatter me and my implements. Behind the wood there is a long dash of evening-lit sky, like a corridor train all lighted up.

* * *

Heavy-bodied clouds glower. It is a cursing sort of day. No sooner had the sun risen than he made cowardly tracks for cover again. A kind of smoky mist comes on in the afternoon and lies like a damp cloak over the world.

We bustle about from dinner hour onwards, intent on catching every minute of daylight: the cow byre is cleaned out, fresh straw spread, the mangers filled with pulped turnips and a mixture of farm-grown grain—crushed oats and barley. The calf-house receives its daily fork of straw (by the spring, the floor level will be three feet higher than it is at present and the dung will have to be cut with a hay-knife), the trough is filled with crushed oats and turnips, and the hay rack stuffed with second-crop clover hay. Rolled oats and hay (and occasionally a few carrots) are given to the mares. The pigs have already been cleaned out and re-bedded; now, before the cows come in, they are fed; it is a job associated with an ear-splitting cacophony. Jimmy gives the poultry their grain ration and proceeds to shut up very soon afterwards, such being the niggardly allowance of daylight conceded these days.

For months to come, all we may expect to see of Old John are his bent knees. He will be concealed under umbrellas of hay and great awnings of straw as he staggers, wind-struck, across the yard to fodder cattle or to bed pigs. If Jimmy is right (and Jimmies are usually right where a man's private life is concerned) John won't wash his face, except perhaps for Christmas, from now until the first of May next, when the cows will be out again at night. The loss of a sight of John's face is not so serious as one might think: he is a melancholy-looking man, with a nose always red and always terminating in a drop, and with a walrus moustache perpetually dewy; no, John's good points are not in his looks. But he is a peaceful and a docile man and, even if he has little or no enterprise, and no ideas, he keeps going, hither and thither across the yard, walking on his heels, his shoulders always hunched, his face inscrutable.

Winter roared in last night, raised Cain, flung bags of leaves about the place, lashed windows and doors, peeled off half the roof of a hen-house, tore up a few trees, and generally made himself obnoxious. This morning the storm is still sulking behind the stripped wood. Every place looks watery-eyed. Tea-coloured leaves are tossing in the wind. There is a splatter of rain against the window and a little water leaks in, making a pool deep enough to float a match. A soughing in the trees outside; the wilted grasses are ruffled; dead leaves whirl in crazy dances; and the birds take panic-stricken flights not much less crazy than the flying leaves.

This room where I sit in solitude night after night would very comfortably seat a dozen people, yet I kneel alone on the hearth-rug, my hinder part to the fire, my elbows on a chair. Less and less do I object to singleness, a bad frame of mind, no doubt. I am too indolent at the moment to thrash out the matter, but I rather think I should like to be married in the winter, if I could be a bachelor in the summer. . . . Perhaps that would be the ideal state of existence, but I am afraid there is no chance of such an arrangement for this orthodox Catholic Irishman.

After all: all the scattering of summer leaves, all

the sad flight of summer visiting birds, all the decay and desertion, it was white-haired, amiable Mrs. Meehan who gave the treacherous death-blow to summer. There on a chair by my bed are my winter flannels, aired, patched and clean, but how detestable, how insolent in their message. Is the splendid, high-spirited summer really dead? Yes, by my pants; yes again, by my vest! Have the swallows really flown and are the flowers gone? Yes, by this woollen underwear, and yes again, by the hot jar in my bed! Mrs. Meehan is determined; summer *is* dead.

CHAPTER II

YESTERDAY I CELEBRATED A BIRTHDAY. IT seems to be a common and increasing occurrence these recent years. If I am not forty, it is not because I do not feel forty, nor that I have not the impression of having stacked up innumerable birthdays. Often I think I have a paunch! I received the usual complement of cigarettes and linen handkerchiefs from faithful relations, but at my age gifts are little jollier than funeral offerings, and I am nothing cheered. If a fellow could skip a birthday once in a while and contrive to celebrate the day he skipped, then gifts would be both appropriate and well deserved.

Every variety of weather has its uses for the industrious and the enterprising. The present frost (first showing of this winter's teeth) allows Mick to start ploughing for wheat sowing and allows me to clean the yard gutters by an original and effective method: one has only to prize up the edge of the frozen deposit in the gutter and, by gentle handling, remove it by yard lengths at a time; it comes out like fruit-jelly, the "fruit" being beech husks, lime-tree balls, sycamore wings, and a great variety of other vegetative fragments, and the "jelly" being the water which should have run through if the gutters had been well laid.

This frost will demoralise the tenacious leaves. Already the chestnut on the lawn beyond the ha-ha has thrown up the sponge and shaken off its yellow garb; every year this tree is the first to bow to adversity. The saw-blade edged leaves of the Morello cherry are going in scores just now. There is still shade in the wood: ginger, hot-red shade created by the tresses of Viking beeches, but these too will soon start flying down in confetti. Perhaps I am throwing up my hands prematurely for the departure of summer loveliness; if the leprosy of frost is in the petioles of leaves, there are still brave survivors of that loveliness. There are roses still (damp, and a trifle mouldy, it is true), marigolds, *Phlox Drummondii*, Siberian wallflower, sweet alyssum, and oxalis. If the grass is blue with frost, the elders are bowed under a weight of purple fruit and the catmint is having a second blooming. There are still masses of night-scented stock which put the constellations to shame, the latter being glorious but unperfumed. Most precious survivor of balmy summer days is eschscholtzia. I pick it in bud, stick it into tepid water, wait awhile, and then I am rewarded with lovely creamy silk on stalks. There are several varieties of eschscholtzia which I must try next year—from pale coral to full orange —and thus extend my present range.

Amidst rows and platefuls and piles and barrels of apples, I am in my element. So is Mrs. Sullivan, who drove up to the Apple Show with me. She contemplates laying down a score of maidens (to be trained into cordons), and I am already committed to at least an acre of three-year-old bush. We are both equally tireless in reviewing the exhibits and in making comparisons which compel us to go back to the first table to look again at those Allingtons which are so different from those exhibited on the tenth table. So consumed are we with our zeal for apples that, had we not met Mrs. Carter, we should not have even noticed the cold (it is certainly cold underfoot in this cobbled, covered-in yard of Lord Iveagh's house) which she so loudly bewails. Although our main purpose is to look at the varieties which we have provisionally listed to be planted, we are distracted by many others. Here are apples which would serve to illustrate Dickens: the Reverend W. Wilkes is Mr. Pickwick without his steel-framed glasses; Mère de Ménage is Major Bagstock very exasperated indeed; here are apples —Adam's Pearmain and Ard Cairn Russet—as unlike apples as Pekinese are unlike dogs; and here are common or garden nightmares such as Warner's King and Ecklinville Seedling. I am relieved to notice a weakening in Mrs. Sullivan's resolution to plant no more than five or six varieties, because I myself have so badly weakened. I long to plant Lord Lambourne, the Queen, and Ard Cairn Russet.

Mrs. Carter's usually-to-be-lamented forwardness turns out to be useful at the Apple Show: she captures a chief of the horticultural branch of the Department and gets him to explain the extraordinary difference between the same variety of apple, particularly in the case of Allingtons and Newtons. We had already surmised two reasons for this variation in a variety: difference in stock, and the presence or absence of iron in the soil; but the horticultural expert adds a third and the most interesting reason: the difference in results from grassed-down orchards and tilled orchards. Filled with resolutions and irresolutions, we depart for our farms, Mrs. Carter accepting an offer of a lift and squeezing herself in between Mrs. Sullivan and me. Conversation is pleasant enough for a time, but the housewife will out and eventually the women lapse into an animated discussion of soups and custards.

*　　*　　*

The approach of Ballynash Fair induces me to waylay Mick on the lawn where he is going through the stock. The division of labour in tending the farm stock is the result of beginning small. Before I got into my present stride, which now forces me along so unmercifully, Mick was factotum, and both the yard and the outside livestock were then in his charge. Now that we have old John as yardman, Mick is almost altogether free to follow the horses. Yet although John tends the pigs, calves, and cows all the year round, together with the stall-feds and calves during the winter months, Mick still looks after the outside cattle. Every day he goes through them, and he also fodders them from December until April. The sheep are everyone's and no-one's care: at yeaning time, John and I do most of the midwifery, but Mick, Joe, and Jimmy are often called in to give help. On field days, when we are washing, shearing, dipping, or dosing against fluke, all hands on the farm are conscripted. On the whole, Mick is in closest touch with the flock; he counts them daily and reports all ailments.

Environment and pasture are the explanation of nearly all sheep trouble. Here we are cursed by those park-like features that are ideal conditions for the greenbottle fly, which is the cause of maggots. Throughout the summer, especially in warm showery weather, no day passes without several sheep being struck. Mick's is the observant eye that notes the symptomatic tail-shaking and the worried look; on his report, the sheep are rounded up, those suspected of harbouring maggots are caught and searched, sprinkled with strong sheep-dip or Jeyes' Fluid from a bottle, or else drenched with water so as to make them shake off the skin-boring parasites; but most frequently the loathsome creatures are one by one picked off the sheep and exterminated in a pool of dip. Neglect maggot picking at your peril: without personal experience of what might happen, I should say that a sheep could be riddled within thirty-six hours of being struck.

The rich pastures account for foot-rot: the land is really far too heavy for sheep, which is perhaps another way of saying that the soil is liable to set up the virus which causes the tissue infection. Paring feet is at least a weekly job from early autumn until the ewes are too heavy in lamb to permit their being handled. Paring in order to prevent the hoof from holding dirt, and applying an antiseptic dressing are the usual remedies to which we resort. The dressing is Butyr of Antimony, which Mick renders as Butter of Antony (as he makes saltpetre into St. Peter's salts—religious man!). Sometimes, however, we vary the treatment by driving the flock into a house of which the floor has been heavily sprinkled with lime, thus hardening their hooves and at the same time destroying the disease-giving germs. With us, liver fluke, thank God, is rare, except in the very wettest seasons. The administration of capsules containing male fern extract is an effective preventative, which is more than can be said for the many supposedly certain specifics for setting up immunity against livestock diseases.

When I catch up on Mick, he is on the point of proceeding from the sheep, which are browsing at the Graigue end of the lawn, to the cattle grazing at the opposite extremity of this division, but on my request he comes back to the sheep. Yesterday he reported one of the blackfaced lambs as very sick; (I speculated in a score of these lambs some months ago). Not very enthusiastically, I instructed him to dose it with a liver fluke capsule (which is rather a preventative measure than a cure). It is an even chance whether one gives medical treatment to a sheep seriously sick, or whether one simply shrugs one's shoulders and does nothing. Sheep do not respond to nursing; they are the least domestic-ated of domestic animals; they seem to be either lucky and healthy, or they are diseased and die. If I could get back all the whiskey and gruel with which I drenched sheep (the patient in every single case nevertheless dying), I should have enough to feed and intoxicate the whole parish for a day.

Between the pond and the road fence we find the blackfaced lamb stretched on a hillock, apparently dying. We make a close examination of him, draw up his eye lining, probe him, and peer at his droppings. We discuss the probability of liver fluke and debate on other diseases, concluding that his chances of life are so small that we will not truck him into the yard for that nursing which is usually so unavailing. Mick, having gone into most of the "horrid" aspects of the case ("horrid" being his favourite fill-gap), makes an enigmatical conclusion: "Well, them blackfaces are horrid sheep for hardships; they'd make out a living no matter what. You'll find now that that lamb won't die until the last minute!"

The effect of continual rain on the countryside suggests a multi-coloured fabric that has been soaked and wrung out. Even the movement of twisted cloth regaining its shape is reflected in the November landscape. When it is sober, the month steams; when in its cups, it is violent; this year, November seems likely to put in its thirty days by boozing.

The hedges marking my farm boundary are fruit-laden: the fruit of ashes, the miraculous burdens of plush-red haws, the black beads of privet and the crimson of hips. Acorns, beech-nuts, and crabs are spilt long since. The elder-berry corymbs are reduced to their wiry frames; spindle-berries have gaped orange and dissolved; snow-berries are growing mould spots and cling sickly to the twigs. The quick hedges dangle beads of perspiration; the furze elbows out to catch wisps of hay from passing carts. But for all the decay, at any time, and on any stretch or clearing, one may come on a tattered banner of vivid beech, fox-red or vermilion, eloquent as a rallying cry, as a bullet-riddled flag, as a souvenir of the wars.

The merest crumbs of beauty are left in the fields: a ragweed that dodged the scythe of frost; a furze blossom that scorned it; a clump of blood-red dogwood; golden willow suckers acting as a spider's web for the tiny flashes of sunshine; trees lashed to earth by ropes of ivy.

Only fur, or things resembling fur, are pleasing in this season. Yew hedges, hayricks, and smoke wreaths from houses hearten the beholder. The bare hedgerows and the naked fields give one cold shivers.

Then comes a squall of wind with a battered rook riding it for symbol. The dead leaves are spurred to wriggling in their beds; the bare twigs yield; tree-tops curtsey to adversity; and the sky-full scuds along. Squelching through a crazy rain-storm in a lurid twilight, with rooks making for harbour as fast as their wings can carry them—how often is it thus in November!

We prowl through the cattle: some are browsing, some lying and cudding contentedly. We stir up the latter and watch them stretch themselves and perhaps lick their flanks, two certain signs of well-being. We steal up on such cattle as we fancy suitable for Ballynash Fair, hypocritically crooning "Sook-sook" until we are upon them, then calm them by scratching them over their tails. Always on this farm we carry a majority of heifers over

31

bullocks. Cloonmore land is heifer land. I cannot explain, no-one can, not even an agricultural scientist with a string of degrees, but there is no disputing the fact that heifers thrive here, whereas bullocks fatten tardily. All the neighbours are aware of this Cloonmore characteristic: they commented on it when I took over the place, but never explained. The result of our survey is that Mick holds Lawlor's white-faced is the best match for the big Derry white-faced, while I champion the merits of the Wart heifer.

As for cattle nomenclature, there is hardly any limit to the length of names that can originate, and no limit at all to their absurdity. The *heifer-out-of-the-cow-with-the-lump-on-her-knee* was recently sold to the Lowtown butcher, but the *missing heifer* is still with us (she was astray for five days, and was eventually tracked down in a field near Cloonlara from which she originally came). Many cattle are described by the name of the fair at which they were bought, or by the name of the man (when it is known) who sold them. Those bred on the farm are known as being out of their respective dams, a name system usually straightforward, though we have had such absurdities as the *bullock-out-of-the-heifer-that-turned-out-to-be-in-calf*, which tells a tale of bad fences, a roaming bull, and an illicit courtship having taken place before the offender was sold to me in a bunch of bovine virgins. Accidents and ailments also account for a large number of cattle names: at present we have in the herd the *heifer-that-was-sick-at-Hogan's* (where last year I rented a grass division), and the *lame bullock*, to

32

indicate two beasts now perfectly sound and normal. Some years ago we had the *blind heifer*, and the *calf-with-the-wart-on-his-navel*. A calf is always described as "he" until it is at least six months old. The milch cows alone enjoy a selection of sensible names. At present there is the *Dublin Black*, *Foxy*, the *Limerick Grey* and the *Limerick Red*, *Hogan's Polly*, and the *Kerry*.

Heaven encourage Mrs. Carter in her forlorn hope of anglicising her husband's herd. She is up against very tough prejudices when she tries to have a grey cow called *Buttercup Roan*, another *Dew-eyes*, and another *Jessie*; the Graigue men, if I know them, will have nothing to do with such fancy styles. I myself had once to come down a peg: to be precise, from *Up-horns* to *Limerick Red*—and I can weep more or less sincerely for Mrs. Carter's failure. There is no help for it: to the Micks and Johns of Ireland, a cow is first and foremost a beast, and after that she may have characteristics of "elder", frame, head, and colour, by which she is described, but at no stretch of the imagination has an ordinary and respectable beast "dew-eyes."

*   *   *

I feel as smug as a wood pigeon and tingling with a virtuous glow in getting our tiny afforestation scheme under way at this end of winter. Usually we are rushed and we postpone our plantings until late spring. I hold with the old adage which says, "Plant in autumn and command them to grow; plant in spring and beg them to

33

grow." Joe and John (when the latter can be extricated from his yard jobs) are at present putting in one hundred silver firs in the wood.

This wood is more nominal than real. It is barely an acre in area, and the trees, which are for the most part old, are set far apart. As I am assured that silver firs will make moderate growth in shady situations, I hope to thicken the coppice (to give the plantation its proper name), and thus lessen that bleak air of transparency occurring annually after the first autumn storm.

Of all conifers, I like least the silver fir, so frequently spindly and meagre, but if it does the job, that is, makes growth in spite of roofing broadleaf, I will not judge it by severe æsthetic tests. We are not making any attempt to keep to a formal plan of planting; my instructions to the men are simply to pop in a fir wherever it stands a dog's chance of obtaining head-room.

When this filling-in planting is finished, there are one hundred and fifty Sitka Spruce and fifty *Cupressus Lawsoniana* to go in as a continuation of the shelter belt in the new orchard. The year before last I plumped for Douglas firs for shelter-belt purposes because of their reputation for fast growth; they certainly made a spring at the sky, but, later on, the lime in the Cloonmore soil upset their digestion; the needles of the trees have gone a sickly yellow, and their resinous wood seems to lack a healthy elasticity.

If there is such an exalted sentiment as labour jealousy, I experience it and heave a sigh when I have to leave the men to their planting of trees. I

have an absurd feeling that they may dig up something valuable which they might conceal from me.
It may be a foolish illusion, but I cherish it in most
sober hours. I believe that the whole of Cloonmore
farm sits tight on gold bangles and bronze spear-
heads, though as yet I've unearthed nothing more
valuable than Wood's halfpence and livery buttons
of the Devon family! I should like to dig all the
holes myself so as to be the first to strike the pots
of gold, or the carved stones.

There is always before my mind the painful story
about the Firlands turf-cutters, related to me by
the schoolmaster. These honest fellows unearthed
a pottery urn when winning turf from their bank.
For a while they regarded their find with suspicion,
then egged each other on to action, and getting
a vision of gold, they gave the urn a mighty swipe
with a slane. Inside it was a parchment manuscript. The turfmen were first vastly disappointed
and then panic-stricken. They made fragments of
the urn and burned the manuscript in the little fire
that bogmen always keep glowing for tea-making.
"Why, it might have been anything," wailed the
schoolmaster, tears filling his eyes. "It might even
have been the lost Book of Kildare, one of the
greatest manuscript treasures of ancient Ireland."
"Yes," I supplemented cheerfully, "or even the
lost Book of Livy!" The schoolmaster told me the
names of the culprits; both of them live within two
miles of Cloonmore.

However, the digging of holes and the chances
of finding treasure are not all left with the men. I
find sites and dig holes too for a dozen fancy sorts

35

of trees and shrubs, in which I indulged myself
when I was ordering the commercial ones from my
nurseryman friend, Tommy Waters. I first find a
home for the Ginkgo, a disappointing tree in its
state of nude infancy; it is sleek and olive green,
possessing hardly any superficial features to distinguish it from the common ash. Yet the Ginkgo
in maturity, both from the botanical and historical
point of view, is perhaps the most interesting tree
in the world. It is the single species in a single
genus that survives from the pre-human era. I shall
have fun showing it to visitors when it is planted,
and telling them its history, although I hardly
expect to live to sit under its shade.

From this I go on to my pretence of a shrubbery
that borders the front gravel sweep, and I embellish
it with an arbutus, a robust and glossy tree with a
flaky bark like that of the yew. I have no use for
the claim which makes the arbutus a native like
the harp, the wolfhound, and the shamrock. The
arbutus may be Irish, but it is no Milesian nor
Irish-Irelander.

Then tamarisk, a feathery bit of shrub, was com-
manded to grow opposite the workshop door; I
expect I was drawn into buying this because of
always reading of its presence in romantic corners
of the globe, but possibly I am a fool when I am
conducted around the nursery walks by Tommy
Waters.

Liquidambar is another specimen which I cannot
now imagine why I bought (apparently ornamental
trees and shrubs go to my head when I have eaten
and drunk at Tommy's expense). On being un-

packed at Cloonmore in the cold light of another day, this tree looks a freak, a sort of sullen, idiotic freak. However, the catalogue states that it will attain a height of eighty feet, so I march with it to the wood and, cuckoo-wise, dump in into a nest which the men had prepared for a silver fir.

For Pittosporum (the Silver Queen variety), I make a special bed which I intend to complete later on with a circle of pernittyia. With its grey-green foliage and black stems, Pittosporum is by far the most useful evergreen.

The last tree which I put in is *Thuya orientalis*, the sacred tree of China, a fit companion for the Ginkgo, the sacred tree of Japan, and so planted beside it. This *Thuya*, being spidery and almost cruel in appearance, sends shivers down my spine; it seems a devilish sort of exotic to introduce among my homely and civilised trees.

All the while I was digging holes, the words of one of the Mass Offertories ran in my head: "Wood hath hope; if it be cut, it groweth green again, and the boughs thereof sprout."

Just for once, the disparaging title of "Planter" may be given a generous interpretation. For all their sins and their alien ignorance, the Devons certainly planted a fine selection of trees in Cloonmore. Between us—the haughty Devons and later my humble self—there are now assembled on this farm all the common trees and many more that are not so common. Although neither hornbeam, mulberry, mazard, nor the wayfaring tree is here, there are walnuts, planes, rowans, Weymouth pines, Spanish chestnuts, spindle-trees, and a box-tree,

37

all of Devon planting, and I have extended the list to include at least a dozen others. When I came here, there was also among the trees that detestable monstrosity, a Monkey Puzzle. Within a week of my arrival (and what a full week!) that thing (I cannot bring myself to call it a tree, for it is more like the product of a tinsmith than one of God's creations) was felled, and then I began to breathe. Most numerous of all the trees here are beeches, and then sycamores, elms, oaks, ashes, larches, aspens, and limes. The thought of Cloonmore bereft of its trees could not be endured. I fancy I could continue to love a love should she shed all her hair, lose all her teeth, and grow sallow-complexioned, but a Cloonmore without its trees—never!

*　　*　　*

Mick is ploughing ley for wheat-sowing. Even in this semi-ranching region, we are bitten with the Fianna Fail Wheat Scheme. I linger for a long time in the Night Park, watching the ship-like progress of the plough. Mick's encouraging "Up, Lil! Up, Kit!" and the soothing swish of the plough were the only sounds that broke the silence of the world. Lovely smelling sod, wet, sticky, almost oily, was left in the wake of the horses. Soil, like the ocean, makes heavy demands on our stock of adjectives; soil being the vast epidermis of our planet. A man driving a ploughshare is rending a veil and altering the world.

Catching sight of Pat Mangan in Flynn's adjacent land, I cross the mearing to meet him. Pat has been sent for by Flynn's man who is a tyro at the art of ploughing. After the usual leisurely salutations are exchanged, Pat tells me that this man had never ploughed ley before, and that he was too bashful to tell his master this fact when sent out to plough for wheat-sowing. The man in question is within earshot and grins amiably while Pat is telling me about him. Evidence of Pat's account occupies the best part of a rood of land: crooked furrows, broken and uneven in their depth, surround a truly ghastly opening. Bad workmen blame their tools, but it took Flynn's *cauboge* to blame the terrestrial globe for his lack of skill. He explains to us that the cause of the erratic variation in the depth of his furrows is due to "Some bloody suck in the land!"

I leave the pair to tightening "boults" and lengthening wheels. ("Measure it there before you loosen it, man!" Pat snaps pleasantly at the amateur. "Spit on your finger and make a mark on the shaft.") But, on glancing back from the Night Park, I can see that, even with the help and advice of Pat Mangan, Flynn's ploughing is going to be the talk of all the folk passing to Mass next Sunday.

The explanation why Flynn employs such incompetent men is not far to seek. He has such a bad reputation as an employer that the good workers give him a wide berth. Jokes about his financial wiles are gossip for the parish. There was a period when he ceased to pay any wages to his two men for a long time, and at length one of them approached him for money. "Now,

Tom," the master gently explained, "I think very bad of not having the money at present, but I have an old sow out there fattening, and when I sell her off I'll be able to give you something." Soon the other man became restive. "Look-it here, Mr. Flynn, I want my wages." This time Flynn got annoyed: "Now, Dan, if you want to keep your job here, stop asking me for money! That's enough about it now."

Across the road another ploughing team is plodding up the field. (What back-slapping, what handshaking this must cause in Merrion Street!) He who drives the furrow was wont to say that no government could ever banish the bullock from its place of honour in the Irish farming scheme. Pat Mangan, who is occasionally inclined to affect the role of "oldest inhabitant," told me a while ago that never before, "in the history of any man living," was either my Night Park or the adjacent field belonging to Flynn broken. These Fianna Fail fellows will grow swelled-headed with the success of the Wheat Scheme if this reddening of land goes on all over Ireland. It remains to be seen, however, whether the Scheme will pay farmers as well as cattle-rearing paid them.

I go to the road fence and linger again, gazing on the pleasant sight of a man and a pair of horses. They turn a field into a tricolour: the green of aftergrass, the deep brown left in the wake of the plough, and the washed-out gold of an oats stubble. Furrow is shouldering furrow like corded velvet, while the stubble is still lustrous. In the next field there are drills of swedes which have been partly snagged: the bulbs lie in mauve rows among a wealth of bright green leaves, awaiting the cart which will draw them to the haggard. The rains have washed the swedes baby-clean, leaving amethyst-coloured tops over cream bases.

I move on to the new orchard to inspect John and Joe snagging turnips. (By "turnips" we farmers invariably mean "swedes"; we stand corrected just as when we say "elder" instead of "udder," and "fast-day" instead of the vulgarly uncomprehended "day of abstinence"!) Our turnip-snagging is a hand-to-mouth affair rather than anything resembling a campaign. Usually we take care to have enough turnips covered in the yard to stand a week's siege of frost. Turnips may be kept in small, earth-covered heaps in the field in which they grow, and there is also a practice (Scottish in origin, I think, but not altogether unknown here) of ploughing in the roots before severe frost comes, and ploughing them out—rather like the way in which potatoes are ploughed out. On the whole, the storage of turnips is only a necessary evil; it would not pay to earth them up or put them into thatched clamps.

I gaze rather dolefully down the drills where the men are bobbing up and down. They have tied sacking round their legs to protect them against the wet and, before snagging, they advance down the drills with long sticks, beating off the rain from the foliage. Again we have too many turnips. Every year I vow I shall lessen my sowing and, curiously enough, every year I do so, and yet I have too many. It ought to be my aim to grow

41

just sufficient to last until the end of January. This year it looks as though the turnip crop will see March in, or at least the remnant of the crop will do so, for, between rotting and shrivelling, time will work havoc on it.

Jimmy will be glad that the turnip crop is out of the ground and drawn to the yard. Every day he takes a turnip sliced into discs on his poultry round. In all the houses he has long nails hammered about six inches above floor level, and upon these he impales the turnip-discs. The hens pounce immediately upon the juicy circles, and soon all the houses are resounding with a loud tapping that is eloquent of poultry pleasure.

Hastening back from the new orchard to the poultry runs, I was just in time to bid Jimmy make a change in disposing of the daily barrow-loads of hen-droppings. Usually he trundles this richest of manures to a dumping-ground convenient to Joe's proposed onion-bed (Joe would sow half an acre of onions if he could get away with it), but the practice is a wasteful one. Poultry-droppings are droppings; in other words, it is not physically a complete manure because of the absence of absorbent matter (the turf mould which we occasionally scatter on the dropping-boards hardly counts for anything). From now on, I will insist on Jimmy wheeling his barrow up a plank and tipping the contents on to the yard manure dump. If tillage is to be the order of the day on this farm, it is necessary to conserve every morsel of manure.

Some day—the same great day on which I shall have a hay barn, running water in the cow byre, electric light in the house, a telephone, and a herb garden—I hope to have a walled-in and covered manure pit, with conduits to a liquid manure tank. No matter how we pack, ram, and build, we lose the liquid manure; it flows away into ditches and thus a splendid fertiliser is forever lost. Deep down in me is an appreciation of the value of liquid manure. "Liquid manure, liquid manure," Professor Wibberley used to chant almost ecstatically to the students of Cork University long ago. "You cannot over-estimate the value of liquid manure. Every farmer ought to put over his mantelpiece a big typed and framed reminder that liquid manure is worth its weight in gold."

* * *

When Tony Donovan had long and vainly pressed the hall-door bell (country-house bells never work), he has the enterprise to try the dairy. He surprises me at the task of finishing the churning. To his way of thinking, I am caught red-handed.

"How long do you intend messing about in this sort of way?" he booms unpleasantly. I gather from his irritated tone and frozen stare that not merely the petty offence of doing the churning myself, but the whole vocation of farming is once more in the dock.

"Always," I answer sweetly.

"Well, if you think you are doing your duty as an Irish citizen, and making use of the brains God gave you . . ."

Tony casts up his eyes to heaven, becoming distracted (I am proud to say) by the flitches of home-cured bacon hanging from the ceiling hooks.

But I interrupt his diatribe on Shirking Life's Business, with which I am very familiar, by calling out to Mrs. Meehan to prepare tea for two.

Then we go through the hen-runs together in search of Jimmy, so that I can tell him to take on the churning where I left off. Tony indicates a flock of Wyandotte pullets with the query, "How do you manage to keep them so white?"

"Oh, they are washed every few days," I answer airily.

"Is that so? I never knew there was all that bother with chickens."

I say no more. After tea, he returns again to the fray. Would I consider going into business? He could find an opening for me in the Agricultural and Dairy Supply business in which he is interested. My agricultural knowledge (when he loves me, it's "agricultural," but when he despises me, it's "farming"), and especially the oddments of certificates and diplomas I picked up before buying Cloonmore, would be useful as window-dressing in the proposed post. I have the business capacity, the "go," a small capital, and "my whole life is before me"!

Well, there is really no motive except kindness in Tony's urgency, though I pretend to believe he regards me as a potential capitalist. He honestly believes that farming is an inferior pursuit, an unprofitable occupation fit only for the unambitious and the feeble-minded. Tony pities me: I don't seem to grasp that farming is sheer waste of time and talents, that the great ideal is to get away from the land and "do something." Tony is typical of

44

hundreds of thousands of Irishmen, emancipated from the land a bare generation or two ago, and now decrying it for all they are urbanly worth. On he rattles, then, pursuing the theme of a man with brains twisting a churn handle, while Ireland's greatest need in Church, State, Commerce, and Society is Business Men.

If Tony Donovan and I were to argue until Doomsday we should never get any further; his hide is as impenetrable to my arguments as mine is to his. This debate in which we have so often engaged now bores me excessively: rural versus urban—oh, stuff for a schoolboy's prize essay! Tony, I know, is not the only acquaintance who looks upon me as a sort of Diogenes of the Irish Midlands, shuffling out my days in unwashed decadence. Disapproval varies with the degree of kinship. Casual acquaintances assume a look of anguish on hearing that I do not possess a wireless. Friends express themselves, sometimes forcibly, as they discover the lack of Cloonmore amenities; while relations nag and bully because I cannot enjoy the same luxuries as they enjoy, and because I do not seem to care. Peace: let them go their way; let me go mine. The world may be on Tony's side, but I cannot bring myself to estimate success as just the making of money, or the building up of a small business into a great one (to the plaudits of acquaintances). If the world lies at Tony's feet, that world is none of mine: he's welcome to it. Let him set out with a light in his eyes and put the Liffey on fire, but Lord give him the sense not to pity me. At worst a happy failure, at best happily inefficient, I go my slow way: a "mad Patsy" if you will, stretched out in the sun and saying he "would not work for any clown."

* * *

To tell the truth, I have little fault to find with this cold season; except that one cannot sit on the grass, one cannot get out of bed in the morning (at least not easily), and one can seldom keep one's feet dry, there is nothing less glorious in it than in July. The beauty of leaves and flowers is in the delight of having them after the contrasting bareness, and the beauty of the stark landscape is in the contrast with its former luxuriance. I love to see the beech-trees nursing their clothing sentimentally; the rounded holly-trees, like fat tradesmen at their shop doors; the efficiency, service, and salesmanship of the robin redbreast; yellowing tussocks of grass; and evening coming in red with diamond buckles on her shoes. The earth smells, hay smells, calves coming home to bed smell; all good and wholesome things have smells. Dead leaves take it into their heads to dance and the stars are positively in their element once November settles into housekeeping. "You won't feel until Christmas now," people say encouragingly to each other, thinking that they are saying something moderately intelligent. In November folk are kinder than at any other time of the year, or else I fancy overmuch.

When I get back from Ballynash Fair, the house reeks from basement to attic with the odour of jam-boiling. So she has broken out again! Already

46

this year, it is the third bout of apple-jelly making. Dinner is slap-dash and tastes of molasses. Jimmy's good-humoured visage is puckered in a scowl: no doubt he is being dogged, and nagged, and abused; no doubt he is being sent out with apple-pulp to the pig-tub (it gives the pigs colic, but Mrs. Meehan will have nothing wasted); or he is made weigh out sugar from the sack; or help in lifting and tying from the legs of inverted chairs the ancient flour-bags now full of boiled apples. Poor Jimmy, how he abhors domestic tasks, how ignominious they seem to the great Cloonmore authority on equine pedigrees.

At present the kitchen is a place to be avoided like the plague, but I know that my ordeal lies before me. Tonight she will summon me to the basement in order to review the array. Flushed, perspiring, and sticky, officiating in such a cloyish aroma that one could cut it with a knife, Mrs. Meehan, I feel, is staging a great hit. The kitchen table (which seats twenty men in comfort at the threshing dinner) will be covered almost from end to end with one-, two-, and three-pound ruby-red pots. There will still be upturned chairs and makeshift jelly-bags around the floor, and buckets half full of muddy-looking juice, which it is difficult to connect with the finished product.

A wiser man nowadays, I will moderate my praises tonight and not get into trouble by flinging commercialism athwart Mrs. Meehan's rural philosophy. On the last occasion, when I saw the array of one hundred and ten pounds or so of delicious-looking jelly, I got a bright idea, and a bright idea

47

in a time of depression I thought something to be prized. If one hundred and ten pounds, why not one thousand one hundred and ten pounds and create a paying side-line? As for apples, there is an almost unlimited quantity of crabs and smalls to be had in the orchard for the picking up. Eagerly I began to enlarge on this theme to the housekeeper; I spread my hands and I warmed up to the subject: I would give her so much on every pound we sold; we could call it some fancy name and we could advertise it: "made from an old-world receipt, of which the secret has been passed down from mother to daughter for hundreds of years!" Mrs. Meehan listened in growing astonishment. "We could call it Sarah—Sarah What's-it Receipt—Sarah *Shaughnessy's* Receipt!" Just when I was about to invent a lyrical slogan, the honest woman cooled my ardour. All she said was her favourite ejaculation, "*Holy God tonight!*" but the look which accompanied this was enough. Sell apple-jelly indeed! One would think it was eggs, or oats, or cattle! She simply did not think my plan feasible, and that was all. . . . City people had money and could buy shop jams, what would they be doing with the like of what we make? Life is too short to reason Mrs. Meehan out of her inferiority complexes, so it grows depressingly clear that apple-jelly will figure pretty frequently on the menu for the coming twelve months.

* * *

These are grey days and bitterly cold. Torn winter is everywhere apparent, trees naked, hedges bared, pastures sickly. The lime outside the study window has gone completely bald. My socks are always damp. There is no sun, no sun at all. The wind and its tortured whistle are desolating; for long it moans, then cries out in sudden rages. Everywhere stripped trees and greasy mud and cold. The lovely holly-berries are hustled off their stage by violent winds before their day has dawned. There is an incessant sough of wind under the hall door.

Cloonmore will be the shuttlecock of winds until summer comes again, gales blowing upon us from east, west, north, and south. The east wind will go on skates, the west wind will tumble head over heels, the north wind will ride on a Clydesdale, while the south wind will mince up to us in carpet slippers. Just now it is a west wind that swings on the tree-tops, screeching like an escaped maniac. The world seems to be blown up like a balloon with boisterous air.

My friends, the Ahernes, on a visit here lately (townspeople at heart for all their protestations), aver that stormy days are invigorating, making them feel like giants; but then these folk are romantic. As for me, I am all earth-struck, for long a plodder in miry walks. I do not see fun in mad winds which may strip roofs, send my straw and hay flying, fell valuable trees, and anyway prevent men, who are drawing wages the farm can ill afford, from doing useful out-of-door work. As a result of years of farming, I am matter-of-fact, calculating, a clod-hopper, a beef-to-the-heels sort of fellow. Except at times: and then I too have seen God

Almighty riding the tempestuous winds, and I have seen archangels throw stars out of their courses (and that too without the aid of music, for with strong music in one's ears anything could happen). Yes, I have seen more than all three Ahernes rolled into one soulful and poetic whole can have seen. But now I am the much sobered farmer, tempered by agricultural adversities. Sedateness has settled upon me because of the slump in the Dublin cattle market, the necessity of paying a gruelling rent, together with the petty persecution of government interference, the decay of liberty, and the disillusionment wrought by close contact with hired men.

Once again the practice of night feeding the poultry comes round. The pullets alone are worth this expensive and troublesome business because they are on the upgrade of egg production. Midway in No. 5 house I suspend the petrol lamp, scatter the contents of a bucket of mixed grains in the litter, and bully the sleepy birds from off their perches. For six weeks at least I am thus booked from 9 to 9.30 P.M. Some nights I endure the half-hour with the scratching pullets, sitting on an upturned bucket, crooning to myself, or in contented silence, thinking my thoughts. Last year I used to read aloud passages from Thomson's *Seasons* for the entertainment of the drowsy birds, but I think they found Thomson's *Winter* rather too dramatic. Most nights, however, I leave the pullets to enjoy by themselves the time snatched from darkness, and I do the yard round in the meanwhile.

"Doing the yard" is arduous at certain times,

particularly now that it means feeding kail to the cows. When I take the lamp into the pulper-house the cows next door recognise my step and my mission; they welcome me with a loud rattling of chains and a lurching up of heavy bodies—a noise as closely related to lip-smacking as bovines can produce. I give a generous armful of the marrow-stemmed kail to each beast: there is a happy munching, accompanied by a cabbagy smell. Cows love kail and it is certainly good for promoting milk. Resolve: grow much more kail. Eh? But I made that resolution last year? Maybe. And the year before? Well, this time I *am* resolved.

I always approach the pig-houses with a pocketful of stones; there is the chance of getting a crack at a rat inside. So far I have never killed one in this way; lately I hit a brute fair on the back; in his dazed state he rushed at my legs but, being flustered, I failed to jump on him. Frankly, I am scared by rats. Where I find feeds left unfinished, I haul out the troughs, cover them up, and resolve to give John a talking-to about it next day, which I usually forget to do. In the loose boxes there may be in-calf cows, or heifers, needing scrutiny. Then there are calves to be inspected and perhaps a sow that is close to farrowing. When in an energetic mood I can find a dozen other things to do, such as giving drinks to lately farrowed sows, tit-bits to the mares, or seeing that the boiler fire really has burned out and constitutes no menace to the hay and straw ricks. I wonder should I regard this night round as such a matter of almost religious obligation if it were not for the shock I got about eight years ago, when a tied cow was found stone dead in the morning as the result of being strangled by the tying chain; not indeed that the yard round is any real safeguard against the occurrence of such an accident.

It is pleasant to get back out of the cold darkness and muckiness to the bright world of my fireside: a composite world which to me means piano, books, drawing materials, farm diaries, tobacco, shrub and flower catalogues, the newspapers, Laddie, and a hot drink.

CHAPTER III

JAILER WINTER HAS SHOT ANOTHER BOLT. His latest gambit is first sensed from the snuggery of bed, and as sleep's pupal stage is cast off, the worst is guessed. A little later, the worst is seen through a chink in the frosted panes. The earth is fettered and manacled by frost, the landscape oxidised.

Through a spy-hole bared by coughing at the feathered panes, I see a Van de Velde frost scene without the figures: vapours crawling on all-fours, trees in shrouds, roofs sheeted in linen, and a background depressed by banks of portentous clouds. The whole house is darkened by the frost-clogged windows. To greet my descent of the stairs, icy whiffs come in under the front door and through slits in the window-frames.

"My wife is up, and with Mrs. Pen to walk in the fields to frost-bite themselves," records the diarist Pepys. To me the benefits of such an outing are obscure, but no doubt it was invigorating to the nerves. Let me take the frost-bite here in Cloonmore: warily I descend the frozen front steps and cross the frost-concreted gravel. Shrubs that were but brooms yesterday are masses of ostrich feathers today; here is something that looks like a swan in flight, and in reality is only a head of kail; yesterday's poultry netting is today like a crochet shawl; hairs snatched by barbed-wire fences from the flanks of passing cattle are now as thick as tea twine; headless stalks of grass look as fierce as crowbars, and disreputable old rakes of weeds have donned shrouds in which they menace us like impish boys dressed in sheets, pretending to be ghosts at a laneway end.

Benvenuto Cellini, despite receiving for his craftsmanship "favours too tedious to detail from popes, kings, and cardinals," could in that silver which was as wax in his hands fabricate nothing so exquisite as the impress of a frosty night on a rank weed.

If the whole effect on the landscape is breathtaking in its splendour, the details are often fantastic. Hoar-frost at its finest is pulverised white sugar; it graduates through ground glass, rice grains, and wheat seed resemblance until it assumes the size of haws; it adheres to every sort of shape, making mountains out of molehills, bearding every perpendicular object, and casting a clothing of goosedown over every flat surface. The motif of the decorative scheme is perhaps the frost-fern, but really rime knows neither rhyme nor reason when it has full play on smooth surfaces. It particularly loves grass blades, dangling straws, or bits of vegetative untidiness usually unobtrusive, and it strings these obscure threads with white corals, just as the necklaces are strung—with the beads side to side rather than end to end. It offers its ornamentation not so much to the proud as to the humble; it rejoices in playing fairy godmother to little mites of weeds; it bedecks the withered and the neglected with greater favours than it bestows upon the robust and the popular. The practice of laying out a corpse is a common art, but the embellishment of a skeleton is left to hoar-frost.

Did Mrs. Pen and Mrs. Pepys ("poor wretch") have to walk in strange fields for the purpose of the frost-bite cure? To me, anyhow, there is the joy of a very familiar scene absolutely transfigured: old tree-friends are in sparkling garments, the little wood is a choir of angels, a yew has taken the veil. The holly-trees, bejewelled with scarlet berries, are in furs of ermine. The cupressus looks like filigree; the beeches are in towering white mantillas; young apple-trees are changed into intricate and elaborate candelabra. A maybush is whiter now than ever it was in any May; and the sweet briar hedge is armed to the teeth with gleaming lances and swords. The garden seat is grizzly, the hen-houses mournfully streaked, the beehives resemble Swiss chalets.

The universal silversmith has done good work. In one night the world has been changed from a washy, drab sort of place into a fairyland. Wet twigs are silver twigs; if there is a Day of General Judgment for vegetation, the blessed cannot expect finer raiment for their eternity. Stark fields are carpeted with crisp and shining matting. Even the silence has taken on a newness—and so has noise: instead of the melancholy drip of trees, there is a fusillade of falling ice when the strengthening sun fires the train that leads to a thaw. There is a salutary smart in the air, an invitation to trot or run (according to your age), where yesterday there was only damp chill, which was a menace rather than an enticement in sallying forth.

My first job this morning is to pick three stone of Brussels sprouts to fill an order from a Ballynash shop. When the plants are frost-starched as now, this is agonising work. I have a good crop of sprouts this year: the secret of success seems to be to sow in autumn and plant out the following summer, allowing eighteen inches between plants. The price is 2s. 4d. per stone up to the present; however, this whack of hard weather ought make all green vegetables advance in price. A robin keeps step and supervises me the whole length of the drill, which is about one hundred and fifty yards. Perhaps I am conceited, but I seemed to fancy something of hero-worship in his beady glances, and a suggestion of lionising in his persistent companionship.

But Mrs. Pen and Mrs. Pepys, perhaps we have not got the hang of it; perhaps we do not gain the fullest benefit of the salutary frost-bite, for we pause too often in our walk back from the sprouts. Had you a powder-blue sky over you, Mrs. Pen? Had you a net of beeches above you, O Mrs. Pepys? A new blue released for the first time from the heavenly satin department, a ravishing, astounding, paradisal blue, with the faintest suggestion in places of the most wraith-like cloud stealing across it. A mass of tree-heads, ivory as it never will be carved, lace as it never will be fabricated, a tangled head of whitest convolutions, beautiful and delicate as a bubble, chaste as pear-blossom. No, we prefer to get our frost-bite by lingering in the frost and gazing up at this blaze of silver glory into which the beech-trees have been transformed, a glory compared with which the cherry-blossom gardens of Japan cannot raise a farthing taper, and in comparison with which Alhambresque is garish. The ecstasy of hoar-frost under a pastel-blue sky consumes us. Heaven need not improve on this unless it likes to instal central heating for the ecstaticised!

*   *   *

This morning, when a certain in-calf heifer threw a fit on being untied and showed every symptom of epilepsy, John made no delay in recommending a "cure" dispensed by a blacksmith in the Conall direction. I know my John, and I have seen fragments of nondescript grease piously kept in holes in the wall of the byre, and, when he was challenged about them, he owned that they were "cures" for "Blasts" and "Starts" concocted by some old woman who "has the cure." I also know that my derisive grin on gaining this information was met by an angry flash from the eyes of the same John. Was I a mocker at sacred traditions?

Thus the blacksmith of Conall falls at first on deaf ears. Then the heifer gets steadily worse, she foams at the mouth, her eyes roll, her limbs are frantic, and it is certain she suffers great pain. The books are unhelpful when, very worried and altogether upset, I consult them about what to do. They have no better suggestions than to bleed the animal, or throw cold water on her head. Then Mick unexpectedly backs up John about the "man with the cure." Now Mick is a different man of a younger generation, served in the I.R.A., associates with the bright young people of Graigue and Lowtown, and sometimes reads a newspaper.

Time passes; the heifer gets no better and, on second consideration, I begin to calculate that after all a cure may be a cure without being a *pishoge*. Mick's moral backing sways my doubting mind towards assent, for he seems to imply that the cure is a herbal one of ordinary establishment, though a dark secret in its composition. Later, I learned that the margin between "dark secrets" and "black magic" is very thin. My education in common sense gives one more kick: I decide to call on Pat Mangan before starting for Conall. But Pat is in bed because of a recent cold, and old Peter Mangan, when pressed for information about the Conall genius, is cautious and non-committal.

Sighing, I drive away in the Conall direction, my tongue with every inclination to stick in my cheek, my good sense tormenting me with the notion that I might be on the Ballinvally road now hastening towards either an expensive but reliable vet. or towards that proved font of knowledge and consolation, Farrell, the chemist. A little voice within me prays that the blacksmith will be out. Over bogs full of bright colours, along a stubborn little boreen. And the blacksmith is at home! He is very much at home, bounding out to meet me with tongs gripping an idiotic little ass shoe in his hands, and saluting me like a brass-horned gramophone.

He is over forty and under sixty, smokes a Woodbine, wears a hard hat with a very frayed brim (headgear that would provoke the derision of small boys in any of the other three provinces of Ireland). When I blow my nose he companionably blows his in a dirty handkerchief. This blacksmith, in a word, is a civilised modern of the English Pale, who dwells within sight of the glare of Dublin lights. I state my errand and give particulars of the ailing beast.

"But isn't this a Wednesday? The days are Thursday, Sunday, and Tuesday," observes the blacksmith, having agreed to help me.

I gasp and splutter incomprehensibly. Rarely have I been so confounded.

"Are you a Catholic man?" This question is put to me with a show of sternness.

"I am, but what has that to do with it?" I answer, now collected and showing some indignation. The man under the awful hat seemed at a loss for a reply. Then he brought out, "Well, a Protestant cannot use it. You see, for one thing he couldn't bless himself, and you must make the Sign of the Cross when you are rubbing it on."

After a few more remarks, the bright man (bright he is and really rather pleasant) makes off to the rear of his house to prepare the stuff.

I remain in the forge. A gawkish boy is hanging around waiting for his ass to be shod.

"Did you ever try this cure?" I venture.

"Oh yes, we did."

"Did it do any good?"

"Oh yes. It was a pig we had; couldn't stir a bit of himself and he was cured by one bottle."

"And did he ever get bad again?"

"Oh no, there was never a sign on him after."

Then a long pause. The foolish-looking boy was not helpful.

"Do many people come here?"

"Oh, they're always coming."

"What does he put into it, I wonder?"

"Oh, he'd think bad of telling that to anyone."

At this deadlock, the subject of our conversation emerged from his cottage with a little bottle.

"This is it," he says impressively. "Draw this out"—indicating the cork (oh, wondrous ritual!)—"when you get home. Sprinkle a little of the cure on your hand, take off your hat, and rub the cure on her foremost leg against the hair, saying, *In-the-name - of - the - Father - and - of - the - Son - and - of the-Holy-Ghost*, then on her other leg, then on her back legs, saying, *In-the-name-of-the-Father*, every time, then along her back, and across her shoulders, and you'll make the Cross on her then, and pour a little in her ears. If you have any left over, don't keep it, because it is no use except on the day it is made, but pour it away in some place where nothing goes near, like an old ditch. Come yourself or send someone tomorrow and I'll give you another bottle, come again then on Friday and I'll give you the last one. She won't be cured with this bottle; it takes the three."

Amazed beyond measure, I thank him and hesitantly mention payment.

"Oh, I'm only too pleased to help you and I wish that your beast was better."

Nothing would persuade him to name a sum of money as payment, he would leave that to myself. I know what this usually means, and the formula irritated me. I proffered a florin. He took it with every outward sign of gratitude, but with a disappointed look at the back of his eye. Finally, with great and very un-Pale-like courtesy, he did the honours of leave-taking. Emphatically, the man is decent and kindly and I'd almost allow him the virtue of sincerity; he seemed to believe in his cure from a religious point of view, if not a medical one.

This glimpse of the primitive leaves me with a stunned feeling as I drive home across bleak bogs. Near my gate I encounter Pat Mangan. He tells me he is on his way to the yard to see my ailing beast. I explain where I have been. Pat smiles broadly and takes a sniff at the mysterious bottle, pronouncing "Turpentine" without hesitation; it is certainly conspicuously present, but appears to be mixed with other ingredients. Pat gets into the car and we drive up to the yard.

"You weren't gone as far as the Cross, sir, when she died." Mick breaks the news.

We make a sorrowful examination of the carcase and say various wise things by way of *post mortem*, before I take the "cure" out of my pocket and place it on a window-sill.

As Pat and I are walking away, I overhear Mick saying to John, who is pulping turnips, "He oughtn't leave it there." The other piously agrees. Resignedly, I go back into the byre and Mick respectfully petitions me to dispose of the unused "cure" in the proper way. Like a fool, I do so, pouring it all away in the grass. Can it be that even I am a little scared by this black magic in religious trappings?

*　　*　　*

After the hoar-frost comes a spell of tunnel weather. All is interminably grey and dank. Daytime is only a little patch like one of those uneconomic holdings that cling to the black walls of mountains in Connemara. Lethargy is induced by these bits of days, mere rectangles of grey wedged in on either side by darkness; one has neither zeal nor energy, not even for apple-tree pruning, which is my favourite winter sport.

Yesterday there were only three leaves on the young crab-tree outside the study window; today there are none. The silence is sepulchral; the year is sunk in sleep. The ploughed land is in a coma; grass is faded a weary yellow.

But I ought not allow grey winter's mood to settle on my limbs and heart. Here by my hand in a jade-coloured bowl are jasmine sprigs in gay star clusters. Through the window, one can glean consolation from the colour splotches on tree trunks. I can see a line of beeches and sycamores spotted in white, olive, and rust, their great round eyes, set in greenish lichen, staring up at the house.

The days are so scrappy, it is hardly worth while tackling any serious outdoor job. By the time the dairy is cleaned up, the eggs graded and packed, and a few letters answered, it is time for dinner. Afterwards I may rouse myself and renew the attack on that shrubbery which I must thin out, or I may make a survey of the men's work. Then comes darkness to scatter my energy.

Drab December, only a time of naked thorns and flowerlessness. The Christian religion dealt a death-blow to this month's individuality by giving it the trump festival. December cannot live down the festive burden of Christ's birthday. For the rest, it is a canvas without paint, though lined, it is true, for the spreading of gorgeous colour when another summer comes.

In the winter one ought to take up the study of astronomy or geology. The modern Irish no longer take kindly to the exact sciences: our winter re-creations consist of discussing greyhounds and the form of our politicians, bemoaning the times, and wistfully describing places as nice in the summer. I know I ought to be making use of these long winter nights learning Irish, or preparing my annual balance-sheet, but I do nothing of the sort. I read a book on pigs; I thump the piano (almost as badly as three years ago when I taught myself to play), and I waste quantities of good paper in an endeavour to evolve a design for a 1916 Memorial. And night steals pleasantly on. Well, God be praised, not only are the longest days not long enough for all I want to do, but the longest nights are all too short for their pleasure's sake.

*   *   *

My greed for more apple-trees shows no sign of abating. I must have at least another statute acre of them. With Joe, I drag a Gunter's chain across the ploughed stubbles that lie next to the present new orchard. Already we have extended the shelter belt: two ranks of grim Sitka spruce thinly inter-spersed with crochet-like *Cupressus Lawsonia* (the latter a nursery surplus at a bargain price). Now we measure for one row of Victoria plums and five rows of apples, with twenty trees in each row, all the trees being eighteen feet apart in the rows, and

63

the rows themselves twenty-one feet apart. The plums are to act as a mild wind-break for the safe-guarding of more precious apples. The plums are to be half-standard and the apples bush. Between every two trees there are to be two black-currant bushes: Boskoop, Edina, and Goliath. All except ten Coxes and ten Worcesters are to be on Type II stock, the exception being budded on Type IX. Fancy this hard-headed heifer-fattening farmer now growing apples on *Jaune de Metz* stock (Type IX), when only a few years ago an apple to him was an apple and nothing more! But the scheme is not so thorough as it may look on paper. Ground fruit does not exist unless I relent and order more than the paltry two thousand strawberries I have already ordered. Yet I cannot see myself furnishing this whole area with strawberries; for one reason, the labour problem is too difficult. I hope to utilise the spaces for plain potatoes, early ones, which will enable me later on to get in celery or Brussels sprouts. And if not plain potatoes, then just plainer mangolds and turnips.

For long the choice of apple varieties wrung my mind before I made a final selection:

On Type II there will be 25 Worcester Pearmains; 25 Laxton's Superb; 15 Newton Wonders; and 15 Charles Ross.

On Type IX I plumped for 10 Cox's Orange Pippins, and 10 Worcester Pearmains.

Seabrook (in his *Modern Fruit Growing*) goes all out for these Worcesters. He commits himself to the extent of declaring that if he were confined to one apple only he would choose this variety.

Although I have placed it on my list, I am never-theless troubled by private fears: Pat Mangan, an amateur grower to say the most, has a Worcester among his dozen trees not half a mile from here, and it produces very small fruit, suggesting that the district is unsuitable.

I have faith in the Laxton's Superb. One reason is that this variety is of noble descent, being related to the superlative Cox; another and a better reason is that their season is said to be from December to March, when apples are dearest and most scarce. I have never seen a Laxton's Superb elsewhere than at the Apple Show.

I have already a nodding acquaintance with Charles Ross, a big handsome chap, easily sold, I think, but dismally slow to come into bearing. Its season is from October to November, which should bridge the gap between the two varieties already mentioned.

In planting Newtons I am acting on the ex-perience I gained in my former planting schemes. Although stated in the books to be a cooking-apple, I have wrapped it in paper and frequently sold it as a dessert apple. The deceit is not so heinous as it might appear: a Newton really has its parts as an edible apple, besides taking on a wonderful gloss with the slightest rubbing, and wearing always an aristocratic air.

If the ten Coxes don't do any good (and likely they won't, as they are temperamental and uncer-tain creatures), they cannot do much harm either. Often in farming matters, one has to be content with such groping.

Perhaps, after all, I am a fussy old fool to give so much thought to the selection of varieties. Should these apples ever arrive in the Dublin fruit market, it is certain that the salesmaster's assistant will flatly introduce them as, "Nice barrel of colours," and the boss will vary the refrain, when addressing the ring of buyers: "How much will you give for the crimsons?"

There is no accounting for taste in apple varieties. Recently I attended a lecture given by the county horticultural instructor in the Tincurragh school-house, which is situated in a remote and boggy district. He concluded his advice on subjects ranging from bees to parsnips with an explanation of the County Committee of Agriculture's half-price scheme for supplying apple-trees to persons under a certain rate valuation. An old man interrupted the speaker: "Begging your pardon, sir, but can you tell me this?" he began, slowly and deliberately. "Will you give the farmers you are talking of there any breed of apple-tree they want?" The instructor guardedly replied that there was a big choice of varieties on the selected list from which to choose. "Well, will you tell me this, now," pursued the old man, "Is *American Mother* on that list?" The quaint name sent a smile travelling round the audience. The instructor consulted his papers and then said he was sorry, but that that variety was not on the list. The old man's face changed. He groped for his ash-plant. "Well, I'll be going," he muttered, more in sorrow than in anger. "I've come a long way, as I live a big distance from these parts." Out he stamped. The instructor looked a trifle crestfallen, but proceeded to take up the interrupted thread of his lecture. As the old man reached the door where I was standing, he caught the lapel of my coat and confided to me in loud undertones: "I had an *American Mother* for twenty-six years until the big wind last January twelve months felled it. It's the best eating apple of the whole blooming lot." And he passed out with his mouth hanging open significantly, and his eyes cast up, as though craving heaven to give these poor inspector fellows a little sense.

*　　*　　*

I seem to pass off as a great wit in Joe's eyes. "Would a knacker take away an ass as well as any other beast?" I asked, putting my second thoughts first, but without any humorous intent. "I suppose he would. But where is the dead ass?" "Oh, there's no dead ass, but if we did away with that stray one, wouldn't there be a dead one then?" Joe exploded into immoderate laughter. The owner of this trespassing beast was up here today with a request for holly. I sourly consented and then added that his donkey has enjoyed free grazing here for several months. I suggested that he should destroy the animal if he didn't want him. "Well, the way it is, sir, we don't want to destroy him, we have him for such a long time." "As far as that goes," I retorted, "I've had him for a long time, too."

There is a second trespasser on my land, even more knavish and pertinacious than the donkey: a

67

stray goat of unknown ownership. Thus I had a twofold object in a drive to Milltown. I wanted to go bail for the sum of £20 for Peter Murray, and I wanted to abandon the goat somewhere. Jimmy effects the capture of the billy at the cost of two full-length sprawls and a torn cap. He had tried to blindfold it with his cap, but the goat brought its horns into action. To farmers and farm workers a headgear is more often a weapon or an implement than merely headgear. When the goat is securely trussed and put in the rear of the car, I set off. The sun is shining softly and the country-side looking sort of sentimental. I keep my eyes open for a stretch of road suitable for goat abandoning, but for long I look in vain. Every time I decide to stop and unload the billy, vehicles or pedestrians appear in sight. I was becoming desperate when within a mile or so of Milltown, and I braved the risk of witnesses to bump off the goat (not in the strict Chicago sense of course) at a spot where a side road branched. Released from ropes, the pest of Cloonmore ignores all the attractions of this briary side-road and determinedly races off before me along the road to Milltown. I could but hope that the brute lost scent at the bank.

The ever-recurring annoyance of trespassing animals forced me to sit down at my desk and review the whole matter of fencing the avenue, to reduce the attraction of the grass for hungry, roving beasts.

There is no question regarding the choice of posts: these must be of reinforced concrete such as are supplied by the County Council at 2s. 2d. each.

The expense will be great, for I shall require 144 of such posts, together with six straining-posts and a pair of gate-posts, but the permanency and appearance of such a job when finished justify the cost.

The wire or wire-netting to run between the posts requires more serious consideration. The simplest plan would be to have five strands of wire, three of the strands being barbed (or "thorny" as we say here), and two just ordinary galvanised wire, No. 7 gauge. The cost of this wiring would be £2:11:3 for the 450 yards that I propose to fence. Alternatively, eight rolls of bull or hinged-joint fence would amount to £7:4s. This article is described as a heavy general-purpose style of fence, forty-one inches high, and is of course in a square mesh. I imagine that it is really too luxurious for my needs and finance. Then there is a thirty-six-inch hinged-joint fence, which would not reach the required height, but with a strand of barbed wire on top, it should suit admirably. The total price of eight rolls of this latter, plus one hundredweight of barbed wire would be £5:14:2. Finally, I could have an ugly, internment camp sort of fence consisting of all barbed wire, which would cost me £3:17:6.

One thing is certain at least, I must have a top strand of barbed wire: it is most useful in preventing cattle from browsing where they have no business to browse, and it prevents humans from climbing over. The issue then reduces itself to this: shall I have barbed and plain wire only, or barbed and plain wire with the addition of the three-fourths hinged-joint mesh? The former is quite effective, easily strained by ordinary unskilled farm men, and costs £2:11:3; but I must admit that it is at no time handsome, and in winter it is apt to become hung with sheep wool, when it looks like a clothes-line decorated with dirty little rags; moreover, not being of a piece, it may snap a strand, which would be difficult to repair. The second kind, on the other hand, is handsome, effective, and permanent; at any rate it would stand, or fall, or sag, as one piece. In a sense, however, it is almost too effective; it would be impossible to get a dog through it, for example; it would give protection to unwanted grasses and weeds which in summer would engage themselves in the squares and tend to drag down the fence; it costs the large sum of £5:14:2.

Yet I find myself leaning most towards this last style of fence. I weaken on conjuring up a vision of a *Lonicera nitida* hedge. With the square-wire fence I could safely dab down cuttings of this shrub from time to time, whereas with the plain and barbed-wire fence, I never could do so. Brave little Lonicera, stiff and green when most vegetation is quivering and naked, what a protection it would be for one's shins from the entrance gates to the house! So let it be. I will write orders for concrete posts and their accompaniments, square-mesh fencing three-quarters height, and the necessary quantity of plain and barbed wire. Thus I commit myself to great expense. My bank balance will sink, but I shall protect my grazing from strays off the highways, and purchase peace and a Lonicera hedge.

This evening I drove away from Cloonmore through Cranagh, and over a switchback road on an errand to a friend's house, all in a winter twilight. Lest I have too roundly abused December, then, let me praise its twilights. Holy spirits roam in them; their colour is blue, a smoky, all-enveloping blue. It is an ideal time of year and day for lovely dying—to melt away into a blue mantle (well if it be Mary's). This evening, there was a stillness abroad, the flitting of little feathered creatures, wrens or robins, and the red-gold of paraffin lamps filling square window-panes added warmth to the scene. The white of cottages took on a blue tone, the brown hedgerows and the stripped trees looked blue also. It was the sort of evening that a mouse would visit a mouse. Scarcely twenty yards away from my front gate, I found a family of tinkers encamped; their fire sent up a column of feathery smoke into a lowering, wintry sky. Further on, a steam-roller was all strung up in the misty beauty of the evening, as though a hippopotamus wore a wreath of roses. How soft became the outlines of rough passers-by: there walked a woman in gauzy veils, and a turf man made woolly and gentle, all plastic and strange in this enfolding December blue.

Beyond the smoke of Cranagh chimneys, greater glories were reached: the moon sailed out and the stars divided the empire of the moonlit sky as I travelled the straight roads. So powerful was the moonlight that a tin roof at the end of a two-and-a-half-mile stretch of unswerving road looked like a brilliant light. The roads themselves were so

71

dazzling that the moonmen must have thought they were the canals that we also think we can perceive on the surface of the moon. The world was all blue and silver like "Love in Venice" pictures (still or motion), or like that landscape described in Walter de la Mare's poem. A path to heaven—or else I am a clod. Little better am I anyhow, though the blue of a December evening can strangely rouse me from clod-dom. All that I might have been in the past: idealistic, romantic, sensitive, poetry-loving, pure of heart maybe, and spiritual, can rise up out of a foggy December twilight and in a thrice fling me off the rung of my age, snatch me from greed and concupiscence, and leave me shorn of vanity.

*　　*　　*

But for Cobbett's *Rural Rides* and *Advice to Young Men*, Darwin's *Voyage of the Beagle*, and Joseph Joubert's *Thoughts*, the long winter nights would be too long by streets.

For an evening's whoopee, commend me to William Cobbett. My feet on the mantelpiece are never so much my feet on the mantelpiece as when I am deep in Cobbett. I puff tobacco smoke at him and chuckle away hours in his company. I like his passion; I like his frank egotism; he uses his "I" without mock diffidence (it sticks out of the pages as prominently as a wireless-pole over a house), I like his venomous hates and rowdy detestations. His enthusiasm is infectious. He rides in Suffolk and he sees a flock of sheep: they are "the best I have ever laid eyes on"; and in Kent he will come on a view of down and woods which "pleases me mightily," and again it will be the "the finest view I have ever seen." Yet in Wiltshire another time, he will see "the finest view I have ever seen." How happy I would be if I could emulate him: ride a horse through Ireland, harangue farmers, chastise foreign exploiters, terrorise financiers with a torrent of invective, foster healthy discontents and seditious ideas in the breasts of the downtrodden and unorganised rural workers, shout at humbugs, and heap scorn on the army of governmental inspectors.

What a loss to Ireland was Cobbett's English birth! Could we but have exchanged prisoners of war in the long struggle between the two nations, how gladly we would have swapped Thomas Moore for William Cobbett, aye and thrown Richard Sheridan into the bargain. If England had offered us their William Blake, how promptly would we have sent them Oscar Wilde. And as for Orage, we would joyously part with all our political economists in order to claim him. For Chesterton, we would give a chain-gang: my selection would be George Moore, James Joyce, Oliver Gogarty, and even our Æ.

Once again I sip Joubert and once again I am amazed at his obscurity in the world of letters; he is apparently known only to Matthew Arnold (in his *Essays in Criticism*), to the translator Katherine Lyttelton, to Mrs. Humphry Ward (who wrote a preface to the *Thoughts*), and to myself. Yet Joseph Joubert increased the light of the world, he had

73

extraordinary penetration and a lofty spirituality. His *Thoughts* are a distillation of Gallic wisdom, with point, with finesse, with delicious aroma. Dear forgotten Joubert, who says that, in giving light, he burns himself away. Yet in what great cause, and how lightsome is the light!

It gave me no great pleasure this morning to hear birds singing as blithely as they sing in February. It is time enough for singing (and the aches I get on hearing bird songs). This is a time of mourning. Summer is dead, and the birds should wear decent crape and hold their little tongues.

CHAPTER IV

WINTER IS EITHER SICK OR FOXING; ANY-
way there is an unwonted mellowness
abroad, making a contrast with the usual
boisterousness and the everyday greyness. I pruned
apple-trees in the old garden, to the sound of the
birds' twittering, and the ring of Joe's spade near
by. So ragged were the clouds that the sky was
like a briar-torn fleece. For flowers, I could see
only a single half-opened dandelion, with a tear-
stained face, peeping out from a tussock of dreary
cocksfoot grass.

High up on a shaky ladder, or swaying from the
branches of the trees themselves, I feel master of
life and death. I can spare, or I can destroy. I can
condescend to tolerations. Snip-snap, and there
goes a mahogany-tinted shoot which would have
borne glossy ovate leaves; snip again, and there
falls a spur which would have had its pied blossom,
and maybe its fat fruit. Can this be dreaded
January? From my ladder perch I hear the cattle
bawling outside the yard gate, and the grating
noise of Jimmy scraping the dropping-boards in
the poultry houses, accompanying his work with
discordant bellowing. "All my dreams," he begins,
then he hums for want of words, and lamely finishes
with, "my heart for you."

There are sounds of industry from the pulper
house, and a thin trail of smoke rising from the

boiler-house chimney tells of pig feeds being prepared. Thoughts race in little mills, their beginnings ending at their starting-posts: if I had three acres of apple-trees and each tree produced five hundredweight of fruit, and if I got an average of 1s. 6d. per stone for them, how much . . . This is the chief thought chasing through the mill, varied, altered, modified, and repeated; interrupted by my own exclamations of annoyance on discovering clumps of lichen which escaped last season's tar-oil spray, cankerous growths, signs of rottenness within. There is the sheen of bright green ivy from the dull white walls. "Did Fred Carter get to set his land yet?" I holler to the digging Joe in the vernacular best understood by him. There follows a shouted conversation about the progress of Hanna's cow, now suffering from a hæmorrhage, rumours of the Land Commission intending to divide local farms, diseases of apple-trees, until the vocal strain leaves me too hoarse to pursue the discussions. Reaching out to the utmost, almost over-reaching, then a spiteful snip-snap, and another strong shoot falls, mortally wounded, to the ground.

I make a dead set on a standard Blenheim Orange. It is so badly diseased that no method of cure could be too drastic. It suffers from scab, canker, galls, and every other ailment that the apple is heir to. So I hoist myself into its middle and ruthlessly saw off limb after limb. That will show it who is boss here! When ringing time comes (that is, while there is blossom on the tree), I intend operating. If bark-ringing does not do it any good, it cannot do it any harm. Of course, I could act still more drastically, reduce the tree to three or four stumps, and these I could top-graft later on. "The only way in which the possessor of an old orchard of undesirable or unknown varieties can modernise his trees is by top-grafting," says the book of words, but I have not the moral courage to follow these instructions. After all, I have only three Blenheims, and it is a fine apple: good flavour, hard and sound. I prefer to give this tree one more chance of life. I love all these old trees, though I do not know their life history, and perhaps half of them are chronic ne'er-do-wells.

I dote on this pruning of apple-trees. From the old garden I proceeded to the front of the house, where I cut the offensive branches off trees that I planted on first coming to Cloonmore. A tennis lawn was sacrificed in that planting, but a fig for sport compared with apples! As I pruned, I eyed the trees and summed up their lines as though I were a Slade student painting them, instead of a farmer pottering about with a saw and sécateurs, for the grace of a tree is a tremendously serious thing to me.

So many creatures are happy on days like these: the ewes wax big with lamb, contentment in their slit-grey eyes; a pair of grunting sows proudly lead out their families, nineteen in combination, and they roll themselves in a dump of turf mould. In the drawing-room, the first chicks bask in the shafts of sun barring the floor. Calves cease their complaining at the gates while the sun bathes the lawn. Birds are blithesome and almost merry in the lush midday hours.

It is a glorious and exceptional day flung down from heaven like a hard gold sovereign, ringing, shining, metallic. I get a craving to sit on the grass, but I pull myself together; anyway I value grass sitting too highly to anticipate the pleasure. Come May for lovely grass sitting! I feel that when the time comes I shall write poems, or make cowslip balls (except that cowslips don't grow in Cloonmore, the land is too good!), or turn somersaults, for with all my thirty years, I have only a threadhold on the proprieties.

*   *   *

Cloonmore this evening is like a familiar face shorn of its moustache. The great Weymouth pine of the front lawn is down. From two o'clock this afternoon until dark descended Mick and Joe swore fit to blast rocks over it, anon cursing the tree, then the cross-cut, or the exudations of resin that clogged up the saw's action. The tree was a noble giant, but showed signs of decay in its riggings; curiously enough, the trunk does not appear in the least dosed. The sawdust is sticky and sweet-smelling. When the tree crashed down there rose up an aroma which inspired Joe to exaggerate the disinfectant virtues of pine (a burnt faggot kept under the bed will ward off flu, says he). This jerks my memory into a trot from present workaday farming to the gaudy past of university lectures, and I hold forth on resins and turpentine for the men's benefit. I view the vacancy among the trees from several angles, and find that I have no regrets. Although the felled pine was mighty and mast-like, it is not badly missed; its touselled head was always a little sere and lichen-clad; moreover, I have two other Weymouth pines for consolation. Supplies of excellent timber for planks and for dray-making, as well as a great stock of odoriferous firewood, are the result of the half-day's labours.

There were wonderful splashes of gold and deep blue in the sky as I closed the hen-houses on the last round before tea. The sun was sinking quickly, but bequeathed deep-dyed colours as its heritage. The earth seemed a very fair place in which to dwell; one could drink a love potion even from a wintry evening.

The two-hundred-egg incubator having been started three nights ago, and the temperature now being steady, I begin filling up the egg-tray. Mrs. Meehan attends the launching of the good work with a tea-cup of holy water, which she lavishly sprinkles over the apparatus, thus causing "Duggie" Sparrow's prominent eyes to bulge a little further out of his head.

It was Mrs. Sullivan who put me on to Douglas Sparrow. (I may call him "Duggie," he informed me with a pale smile.) He had been recommended to her by the Oaklands Poultry Farm, where she had been lately buying an expensive and be-medalled breeding cock. She had no immediate use for the little Englishman down on his luck, but she did not wish to lose sight of him, and promised to take him off my hands in a fortnight. Meanwhile, I am giving him a temporary job as poultry assistant at a pittance of 10s. a week, with bed and board, the former being in the attic, next door to Jimmy.

The new assistant and myself cannot be said to be congenial spirits, but as he is supposed to be a poultry expert he ought to take some of the petty jobs off my hands.

Duggie is a pathetic little chap. From his own story he must be now in the fifties, though he does not look so old. Before the War he was a Post Office clerk in Cardiff, and he described to me with a surprising amount of emotion that deadly occupation, its ghastly routine, its monotony, and the feeling it induced of serving a life's sentence. Then the War came, a Peace for Duggie. He joined up as an army telegraphic official. He told me of the joy he felt at first in his new work, of the sacrifices and heroism he witnessed, the misery and suffering, the Christian lives of some of the soldiers, and the lives of sin and blasphemy lived by others. Though tackled to a telegraphic instrument he observed the ways of men and the ways of God with men. As he ticked off codes he was thinking out human problems; and as he read official communiques he was recalling Biblical consolations; he was knotting red tape and unknotting human mysteries; he was living for the first time. Demobilised when the War was over, he found that he could not endure to return to his former job, so he took up poultry, like so many other ill-advised ex-soldiers. After a couple of months spent in intensive theoretical study, he plunged all his carefully garnered capital and started out for himself. Despite his expert knowledge, however, he failed to make a success of his farm. He had to sell off later on for considerably less than he had invested, and since then he has been drifting from job to job. It is an old story. There are almost as many graves of wrecked poultry farms as of dead soldiers; in fact, the blasted hope of a poultry farm is almost a symbol of post-War rural England.

In practice I find that Sparrow is positively hampered by his poultry knowledge. He has a great head, but he is a poor hand at work. Thus he knows all about the physiology of a hen, but seemingly nothing about plucking one (Mrs. Meehan's face was a study when confronted with his finished article!) He knows the whole theory of hygiene, but nothing about scraping a roosting-board in an expeditious way. Fowl seem to be to him what the Phœnicians might be to a classical student: something as abstract and as remote from the world of real affairs as astronomy might be. He has a bundle of diplomas and certificates for poultry knowledge, yet he catches a hen with the greatest awkwardness, and holds it gingerly with a look of helplessness in his eye.

Sparrow is cruelly well named. He has a large head, with a great dome forehead, above a miserable little body. When he wears a canary-coloured cardigan, which seems to be his favourite style, I cannot pass him at his work without suppressing a grin, and as for the rude Jimmy, he gets "the stitches" far too often. Sparrow's movements are bird-like jerks, he has bird-like legs, and he almost seems to chirrup like a bird. His mild and humourless eyes stare at me reproachfully if I speak tersely or make a frivolous or cynical remark. He strongly recalls H. G. Wells' "Moon-man," with his monstrous head and his little insignificant body. The other day this odd man told me solemnly that he "had, through his deep study of biology, come to the conclusion that sexual attraction, mating, and fecundity were enormous factors in animal and human life!" He told me within an hour of his arrival here that he feels at home everywhere there are Plymouth Brethren. As I am positive there are none within at least thirty miles of Cloonmore, I do not think he will feel as much at home here as he hopes. He is an amazingly religious man; for solid virtue his equal would be hard to find in Catholic Ireland. He dropped the information the other day (simply, and without a thought of boasting) that he had never been inside a theatre, or a cinema, and that he had never read a novel. Strange paradox, that a man can contain so much goodness and yet quite lack the glow of spirituality, as we define the word. He spends his evening leisure over the *Confessions of St. Augustine*, a fat blue pencil in his hand, reading slowly, and so sunk in his armchair that from my desk I can see only feet, large ones too considering the size of the man.

He is the despair of Mrs. Meehan, whose motherly concern about him knows no bounds. "Sure, you could blow him off your hand," she says. She is bent on fattening him up. As he was suffering from a slight cold when he came here, she suggested a good glass of strong punch before going to bed. My back was turned to the pair when the good woman proposed this common Irish cure, but I could feel the shock to Duggie's soul. "Or a hot sherry and egg flip?" I put in for devilment. He smiled wanly, but how he inwardly squirmed at the mere mention of alcohol!

Sparrow, according to Mrs. Sullivan's information, is a fairly efficient carpenter. I am to get him material for making a double breeding pen-house with a capacity for twenty-five birds, which will later serve as a brood-house for chicks. He told me that he already made just such a house for the Oaklands Poultry people, so that he could knock up another one for me without delay. Besides this constructive work, Sparrow is to look after the first batch of chicks, attend the incubators, and collect and grade all the breeding-pen eggs.

Beyond what he knows about the care of poultry, it seems that farms are largely foreign territory to Sparrow. Things are different in England, apparently, where a man could spend his lifetime at poultry-keeping and visiting brother poultry-keepers without learning anything about general farming, or work on the land. When I was showing Duggie over the place on his first day here, I brought him into a loose box containing a cow that had calved the night before; the calf was on its reedy legs, suckling. Duggie gazed so intently and solemnly that I expected some valuable pronouncement on the merits of the cow; instead of which, he naïvely volunteered that they used to have something like that at home long ago—in china on the mantelpiece! I was tempted to send a note over to the Sullivans thanking them for the live specimen

Englishman duly received in good condition, and now undergoing tests and analyses.

* * *

"Cool times!" jerked a grizzly, bleary cattle-drover, proving that the Irishman is still the greatest satirist, the greatest optimist, and the greatest poet that the sun spies out. For an icy wind whined and a rain spattered and a coldness caught the earth by the throttle, freezing its very plucks and lights, and numbing its innermost plasm.

Truly Ballinvally ought to be erased from the earth; it is a splotch on the map like a tear on a letter; it is the missing link between the Glacial and the De Valeran age; it is as snug as the harp that hung solitary on the deserted walls of ruined Tara; it is as smiling as a Weeping Erin. No need to look far for explanations of its bleakness: the canal lock is at least twenty feet above the street level. Beyond this wind-path, this canal, there is a railway which is another cutting for the harsh winds to blow through, a track for blasts, a permanent way for frigid evils. Ballinvally is scourged and whipped by every wind from west to east, by every fat-cheeked rogue that cares to puff: it is the blow-ball of Boreas, the fluff of Notus, the dead leaf of Eurus, the feather of Favonius, Argestës' fag, the butt of Corus; and the tea-cup of the proverbial storm.

"One crack of the whip! Give me your price in a word." Calves bleak and watery-eyed, nibbling hay from a crib; bullocks bent before the wind; intense cold. Men with blue faces; dealers going about with the air of gods, wearing lawn coats and carrying umbrellas instead of the common ash-plant. There is a bunch of three-year-old bullocks being driven to the railway bank for shipment, steam rising from them, their heads lowered.

A train hisses past us. "Make me an offer. What will you give in a word?" The crack of a stick on a beast.

The wind singing in the wires overhead; cattle rising on one another; men reeling in the wind down the street; a cow lowing for her calf that had just been sold. "What's between ye, men?" some-one shouts. The sky is scudding; there is a flooded field shining down the road. "Nothing, Paddy, only love," the seller retorts, by which he means, "Don't you butt in on what doesn't concern you."

Two farmers, neighbours and friends of mine, get their teeth into a seller of calves. The bargain-ing goes on for hours. How they love the battle, how they glory in giving and receiving darts, how they linger in this delicious warfare. I listen for a while. I leave them. I come back and listen once more. Two calves are the subject of the barter, £10 asked for the two and £7:10s. offered. I go off to purchase a few things at the chief shop and to in-spect a second-hand chaff-cutter advertised in the local paper as for sale here. After this I return to the fair and get into grips with a dealer in ring calves, and without much wrangling I buy a red heifer from him for £4:5s.

On my return to my friends, I find things are more or less as they were: two calves, £9 asked and £8 offered. "Couldn't ye make a divide?" I chip in, but my kindly interference is unheeded by the intent bargainers. I go away and transact business at the bank. I return to find the same two calves, £9 asked and £8 and a half-crown offered. I go to the other side of the canal bridge, hoping to meet Peter Mangan and suggest to him that he might drive home my calf if he has made any purchases himself. When I come back, I find the same two calves, the same tireless children, £9 still doggedly asked, and £8 : 5s. offered. Once more I go off to the bank and to the shop. Here I encounter Matt Sullivan and bring him to view the chaff-cutter, which he contumeliously rejects as hopeless, thus flooring the man who had expected to sell it to me. After this interlude, I return to the two calves now surrounded by three grumbling men: one of whom took too little when he accepted £9, and the others who gave too much when they tendered £9. A pub swallows them up for the completion of the business. One of the buyers pressed me to join them, but I excused myself firmly under the pretext that I had to go to the station.

Is there any spot more unlovely than an Irish country railway station? In winter there is none so gloomy, cold, and sepulchral. Here is existence dragged out beyond its time of usefulness; like man, the railway system seems to be limited to the accustomed span. At this stage, Ballinvally station is a nonagenarian, too old by a score. It is in a senility of neglect, dirt, squalor and dribbling dotage, left disregarded and friendless. The ravages of the years are unrepaired and the guardians of the old public servant are stony-

86

hearted; they will not supply even a rouge pot. They allow the miserable ancient to decay under one's eyes in its lampless old age. By means of lights, paint, and the making of some repairs, the doddering old place might recover a great measure of its former glamour, but that is not the Company's policy. Perhaps the adage, *Easy come, easy go*, applies to this position with a little twisting; perhaps inventions tumbled out too quickly in the current hundred years; breathe it not, but perhaps the Gael and mechanisation are really inimical.

It is two o'clock: nine until two in order to purchase one calf, to feel the pulse of my feverish bank book, to make a few purchases in the shop, to make a fruitless call at the station which only inspired pessimism, and to get starved with hunger and chilled to the bone.

Half a mile outside Ballinvally I am hailed by a man who wants a lift. I oblige him and find I have for companion an old cattle-dealer. According to his own account, he has been in the cattle-buying business for thirty-five years. Like most cattle men, and indeed farmers in general, the period he chooses to dilate upon is that affluent era comprising the last two years of the European War and the year following the War. How often have I heard the story! This fellow's eyes gleam hungrily when he tells me of the prices ruling in that golden epoch. I utter exclamations and say *Tut-tut* and *Phew* all at the right places (for I begin to notice that my companion is just drunk enough to need humouring), and I incredulously repeat the prices he so exultantly details: "£56 for a cow! You don't mean it!" and "If I were offered £90 for two unfinished bullocks, I'd go and see a doctor about my ears!" (Duggie is having the effect of Anglicizing my idea of the humorous.)

The first public-house we passed, my companion said almost in a whisper and making a slight motion with his thumb, "Would you care for a drink?" I thanked him, but declined. He was sad and silent for a while. Approaching the next pub, which is outside Cloonlara village, he made another effort: would I care for a mineral? Again I answer, No, but seeing the misery in his red eyes, I suggest that I could let him down. . . . "Oh no, oh no, oh no, not at all!" he protests. No, he would not desert me; he would not drink alone; we stand or fall together. That is his code and, drink-fuddled as he is, he lives up to it. He is decent after his own queer lights.

But the gods favour his thirst. A hundred yards or so outside Cloonlara we get a puncture. At first my friend is all for helping me, but I persuade him to take things easy; that changing a wheel is a one-man job. He looked on at my labours for a minute, then glanced towards Cloonlara. I was expecting the announcement that came: "I think I'll go back there and see an old woman who used to be great with my mother, God forgive her! Maybe if you're here when I get back, you'll take me the rest of the way?" I warmly agree and off he goes in good humour. I suppose it is part of my code to honour such an agreement, though it was very doubtfully binding. Thus, when the punctured wheel was changed for the spare, the latter inflated, and all the tools stowed away, I drew out a cigarette and strove to forget the pangs of hunger while I abided in patience the return of my companion.

To give him his due, he did not delay long in Cloonlara, but as soon as he appeared around the corner I knew that the old woman was dead and that he who was to have called on her for old time's sake had drowned his sorrow! I opened the door for him, fixed him in the seat, tucked his frieze coat out of the way of the gear lever, and we drove off in silence. I asked him no questions, but of his own accord he suddenly leaped the barrier: "I had a few drinks at Ryan's and the boy in the shop told me that me mother's friend is dead this many a year. I'm a foolish man, anyway." He repeated this last over and over again to himself. Then he suddenly gave a roar: "Do you know what it is, young man?" grinding the point of his ash-plant into the rubber mat at his feet. "Do you know what it is? A man would be better off if he never took a drink." Having rid himself of much maudlin remorse, he changed his key and was talking sensibly and coherently enough before we reached the parting of our ways (he was to meet a man at Derry cross, who would drive him to catch the train in Milltown). He discussed with disarming frankness the whole matter of the drink craze as it hit him, clearly gaining relief in finding a confidant. He spoke of his temptations caused by a hard life: attending fairs either as buyer or seller five days out of every week, standing drinks and being stood drinks, for from the custom there is no escape. He was a single man, and all his non-drinking days were lonely. He told me his story in a thick, halting voice, and with the face of a man living in a bad dream.

Grateful for the lift, as we approached Derry cross, he began to cast about in his mind for some means of expressing his gratitude. Finally, with the air of having received sudden illumination, he told me impressively that he knew a sure cure for piles. He said he would give me the formula if I wrote it down. I demurred somewhat, but it was no use. He insisted that it was a positive cure and ought not to be declined! So before he alighted I took my pen and gravely wrote out the formula at his dictation, while he peered over my shoulder to make sure I wrote correctly, and he continued to impress on me all the while the value of his gift, which read:

1 teaspoon of (tinc.) "Golden Seal."
4 drops of (tinc.) Witch-hazel.
Mix with 7 oz. Water.
Dose: 1 dessert-spoon six times daily.

*   *   *

Returning up the avenue, I meet some tinker children coming disconsolately from the house, where probably they had been vainly knocking. They are not interested in me. "What do you want?" I ask. "We want to see the lady of the house," they tell me. "Well, I'm the lady of this house."

Sadly I thought of their innocent query next morning when I awoke and found myself the victim of a smothering cold, for a sick bachelor is a sorry object. I felt as if I were under mountains of feather mattresses. My legs ached. My spine felt spongy. My ears pained for their singing. My eyelids weighed my head down, and only occasionally could I breathe through my nose.

Mrs. Meehan discovers my absence from breakfast. She brings me tea and toast; she hectors me and, short of taking away my trousers, she does everything possible to make me consent to stay in bed for the day. Well, I reflect, the skies lately opened and dropped Duggie Sparrow into my lap, so I may as well make use of the gift. He can surely do duty for me for at least one day. I send for him and instruct him on how to run a farm for twelve hours in the master's absence. The biggest item of the day is to tie in for stall-feeding two heifers which have been already marked out, and I inwardly pray that he will supervise this job carefully: beasts tied in for the first time are liable to strangle themselves. When he is gone I lie back and contemplate the cracks in the ceiling, feeling sorry for myself and beginning to doubt my self-sufficiency to entertain myself for the day. Mrs. Meehan is a woman of parts, no doubt, but . . .

Well, "but" the devil! I fling myself into Burton's *Anatomy of Melancholy*. Only for Burton, all would have been a cold, dry distemper. Without his good company an evil humour would have engendered in my body; perhaps my heart and liver would have gone hot, my brain moist, and my belly cold. It was Robert Burton who wooed me from the megrims by his drollery, and led me smilingly through a severe cold without unbearable boredom, and this despite the fact that the age of thirty is assigned by him as the age most prone to melancholy. For a desert island, for prison, for a long illness, commend me to Burton's *Anatomy*.

By and by Duggie comes creeping up (if there were much more of that creeping business, I'd get panic-stricken and send for the priest). He tells me that a woman has come to the yard looking for bonhams ("little pigs," he says. The English language has many excellent points, but no word for a pig which is neither a suckling nor a store). I am deep in Burton and, before settling the matter of the woman's need, I perversely insist on reading out a passage to Duggie: it was not a particularly ungodly extract, but Duggie goggled at me in misery, as well as grief at my delay in telling him how to sell a bonham to a woman (obviously, there are two methods of conducting a bargain, one for males and the other for females). He departs looking perplexed at what the lord of the bed enjoins: "Ask 25s. Don't let her have two hogs, if it's a pair she wants. And don't take less than 19s." Then, when he is half-way along the corridor, I yell after him: "Sixpence luck for each bonham! And next time you come up, bring me the newspapers."

It was much later in the day that I began to wonder what transpired between the Englishman and the Irishwoman who strove to make a bargain. All I know is that there was no sale. Duggie gave me no details. Nothing would induce him to get talkative on the matter, or to appease my curiosity. No sale: I suppose the honest fellow stuck to his guns and would not budge from 25s. I'd give the best part of the 25s. to know what really happened.

I wonder did Duggie go scooting all over the slippery floor in pursuit of fleet bonhams? Did the prospective buyer come out with the invariable, "Ah, sure they're very small," to which the time-honoured response is, "Ah, sure the price is small too." Did Duggie catch a pair and hold a hind leg of each in either hand, saying with the correct degree of impressiveness, as he looked the buyer full in the face, "Sure, they'd plough for you, Ma'am!" Somehow I feel he didn't!

Laddie is to me abed what the old night-watchman used to be to sleeping citizens. For the night-watchman's "Seven o'clock and all well!" Laddie goes into a fit of barking to mark the arrival of John at the dairy door for the milk buckets. At 8, Laddie chimes up again to notify that Joe and Mick have arrived and that John is bringing out the separated milk from the dairy. At 8.45, ever-vigilant, he announces the return of John from his breakfast. At 10, his barking has a nasty tone, and that must be the postman (whom he detests: all dogs hate men in uniform) coming to the front door. At 10.30, his renewed outburst of yelping tells me that the cows and calves are being driven out from the yard for the day. But he reserves his most prolonged and furious paroxysm for the dinner hour, when the men go down to the kitchen to get hot water for their tea cans ("Think of these fellows coming into our kitchen!" he seems to snort). Mrs. Meehan usually grasps him at this juncture and hauls him by the scruff of the neck into the dairy, where he is imprisoned for a while. Being human, she enjoys a

93

gossip, and she could not hear a word of the news with his incessant yelping, which he varies by angry dives at the men's boots.

After dinner Laddie continues to enliven the day from his post of observation on the front steps, allowing no caller to pass unchallenged. He is a stickler for social grades, snobbishly tolerating motorists, growling at cyclists, and barking at pedestrians. When a poor man of the roads comes up for "a little help," Laddie has to be either locked up, or threatened with a stick, so savage does he become. He gets beside himself with rage at the mere sight of raggedness.

Duggie brings up the post and papers, reports progress on his hen-house, asks where he could find some Jeyes' Fluid, glances nervously at Burton (possibly the very word *Anatomy* is taboo to the hyper-sensitive Duggie), and leaves hurriedly before I can fling another extract at him.

Possibly my temperature *was* normal, my pulse regular, my cough not of a fatal character, but that was before I unfolded one of the newspapers. Now things are different. *The Irish* —— makes me sick, almost literally sick. Ireland is celebrating a national centenary of the first importance, and what must my precious paper do during this week of commemorating but fill its dirty craw with praise of its own circulation. Its flea-bitten front page is an ugly gash of self-adulation: its ribs and hind-quarters, its liver and bile ducts are bursting with swanking ooze. The mean, pettifogging, bum-sucking fish-wrap; the slimy, dribbling, dish-licker; the thumb-sucking tell-tale; the nasty, snobby, venomous vermin bait; the caterwauling sneak! So much for this daily paper. I'll read it no more! Aye, and I am not quoting Burton: I out-quote him; mine is tinker's parlance.

The long grey day, attended by painful coughing, fits of sneezing and, on the whole, horrible boredom, was mercifully illuminated towards its end by a visit from Tom and Sheila Egan. Mrs. Meehan showed them up and they sat on the cold corners of my bed for over an hour. They were very nice and exceedingly sympathetic. Tom, who shares in most details Tony Donovan's contemptuous views on country life, evidently felt genuinely sorry for me. "Fancy being sick up an avenue of that length!" he seemed to say, as he gazed dolefully out the window. He went so far as to suggest a game of cut-throat bridge to while away the time, but I wiggled out of the suggested entertainment; even though sick, life is still too short to waste on bridge.

Duggie Sparrow is good enough to sit for a few hours with me at night. He stares hard into the fire, but his stare is not vacant. He does not smoke, nor even put his hands into his pockets, so good and earnest is he. He asks me many questions about Ireland and the national struggle, which I find hard to answer. It is so long since Boswell worried about the freedom of Corsica, or Lord Byron about that of Greece and since then Englishmen have mostly forgotten that oppressed nations yearn for freedom from their bonds. It seems Duggie got talking with the men in the workshop after their dinner today, and in fifteen minutes he heard more about the 1916 Rising than he had heard in the whole course of his life before. Mick showed him a copy of Pearse's last letter to his mother (he keeps the cutting in his watch-case); it is a document that would wring tears from a stone. The original is now in the NationalMuseum. Apparently it had a startling effect on Duggie.

"Who was Pearse?" asks the earnest Plymouth Brother at his most earnest.

And I am at a complete loss how to answer!

How can one explain Pearse to a citizen of the British Empire—the Empire upon which the sun never sets; to a member of a proud imperial race that has never in the memory of man suffered defeat? There was Kosciusko of Poland, General Paoli of Corsica, William Tell of Bavaria, Washington of America, but who of England? Our noble Padraic Pearse, who deliberately gave up his life in order to rouse a nation, who took up arms almost single-handed against the British Empire; the poet Pearse, the cultured, gentle, idealistic Pearse, dying for a heedless country that was settling down to profiteer out of the War: Pearse, the heroic. How can one topple out the contents of a full heart into an Englishman's lap?

So I answer off-handedly from the bed: "Pearse? Oh, he was the whole doings!"

*   *   *

These last two days timbal music has been coming from the garden, John making short strokes with the pump-handle, while Joe moves under the trees, directing the spraying lance, his eyes blinking. There are tricks to be learned in spraying, such as attaining that distance from the tree to be sprayed which will give maximum results, and also making use of the slightest wind inclinations. Our present spraying outfit is only a poor thing of low pressure and limited reach but, as the days are almost windless, I hope for good results.

I am summoned from the spraying by Jimmy, who tells me that the Poultry Instructress wants to see me. Reluctantly I hand back the lance to Joe. The instructress has come to pick out birds for breeding-pens. I rout Duggie from the workshop, where he is rooting for three-inch nails for which he has a mania, and request his help in singling out birds. He grumbles a little, but follows me.

The girl awaiting us is tall, handsome, and shy, with eyes evergreen in colour like a December shrubbery, clear glowing skin unspoiled by cosmetics, a brilliant smile, and an attractive way of stooping as she passes into the hen houses. Even Duggie (who seems to walk in fear and trembling of the gentler sex) is not too embarrassed in her company. She comes from Donegal: all the bright people on the loose in the midlands always seem to come from the maritime counties; there are more brains in one square yard of any sea-bordered county than in a square mile of the central plains (because there is less intermingling of English blood in the maritime counties, as I explain to poor Duggie afterwards). We set to work at once on the Wyandotte pullets: Duggie sprawls about the straw catching the required birds; the nice girl handles them, explaining to us how it is necessary to get the full of one's hand here, and the flat of one's hand on some other part; while I put metal rings on the legs of the successful candidates and hand them over to twinkling Jimmy, who bears them away to the run selected as a breeding-pen.

She takes tea with us. Duggie overcomes his nervousness in the sustained warmth of her charm. He discovers that the Poultry Instructress has as much knowledge as himself of such subjects as the composition of dry mashes, sex-linking, Mendelism, and the deuce knows what else besides. At the second cup of tea I find I am fading out of the picture. Then she accepts one of my cigarettes and has a momentary fall from favour in Duggie's eyes. But they go at it again, hammer and tongs: feeding for egg-production, white-eye in Leghorns, roup and bacillary white diarrhœa. Mrs. Meehan then beckons to me from the dining-room door. I excuse myself, though my exit is scarcely noticed so thick has the atmosphere grown with the merits of Sussex Ground Oats, and White Bran as compared with Red Bran.

Mrs. Meehan wants to know if she can go to the pictures in Lowtown (a travelling show of the primitive sort) with Jimmy, and take the kitchen key with her. I have no objection. Incidentally, I am amused at the friendship that is growing up between Jimmy, aged sixteen, and Mrs. Meehan, aged sixty. I am about to return to the tea-table when the housekeeper chuckles as if she has a funny story to impart. Knowing the signs, I encourage her and out she comes with it. Jimmy is the tell-tale and Mr. Sparrow his victim. Jimmy was in the workshop helping Mr. Sparrow before dinner, and at that time the four sides and floor of the new hen-house were leaning against the workshop walls. A few hours later, Jimmy saw Mr. Sparrow bolting the sections together, thus completing the house except for the roof. The next thing was the sound of terrific hauling and shifting. It is alleged that Duggie was striving to drag his fourteen feet by seven feet house from the workshop, through a door three and a half feet wide! After that the prying Jimmy perceived Mr. Sparrow swiftly sundering the sections and hastily putting them where they stood before dinner.

"That's a good one, Duggie!" I shout at the top of my voice, having almost slammed the door in the housekeeper's face. All "our British Poultry Breeds" then under review were scattered squawking to the four winds at my interruption. "You put your hen-house together in the workshop and then couldn't get it out the door!" Duggie turned scarlet, and the instructress smiled prettily . . . but I wonder have I really gained much in the lady's favour?

*　　　*　　　*

This open, cheerful weather is a boon. The ewes are due to yean. Every evening Laddie and I round them off the lawn and steer them up the sod-bridge over the ha-ha that leads to the house lawn, where two barrow-loads of mangolds have been spilt for them; admittedly not good food, because it makes their milk thin, which in turn is apt to scour the lambs, but we can spare nothing else.

The tops and tails of days grow more dulcet with bird song. It is pleasant to stand on a knoll of the lawn in a pool of wan evening sunlight, a fillet of bird song about my bared head: little unmusical birds mostly who are thus vocal and scattered on all far-away sides, yet a rare blithe choir. I hearken with a pipe clenched between my teeth as the ewes file slowly through, Laddie sitting alert and observant beside me, green blades of grass under the bronze trees, gruntings from a hungry sow in the pig field, and the church bell ringing out its summons unheeded—at least by me. Away up stands the tall house, almost poised on its knoll, massive Georgian house, severe, always handsome but by no standard either pretty or charming. Cloonmore House, with the good looks of a serious and moral man over sixty, will now reflect the setting sun-rays in its glass-panelled hall door. How idiotically proud I am of having recaptured this property from English planters!

CHAPTER V

I GUESS I'LL ACQUIT MYSELF FROM MIDNIGHT duty on ewes tonight. What a villainous job it is! That interminable interval during which conscience nags sleep into half wakefulness, then the misery of throwing off the bedclothes and stepping on to the ice-cold floor. Miss Mitford slithers out of the other side of the bed with an unmaidenly bang: she did little to prolong wakefulness last night. The candle is lighted, trousers hitched up; I thrust my feet into socks and dig myself into a dressing-gown. Creeping down to the silent hall, I there add to my attire an overcoat, muffler, hat, wellingtons. Then I collect the flashlight and storm-lamp.

I vault the fence into the house lawn. Overhead, the stars are all mixed up: Auriga sailing at a ridiculous height, Gemini gone altogether aloft, the Plough standing on its silly tail. There is a black frost which numbs the very trees. White blotches scattered here and there are sheep: I make the count by wagging the flashlight ray on each one: forty-six ewes, the ram, the superannuated lamb of last year's crop, and perhaps Kiely's damned goat. Then the warning bleat is heard, a sound unlike any other sheep noise: there is a ewe about to yean. The nervous bleat is identified with a moving white rectangle. By velocity or cunning, she is caught and thrown: she kicks, grunts, bleats. The lamp is placed in position. I roll up my sleeve and gently explore the lamb-bed: two hairy legs, the head, my finger recognises an eye-socket, a semicircle of little teeth. My hand closes on a leg and I slowly draw; then I go back for the second leg; if successful, the two legs are just protruding from the mouth of the womb. I dry my hands on the ewe's fleece; then for the pull. How the poor old creature baa's at this juncture. But it is all over in a minute (if angels aid), with a flop of water and a trace of blood. "Here he is for you," I say reassuringly to the suffering ewe, and I drag the sneezing, head-shaking morsel up to its mother's face. Then I make a further exploration of the womb for the chance of a second lamb.

When a few additional more or less tender offices are performed, I am free to return, holding off my reeking hand from my respected clothes: incidentally, a hand that would suffer severely if the frost played too long on it. Indoors (my hand still in quarantine), I pull off some external wrapping, glance in at the incubators and the cheeping chicks in the drawing-room (more sleepy than I am myself), steal upstairs, wash well my offensive hand, smell ewe from all myself, punish the candle flame with a malicious pinch, plunge into a bed that has disappointingly cooled, and fall asleep. Ah, how good that brevity, falling asleep!

(In parenthesis, I must boast that Miss Mitford, who took her dog, Mayflower, for rambles in Berkshire lanes, discovering violets to the tedium of posterity, is nowhere in competition with me when I describe midwifery among the ewes in the small hours. Country life as I live it makes her vernal primroses and violets look silly.)

*　*　*

Well, it is over now; all is silent as the tomb, and a charming fire laps the grate. But what a night and a day we have had! How long more will this hardship, this anguish, and this fear last? Kind God, spare us from greater losses and from worse terrors. The silence outside is ominous: the muffled silence of continuously falling snow. On it comes from the east unceasingly, unrelentingly. What will snap? Something must: our courage, our hope will go, if nothing more material. This evening, when John set off down the avenue for his house, Jimmy and I bade him an elaborate farewell in which there was little raillery: a journey which ordinarily ought not take four minutes will take him ten or fifteen. Shall we see him in the yard tomorrow, or will the absurdly short journey prove really impossible with blocking snow?

Providentially waking in the small hours this morning, I set forth to practise the usual obstetrics on ewes. There was less than half a foot of snow on the ground at that time and it was not snowing. Under the holly-trees the ewes had tramped out a clearing for themselves. One is discovered on the point of yeaning at a part of the enclosure furthest from the gate. It takes the last ounce of my strength to drag and shove her into the cow-byre. I am dead beat and almost fainting. I throw myself on a box, panting like a railway engine. Recovered,

I seize the ewe, knock her, probe for the lamb, get a grip on his slimy fore-legs and pull him into this snow-sick world. I fix up ewe and lamb for the night, placing a hurdle between them and the tied cattle. It is ten past four when I put out my candle.

At waking hour the snow on the ground seems higher, but its depth has hardly doubled. A blizzard blows from the east. The hall door permits of opening, and parts of the gravelled front are only dusted with snow. John has gone home to breakfast. I go into mine after a brief inspection of the yard. Afterwards I lost priceless time by searching the Little Meadows for a ewe that was not there—she and her lamb having been removed to the main body of yeaned ewes yesterday when I was away. But Heaven forgive my dalliances, brief as they were.

The blizzard is all the while increasing in velocity, the snowflakes small but myriad. A fusillade of bitter ice meets me as I plunge head foremost down the avenue. Idiot that I was for seeking out John before I investigated matters among the ewes with lambs in the Stream Field. He comes with me, long-drawn of face and pessimistic. Across the marbled fields we go, caged in lashing eastern snow. The landscape is so blank of feature that what can be discerned might be sketched with a few dashes of an H.H. pencil on white blotting-paper. The upper world is a nothingness, a monochrome of clamped-down lead: more sky feeling could be found in a wine cellar.

Lowland sheep set their tails to the wind in storms, so we make for the western fence. All that meets our eyes is barren whiteness punctuated by barren thorns. Then a dirty blotch—a sheep's head, like that of a creature swimming in a sea. Further on, another; then a third; and no more after that. John is listless with despair. I fall on my stomach beside the covered ewes and scratch up snow like a dog at a rabbit burrow. John gives reluctant help: for him affairs are too appalling; he would wring his hands over the dead and neglect the quick. Sheep are fools but they excel in maternal instincts: beneath each ewe is a lamb, sheltering under its mother's belly. We haul them to the other side of the ditch, where the ground is somewhat higher.

Jimmy arrives from nowhere, a scared face protruding from snow-plastered clothes. We separate, each following out his own crazy notions on resurrecting sheep out of the snow. I go about on all fours, and every few yards send an enquiring leg down as far as it will go. The drifts were already four feet deep, and in places five and six feet deep. John moans about sending for more help. I scoff at him. Who is going to help us in a hurricane like this? Will not every farmer have his own troubles? Then heaven conceded us a glorious sight: seven ewes with a bunch of lambs huddled together on the safer side of the thorn fence. Soon afterwards we collect six more sheep from the fatal drifts. While hauling out a sunken ewe, my foot, which is about two feet under snow, encounters movement, palpitations—it is a lamb! Half dead, almost completely frozen, our six ewes and their lambs are added to the others and placed in comparative safety.

We go back to the yard for shovels and tools for

cutting the wire fences. Jimmy has gone so pale in the gills he requires to be revived. "Holy God tonight!" cries Mrs. Meehan, "it frightened him out of a year's growth." I order whiskey and make him sit at the kitchen fire for ten minutes. Then we go back to the marooned sheep, which were almost buried in our absence. The blizzard is blinding us so that we stray hundreds of yards out of our track. Recognising ploughed land under my feet, I find that we are pushing northwards instead of brazing out the heathen east. On reaching the rescued ewes we first dig an indifferently good path from where they are gathered—a pathway which is really only a snare, as it leads to deep snows and wilderness. Jimmy cuts the wire, I thrust lambs through, John gets them moving. Some of the ewes follow their lambs in frenzied terror, yet burning with a mother-love that is surely part of divinity. We get across the new grass, then reach drifts which we know to be the turnip drills. Here the ewes will not advance another inch, so we capture the lambs, plunge onward with them knee-deep, and the ewes follow us. This batch is left in the security of the tillage-field road on the lee of the garden wall. Back we trudge; our five-minute-old tracks are already quite obliterated. A second path has to be made for the remaining ewes, more wire cut, more coaxing and goading. The snow sheets are serrated by the lash of the wind, the sky is riotous with liver spots. Finally, from the tillage roadway to the haven of the yard is an easy journey.

Going into the yard, I see that the entire back portion of the calf-house is swinging in the play of wind; the roof is made of flat tin. Charming weather. We gather in the kitchen: Mrs. Meehan gives us tea; we joke a little, but not with much zest. Then out once more into the fierce white world. The ewes that have not yet yeaned are next driven into the yard for shelter. On our final count we find that one ewe and four lambs are missing: these must be buried in the Stream Field. Armed with shovels and hayforks, we again brave the vortex of the open fields. We probe the drifts with the handles of the forks, barely touching bottom in places. The snow still falls, or rather sings through the air like barbs from bows. No trace of the missing sheep, but God be thanked for the smallness of our loss.

Cloonmore is liberty farm now. All gates are thrown open. The cattle are invited into the house lawn and there given hay, in a location where they may well eat down my briar-rose hedge at will, or trample upon the rings of sprouting daffodils. Certain ewes enjoy the hospitality of the motor shed (and of the motor car also, if they should so desire). Some stray bonhams are permitted the run of the feeding-house for a short while. Two cooped-up hens are allowed the freedom of the pulper house with their chickens.

Later, the blizzard having abated, I pioneered a passage as far as Lynch's, which is the nearest dwelling-place to my own, so as to gain a little consolation from human companionship. I found that Johnnie, the man of the house, was not over-alarmed, nor inclined to sympathise, but then he has no sheep. He said he remembers a far worse snow-storm in the 'nineties. Trudging back, I met Mick Coyne, pulling his knees up as he walked, with an action more like that of a cyclist than a pedestrian. He told me that the road to Milltown is completely blocked and impassable. He was then on his way to Lynch's for the water he usually draws from a pump a little way along the Milltown road, Lynch's being three times the distance of his usual source of supply.

It began to snow once more as I plodded homewards. It is still snowing as I write. Just now there was a flash of vivid lightning. I renew the fire and close the shutters. It would be impossible to imagine a greater silence than that which surrounds me. There is not even a stir in the kitchen downstairs, as Jimmy and Mrs. Meehan have gone to bed. The soft sound of burning turf in the grate and the scratch of my pen serve but to emphasise the stillness. Uneasily, I take down *Lorna Doone* and read Chapter Forty-two, thus filling myself with fresh fears. I cannot even muster a sceptical smile when I read of John Ridd's feat of excavating from the snow and carrying home one by one under his arms sixty-six sheep in succession. The awful silence and, above all else, the loneliness besetting me must not be thought of now. What fear can grip a body because of the elements' fury, for all our boasted progress and enlightenment!

*   *   *

Two days later the sun is blazing down on a mere two feet of snow (drifts of course are still holding their four and five feet of depth) as I drag my way along to late Mass. Advancing up the Milltown road comes Bill Liddy, leading a bunch of Moorstown boys like a string of ducks. I take the head of the column, and in this rather uncomfortable line-out we discuss the snow-storm. I am given news of tragedies amongst my neighbours' flocks, the plight of homes where some of the family were ill, and stories of the stoppage of buses and mailtrains. Then we switch on to politics. The five roads leading to the church are patterned by Indian files like ours on their way to Mass.

The P.P. is merciless this morning. Not satisfied with reading the Epistle and Gospel, and preaching a sermon on the Second Commandment, he lectures parents for not sending their children regularly to school, apparently unconscious of the humour of this reprimand under present conditions. He goes on and on and on, as though it were midsummer, or as if all the clocks had been silenced forever. I walked home along the track in front of Peter Mangan and chatted over my shoulder with him about snow-storms past and present.

Soup, or hot milk, is more in my line after the ordeal of walking to Mass and back, but all the same I step aside from the avenue on my homeward way and make for the dyke where our lost sheep are presumed to be. I probe about diligently in the snow-drifts with my walking-stick. Soon Jimmy joins me. Together we make a more or less desultory search. The sun flames out, but there is little thawing. Every step is a plunge amidst the drifts; on the level ground one's feet go crunching down a foot or two in depth. Sprawled out upon the snow, I poke my stick down its full length; at a certain point I receive a check and find that I am poking a lamb's hind quarters! Quickly I tear up snow with both hands. Jimmy comes running at my excited shouts and helps in the work of excavation. Up we pull the creature by his hind legs and find he is as alive as a bee! Poor little lamb, dazzled by the flaring whiteness of the world, hauled a second time from a womb. We peer down and examine his shelter: it is a cosy room enough and was probably provided with a ventilator, although we could not trace this in the wreckage we had made. Leaving Jimmy to carry on, I shoulder the lamb in biblical fashion and make for the yard. I turn round in the avenue to shout down to John at his house (the snow stillness enables one's voice to carry far), bidding him come up and help at the work of digging for sheep. In the yard I catch the first available ewe and treat my resurrected lamb to a drink. Then, armed with implements, I return to the others and we work away with spades for about half an hour without any further luck. "Wonder they wouldn't bleat," I remark idly to John. "Ah, sure how could they? Sure sheep are useless in the snow; they stay just in the one place until they die and they never let a bawl out of them," he answers morosely, for he is an incurable pessimist. At that we hear the faint bleat of a snow-buried lamb! In a frenzy we set to work again and soon the youngest lamb of the flock is landed up on the scintillating ground, apparently none the worse for his forty-eight hours' entombment. But here our good fortune left us. No matter how deeply we dug, nor how energetically we plunged cob-web brush handles into the snow-clogged briars, we found no more missing members of the flock.

The Irish yew before the front door, usually so proud, so scornful of hardship, is now like a turnip-top, its noble plumes lying this way and that way, with an effect as though one had dashed a wet camel-hair brush on a hard surface. The yew in the garden, a poor specimen anyway, not vase-shaped, but jutting out on one side like a pent-house, has suffered considerably, several of its limbs having been broken off. Even yet, I am too timid to make a tour of all my new small shrubs because I fear that between the storm and the hospitality extended to the cattle, the damage is bound to be huge. Juniper, cupressus, broom, laurel, and all the small shrubs are bent right into the ground. First aid is misplaced energy: the rosemary crackled as if snapping when I gave it a friendly kick to relieve it of its snowy burden.

Branches of firs and hollies have snapped off everywhere. The box-tree is all tousled. The branches of the young apple-trees in the hen-runs are so bulky with snow that they are like restaurant hat-stands. Water-barrels wear a stomacher of drifts; the windows of the house are snow-smudged. Shovel work was required on all the gates of the hen-runs before trafficking could begin. Some of the yard house-doors were so choked up that we did not even try to clear them until today.

There are interesting little phenomena to be

observed on every side after a heavy snow-fall. Wherever the snow wears the least bit thin, the sheep burrow avidly for grass. When one enters the hen-houses, the poultry make a wild dive at one's snow-covered boots and greedily gobble up the snow. Hares leave a three-cornered track. The snow melts most quickly on the roofs of houses containing stock, because of the heat given off from the animals' bodies. The strangest thing was the curves we described in our journeys around the place, when we were trying to make a bee-line from one point to another.

We all returned to the Stream Field later in the day (when our shadows were china blue cast on Carrara marble), and continued the work of excavation. For long spells we leaned on our shovels in business-like silence, but no bleat rewarded us. The drifts on the lee side of the dyke where the sheep had taken refuge were poked thoroughly from end to end; the dyke itself was jagged from our shovelling; we cut back the thorn bushes; we poked under all the stumps, but without any success. Eventually the others have to go up to their yard work. I remain on, shoving my pole in every drift around the field. The sky wraps up half a dozen sunset colours in a gauzy rag and streels them through the west. From all over the countryside one hears the bleating of ewes and lambs, speaking of tender scenes of family re-union after the sack of snow. Small birds sing bravely voicing the courage of their conviction that fine weather will surely come again. How blue white can be! How lovely this desolation looks flung across

Ballinamona bogs, Lowtown plains, and far-away hillsides!

*　　*　　*

What a wide berth the townies give to their country friends in winter! From May until September they will come in scores, chock-a-block with advice on making fortunes out of mushroom culture or the breeding of silver foxes, but now they bask beside their electric fires and their radiators, pitying all benighted farmers in God-forsaken parts. During the last twenty-four hours my only caller was a happy old soldier who trudged up the rough quarter-mile avenue with coloured paper gewgaws, assorted ornaments, and a cross in a bottle. Questioned about the latter, he told me that he can put crosses into bottles at the rate of three per day. The sample he carried was an elaborate, almost scenic cross, festooned with a decade of a Rosary beads, flanked by sprigs of yew, and footed by a Sacred Heart badge. He did not ask me to buy, but on receiving a gift of fourpence he was willing to talk and even to initiate me into the mysteries of his craft.

He explained in detail, but by no means lucidly, the difficult technique of putting crosses into bottles. It was the French who originally invented the art of building ornaments in bottles—so he has always heard anyway. There are bottles and bottles, it seems, but ordinary four-noggin gin bottles are the best for the purpose. The rest is a matter of wangling very slender sticks through the narrow neck and the possession of superhuman patience.

He knows where the real masterpieces of this craft can be viewed. There is an ex-soldier in Derry who has a ship in a bottle, which I really ought make it my business to see. A certain Wilson who lives in Cranagh also possesses one: you couldn't ask for a more beautiful ornament, you'd swear the ship was sailing, and he has the whole thing in a lovely frame. Wilson would bring the treasure down from the bedroom if asked, and he is a well-schooled boy too! Then the mystery of the apple in a bottle is explained to me: one has to rig up elaborately the right kind of bottle in conjunction with an apple blossom which has just set, but successes are few. I am told where I could see specimens of this art and earnestly pressed to make pilgrimage to the shrines of bottled apples and pears.

According to the ex-soldier, the grandest example of the art he follows is preserved in a London barber's shop, whither my craftsman repaired to be shaved while on leave during his service in the Great War. It was a "chapel" in a bottle, and "you never saw the like!" He whispered to his commanding officer, also getting a shave, that they were in the presence of a masterpiece and urged him to ask the barber to sell this glorious specimen, but no sum of money in the world would persuade the barber to sell it. Having imparted all this information to me, the cross-in-bottle man went off as cheerful as a bird, with a sort of skipping walk and humming to himself. How delighted he is with himself and with his talent in a rare art!

I spent several hours of the night in making out the vegetable and flower-seed order. It may seem a lot of time to devote to so slight a task, but I twice changed my mind, which necessitated tearing up the list and making a new start. At the first attempt I was wildly extravagant; then I was too economical; and finally I hit on a golden mean which did not include the scorzonera of the first list (which I included simply to irritate Mrs. Sullivan, who grows salsify and therefore believes herself to be the last word in vegetable enlightenment), and which included the second list's broad beans, which I really abominate, but which sell like hot cakes in Bally-nash. Nothing will cure me of horticultural optimism. Already I have had two failures at propagating St. Brigid anemones from seed, but I persevere; this year I am determined to sow the nasty woolly seeds with the merest suspicion of a cover; probably my error before was deep sowing: as the bulbs cost about 1s. 6d. per dozen, the only means of having a great spread of these bright flowers is by sowing the seeds. Unless brachycome and kochia are reckoned as novelties, my selection will be un-original enough this season. I classify annual flowers into luxuries and necessities. Antirrhinums and asters are luxuries; clarkia and stock are necessities. Wallflowers, larkspur, godetia, mignonette, and a host of others can be dispensed with, but I'd as soon forswear tobacco or cursing as forgo sweet peas, cornflowers, candytuft, cosmea, eschscholt-zia, swan poppies, and night-scented stock. Joe's face will drop yards tomorrow morning when I tell him that I have only ordered one ounce of Ailsa

Craig and a sixpenny package of James's Keeping onions.

*   *   *

Mick, Jimmy, and myself were several hours endeavouring to help a ewe to lamb, but without any good result. Mick was the first to notice that this ewe had difficulty in yeaning. He stood by for some time watching her, then caught her and explored her womb. Finding something unusual, he hollered for me. On investigation I found that the lamb's head was twisted under its body, so that no amount of pulling at the forelegs, which were normal in presentation, could succeed in releasing him. Jimmy joined us and Mick muttered to him that this was the "horridest case he ever seen."

The ewe was in pain: at first she moaned piteously, then she ceased, as though her pain had become too great for expression. Her grey eyes with their narrow black slits were eloquent of intense suffering: poor, frightened eyes; eyes which could see things in the wind, and make shapes and colours out of every breeze unnoticed by us. Mick and the boy pulled at the lamb's legs, while I held the ewe down by putting my knee on her neck, so as to give them leverage. From time to time we would desist pulling, while Mick or I again explored the lamb-bed and endeavoured to the best of our clumsy power to get the head into the right position. Soon blood appeared. We had penetrated the womb. Charity forgive us. The ewe suffered silently.

We hardly spoke over the business. The boy

was visibly pained at the sheep's agony; I would have sent him away, but his help was needed too badly. Mick occasionally ejaculated, "Doesn't that bate all?" The ewe bled profusely; Mick was blood to his elbow; my wellingtons were smeared, my hands red. It was harrowing to see the suffering of the poor, unheroic creature. None of us were capable of making the Cæsarian operation, nor had we on the farm an instrument that would serve for such a purpose. We sent the boy for a rope and knotted it to the lamb's legs; again two of us pulled the rope while the other steadied the unfortunate sheep. She suffers from our ministrations and the lamb remains unreleased. Much more of this kind happens than is good to describe. Several times we agree to give up and destroy the animal to put her out of her pain, for she seems already in a dying condition, and again one of us makes a fresh effort. Finally, Mick pulls the rope by himself; at the moment it happened to be attached to only one leg and the leg comes away. "That ends it," I say decisively, "we will never get the lamb from her now. The best thing you could do, Mick, would be to give her a good crack on the head with the sledge." Mick looks miserable. "Or I could get my gun," I continue, noting his reluctance and remembering that to kill a dying beast is a taboo amongst the men. "Better shoot her, sir," says he, gladly jumping at the alternative.

I return to the house for my gun, run the ram through one barrel several times, pocket a cartridge and go back to the garden. Mick and the boy have gone off to their respective jobs. The office of executioner fills me with extraordinary repugnance. I see the ewe moving her legs in agony, her head swaying a little. She takes no notice of me: she is past fear, almost past feeling. I load the gun, raise it to my shoulder, and lower it again, overwhelmed with nausea. I am aware that Mick is probably keeping his ear cocked to hear the report which will tell him that the sheep's pain is ended. Shall I just fire into the air and let her die naturally, as no doubt she will within an hour or so? I move about the dying animal; she is quite quiet. Then I put my back to the garden wall, raise the gun, point the muzzle at her head, steady my hands, and involuntarily close my eyes as I fire! When I venture to look again at the ewe, I see that she is moving her head up and down— not dead, perhaps hardly a single pellet penetrated. Impulsively, I rush to her and hit her forcibly on the head with the stock of the gun. Then I go away hurriedly, filling a pipe and telling myself violently that I am a soft fool.

* * *

If there is a machine that flits about hen-runs, bending, carrying, lifting, moving, opening, closing, filling, emptying, and swearing under its breath, then I am that machine. True, Jimmy does the scraping of the dropping-boards, as well as the feeding, and the replenishing supplies of water and grit, but I maintain that I am the real slave of the poultry. Every day there are ten stubborn, crass, and stupid hens to be taken off ten clutches of uncountable or, more honestly, uncounted chicks, and placed in a cage for feeding. How I detest this job: ten hens mean twenty journeys between the brood-house and the cage; in that short distance there are enough steps, snags, and obstacles to slow down the charging of a bull. Sweat pours off me as I extract the angry hens from their coops, each one so puffed up with her own importance, so fussy, so distrustful of my good intentions. All about the cage in which the clucking hens are confined for feeding congregate the envious laying hens, who belong to the other section of the brood-house; ever hopeful of an aperture, these keep on a continual flutter around the cage, or squabble together over a stray morsel shot out by the favoured ten. When the feeding is over, each mother hen is returned to her chicks, the correct combination of hen and clutch being established by a numbered leg-band and a numbered coop.

Indoors, I do all that has to be done in connection with the incubators, although Mrs. Meehan lends a hand in tending the smallest chickens. Day-olds are fascinating: they squat as close as they can get to the heat of the blue-flame hoover, prim, smug, slightly reminiscent of Winterhalter's group of Queen Victoria with Albert and children. Chickens go through three stages: at first they are little ducks; then they are little monkeys; and finally they are little fools. My first batch, now advanced from the drawing-room to No. 6, have reached the monkey phase: they fly over the wire hurdles, paddle in the drinking-water, and make pigs of themselves at feeding time. Four times a day (unless I forget, which, alas, sometimes happens) I feed the little indoor brats with pinhead oatmeal. This season's batch ought to be healthy, owing to the five-gallon drum of cod-liver oil that I bought, and which I am putting through the dry mash. When the next cow calves I should be able to spare a little separated milk, which has the effect of making chicks grow amazingly.

John reports a "sick" ewe when he is bringing in the cows for milking. I accept guardianship of the creature. From a respectful distance I watch her uneasiness; she gets up and lies down, paws the ground, makes short runs, and gives distressful glances at her flanks. Nothing happens; the expectant ewe wins the siege. Having spent about twenty minutes in her uninspiring company, I leave her for the poultry shutting-up round. On my return I find a lamb just struggling on to his long legs, but I am forced to leave the pair to their own resources because of the four pocketsful of eggs with which I am burdened. Later on, I join Mick in a review of the flock, and this time notice that my charge has yeaned another lamb. Half an hour afterwards Mick shouts to me when I am crossing to the workshop: "She has another!" I chase down to the big beech-tree, where the silly sheep stands surrounded by three little knock-kneed mites, all confused by the light, height, and breadth of a bewildering world. I sling the weakest of the trio around my neck and dump it in the kitchen, much to the delight of Mrs. Meehan and Jimmy, who are about to sit down to their tea. The first pet lamb this season has certainly found a welcome.

*   *   *

Will miracles ever cease? With a string about the dirty neck of Kiely's knavish goat, I set out to lead it off my land. Docile and mannerly enough when confronted with my determination to be rid of it, I succeed in thrusting it through a gap on the Night Park road boundary, after which I saunter home by the ditch where the ewes were lately snow-bound. I took a short cut through a now demoral-ised snow-drift between the decayed thorn fence and the wire fence. Although the snow has now practically vanished from the rest of the farm, it is still thick along here. As I sprang over the drift, I was almost petrified to hear a rustle under my feet, and at the same time see the snow heaving! Good God! Can she be alive after an entombment of six days and nights? I yell for John, and rush for a spade left near by after our last search. I dig like fury and in a very short time uncover a live ewe, with a dead lamb at her head and another behind her. I try to raise her but she is too weak to move, much less to stand. No-one hears my shouts. I set off to the yard for a wheel-barrow and encounter John coming from Little Meadows. I point back to the drifts as I run into the house to order Mrs. Meehan prepare gruel with a whiskey splash. John and I lift the ewe out of her hole. There is an abominable smell. We trundle the poor wretch into the yard, and cover her with hay in a railed-off part of the calf-house. The real miracle will be if she lives.

Jimmy is all excitement and insists on having full details of how and where she was found. God has been good to us: the big snow has directly caused the death of only two lambs; indirectly the death of a ewe later, and no doubt the milklessness of several others may be traced to the same hardship.

* * *

Thunder of north wind, shouldering at the door, testing the windows, charging down the back steps and shaking the kitchen entrance. Express trains roar outside; the house trembles; I shrink from a tour of the attics lest I see the roof ballooned. This morning the poultry runs were serene, but in a thrice they went down in a storm of dead leaves before the onslaught of the furious gale; the leaves clog the netting and the posts bend under the wall of wind; one whole side of the runs was down before dinner-time.

I fret about the hayrick, the smaller hen-houses, the mighty ash-tree on the mound, the old tumble-down garden house (terribly weakened by the removal of ivy) and all the outhouse roofs.

I have flung a mat at the bottom of the study door, invited Laddie into the hall, and piled up the fire. What violence can winter do which it has not already done? All day long the wind roared in tree-tops, flung itself against the house and outbuildings, pounced on dead leaves, and made knots out of the smoke from the boiler-house chimney. We have a cupressus which, in a time of wind, sways like a very tipsy lady. On the parapet just outside the front door is a water-can quarter filled with water; it whines like a dog in acute pain until, annoyed beyond endurance, I rush out and turn the spout in another direction.

An hour before dinner-time Mick comes in from ploughing and declares it is impossible to work any longer in the "horrid" wind. Joe gives up out-door work after dinner; together with John he had been straining "wicket" wire on the new avenue fence. I put Mick and Joe at white-washing the farrowing-house; before they make a start, I am irritated by their slow and elaborate toilette (which consists, among other things, of cutting arm-holes and a head-hole in bran bags). John is nicely caught out having been seen by me idly leaning on a yard-brush when I made an unobserved and wind-silenced entry through the wicket-gate. Deprived of the plea that he has yard work to do—stall-fed feeding, byre cleaning, pulping, or boiling—he is made to wash the sows. A bucket of boiling water, to which is added a dash of paraffin-oil and a dab of soft soap, does wonders on a pig's hide; in fact, except for an occasional rub with a rag soaked in motor-sump oil, which has the effect of making the lice glide off for their dear lives, this will be the only effort of hygiene my pigs will experience this year. I take pity on Jimmy and withdraw him from the gale and rain of the poultry runs to the shelter of the pulper house, where he picks out sacks. There is one way and one way only of storing sacks so that they may be safe from the plundering of mice, and that is to close them into a metal container. Our bin capacity is very limited, but we allot one portion of a galvanised bin for bag-storing. It is not for want of trying other methods: we have hung up bags in bundles from rafters, and we have slung them on a wire line run through a pair of paint-tin lids, and still the mice got at them and wellnigh destroyed them. When Jimmy has all the bags in order, he is bluntly told to prove by turning a pile of barbed-wire reels into milking-stools that he was not wasting his time in skittish behaviour when he attended the carpentry class in Lowtown. He eyes the material dubiously. "Who's going to sit on them stools?" "John Kelly, of course." "Well, it's not my affair, but don't blame me if he goes through them to the ground." Maybe Jimmy is right; the reels are made of very light timber. My predominant passion is making use of by-products.

Indoors, I fasten myself to the hitching-post of long tots in an effort to draw up an annual balance-sheet. Through the windows, I can see the wind-tormented trees in a cage of rain: depressing scenery for a depressing task. Expenditure towers over Receipts. Great big bloated Expenditure quite dwarfing the other with his head and shoulders of Wages, belly of Fodder, thighs of Rent and Rates, arms of Implements and Equipment, legs of Constructions and Repairs, and twenty disgusting swollen fingers and toes formed of Taxes, Insurance, Licences, Subscriptions, House Expenses, Personal Expenses, Fuel, Light, Petrol, Threshing, Milling, Hire of Implements, Seeds, Artificial

124

Manures, Haulage, Forge, Harness Repairs, Service Fees, Veterinary Fees, and Sundries. What chance has poor little David Receipts against that monstrous Goliath? Sturdy little chap, ill-equipped but game for going into battle against the ogre, affecting ferocity, bristling up and exhibiting all his comic features: his butter fingers, his bull-neck, his chicken chest, his strawberry nose, his sheep's eyes, and his well-developed calves! When the tot is completed, David loads his sling and lets fly at huge Goliath. Down topples giant Expenditure to sprawl on the ground; the little chap, the tiny tot, used a very special stone in his sling, not even a colossus could withstand its whack: it is the philosopher's stone.

The last ewe to be resurrected from the snow died yesterday. She lingered for over a week, almost completely paralysed and all the time listless. We threw cart-ropes over the rafters and slung her up in a sort of cradle, with her feet barely touching the ground, but she never regained the use of her limbs. We fed her with ivy and pulped turnips, but for these delicacies she showed no enthusiasm. There was something ghastly about the propped-up corpse that I discovered yesterday morning in the calf-house.

Wild winds screech around Cloonmore House tonight, trying the strength of down-pipes, rapping the slates, whining and wailing now at upstairs windows, now along the area passage, roaring and shrieking from front steps to chimney-stacks. I fold in the shutters and pull their bars; with a flash-lamp I make a tour of the attics. In the kitchen Mrs. Meehan sonorously gives out the Rosary and Jimmy answers; may their prayers ward off danger and keep on the rotten roof. Laddie gives me a solemn, sidelong look when I get back to the hall: a shower of soot has come down the chimney since I left the room. The cat alone seems unperturbed, and blinks serenely at the fire; in a crisis, rally around your cat, for she is never scared. Oh, to live in a mud-walled, thatched cottage built in a dell!

CHAPTER VI

THE BORROWING SEASON IS NEARING ITS
height. Blackledge sent up for a loan of
the stone roller, and Pat Mangan came in his
ass and cart for the chain harrow. Time is wasted
more profitably in chatting with Pat than in any
other way known to me. I gladly left off tarring
a water-barrel when he clattered in, and spent
three-quarters of an hour leaning across the
donkey's back in conversation with the man
perched on the driving seat. Having reviewed the
weather from the big snow until the sharp sunshine of today, having dwelt on most of the bargaining episodes of the last Ballynash Fair, Pat
gets on to the Devons.

The Mangans were tenants of the Devons in the
bad times, and although they paid up their rent on
the nail, they were evicted from the greater and the
best part of their land. Faced with emigration, the
workhouse, or eating humble pie, Pat's father
chose the latter course and he and his sons became
farm labourers on the Devon property, the father
at 12s. per week, and the sons at 2s. 6d. each.
Heaven knows where the descendants of the
Devons are now, they have gone like a wisp of
smoke, but the Mangans have been restored to
most of their land and enjoy a share of prosperity.
This is not the first time that Pat has told me his
yarn, but on this occasion he holds forth, greatly to

my liking, on the lay-out of Cloonmore farm and farm-yard over fifty years ago. The Protestants held their services in the little house now used as a workshop, after their church was burnt in 1798. A gardener of long ago reared a large family in the old ruined house by the garden gate; it is twelve and a half feet square and used to be two storeys high; last year I re-roofed this same house and converted it into a pig-house. There was a smithy in what is now the boiler-house. Mrs. Meehan sleeps in the room once occupied by the insane Devon uncle!

Before going off with the chain harrow, Pat urges me to take a trip to my bog division, as he has been told that trees are being stolen there. An hour later I set out across the fields on what is to prove, I hope, a punitive expedition, Laddie following at my heels.

My black curse on the tardiness of this midland spring! I have not yet seen a daffodil and scarcely a primrose; the snowdrops are still in their prime and there is not a speck of blossom in the orchards. What a latitude anyhow! A damned Danish climate, an outpost of the Frigid Zone. Why, daffodils by this time must be sick of the sight of each other all over Munster. Truly, I left Ireland when I removed from the south to live in the midlands. Today if dry, crackling sunlight abounds in a chastened bowl of sky, there is still no growth or any sign of vernal awakening. "A fine, open time," is the agriculturally correct greeting these days, to which the answer is usually, "Aye, but feeding is getting scarce."

A bog in early March is desolate enough. I walk my undesired twenty-two acres of this area and discover that two or three small larch-trees have been recently cut down; signs of older damage also can be seen. Apparently my bog is regarded as commonage, and the right to take timber for fuel and fencing seems established.

When city visitors remark that Cloonmore farm is silent, I politely agree, but I make a mental reservation: yes, but you should hear the silence of my bog! The stillness is absolute here. I cannot discern even the chatter of distant fowl, nor the rumble of a dray, nor the songful persistence of blackbirds.

I sit down under an elder partly dead and bearing many bone-like branches, fill a pipe, revel in the quietude, and review the situation. Primrose leaves are in clumps all around me; nettles are forcing their way up through the dingy humus, and the tiny cupid-wings of new honeysuckle leaves have appeared. A bulky person in hairy, baggy tweeds enjoys silence and mildness on a tract of land that belongs to him but which provides firewood, turf, free grazing for jennets and goats, litter from bracken, and some rough gravel for the neighbourhood. What can I do? Bog and farm are sadly disconnected. I cannot establish a patrol here. The bureaucratic landlord, meaning the Irish Land Commission, will neither take the place off my hands nor cede me the necessary permission to sell it. I see no way out of my difficulties. The cost of fencing the entire division would be more than the value of the land itself. The nearest Civic Guards are four miles away, and I have already learned the uselessness of apprising them of the trespassing and thefts which are such an unending annoyance.

Squatting amidst the tardy vegetation goads me to satirical thoughts on the compilers of those Nature Notes now a feature of most newspapers. All these notes have two characteristics in common: they are perpetually anticipating growth, and they bewail the passing of each season long before it has reached its zenith. The newspaper naturalist will invariably come into print several weeks ahead of the flower, bird, or insect which he tells his readers to seek for there and then. Not content thus to fly before Nature, he makes a point of talking about rare flowers rather than common or garden specimens. Even the Irish nature note-makers (who ought to be better acquainted with the limitations of Irish flora and fauna) bid us watch out for such things as herb Paris, or wood warblers, or Camberwell Beauties. A restless race, these newspaper naturalists, they are never happy unless it is the month after next: they spend the whole winter on the lookout for breaking buds and hearing the birds make calf love; they spend the spring acclaiming the fulness of summer, while in summer they begin to crane their necks for "burnished foliage" and "coral-like berries." I detest this unmannerly haste in treating of Nature's mutations. I suffer discomfort when I hear that spring has made advances not yet possible according to the calendar, and I am consumed with misery when I read about the departure of the swallows, or the falling of leaves, before their due time.

Since there is nothing to be gained in the cause of property protection by sitting on cold clay, I whistle up Laddie and walk home through the naked fields.

*   *   *

For farmers there is no busier season than the present one. I have not an idle moment all day, nor any day (despite my recent dalliance amidst primrose clumps). Preparing for sowing is of course the main cause of extra work and worry, but my notes lengthen too on smaller jobs to be done, item is heaped on item unpityingly and I stagger, the pack-ass, under fifty commands from myself: to order seed oats, to read up the oat variety experiments in the County Report, to answer letters, to purchase pin-head for chicks, to go through the apples in storage, and to set mouse-traps: memoranda that lower me to the status of a dog with a tin tied to his tail. Meanwhile the harrow is going hither and thither in the fields, drudgery for Mick and the snorting mares, and a sort of mental cruelty to myself—there being so little in readiness for the sowing campaign.

Oh, give me haymaking: with decent cool weather, long hours in meadows, and a wondrous thirst! These strenuous March days would kill eels. Lambs to the right of me, lambs to the left, chickens in the rear, and a torrent of bonhams, cows due to calve, apple-trees waiting to be planted, and nothing but the same stark slavery for future prospect. Give me wet weather and easy-going summer routine, give me even the churning of a couple of stone of butter, or the thinning of turnips, or—most monotonous of all—the picking of black currants, rather than this feverish spring rush.

Truly I have no rest or leisure. I have not a moment for appreciating the empurpled Hill of Allen (which is the limit of the landscape) at sundown, like an innocent old woman's idea of paradise. I have not a moment for the pilewort (not for me the genteelism of Lesser Celandine) now spread in the coppice, no time to read spring's advance placards in the hedges and swampy places, no time to note the tiny regiment of snowdrops arrayed between the mossy feet of beeches, nor to watch the sun playing King Cophetua to a daisy Beggar Maid. However, the days lengthen merrily and maybe time will yet catch up on toil.

Joe and I put down rhubarb stools in the garden. He forks and I follow, deepening his holes by digging. When he has the ground all forked he follows me again, sticking down the stools. I leave him to finish and proceed to a patch of ground where the garden is most jungle-like, and there I begin excavating a site for another beehive. Brambles, chervil, nettles, and ropy grasses are hewed and hacked, sods are turned face to hell, worms waggle mutilated halves, ground beetles remember appointments, while the sun shines staringly. The ivy on the walls is glossy, starchy, and crisp to the winds; not indeed that it should be there at all, for I paid a man to destroy it root and branch three years ago. Dandelions speck the grass with their round yellow faces; they are vulgar, nasty little things, I'm sure, but very pleasing. Around me the earth is thrown up in blackish clods, speckled with pebbles and bits of broken china; there is a smell of fresh earth for those who have noses long enough. The birds make the garden a city of bells (except the blackbird, who sometimes mimics the boys calling the evening newspapers). I hack and hew intently, silently, thought-free, for the sake of establishing more beehives so that my apple-trees may be the better fertilised: honey I scarcely consider.

When the clearing is made I lean against the grandsire of the garden, an ancient and unsprayable pippin. The sky is tricked out in vermilion. Birds singing in March twilights are as the humming of God in heaven. Why, I could not drag away my creaking body from the bole of the tree, though the evening became cold and damp and almost dark, because of the choir about it, each jesting bird daring his rivals from his post: on up, on up, swing high like a thurible, swing low again, let the notes dance as the Spanish acolytes dance before the altar at Eastertide. Lord, didst Thou give birds the gift of song just because Thou wished man should know it is not good to dwell alone?

*   *   *

Willie Hogan drives up and bears me away to an implement auction. As we turn out the gates he talks of what is for sale and expresses a hope that the corn-drill will go at a moderate price. He proposes that we two should go halves in buying it. "And we won't lend it to anyone," he declares firmly, to which I agree with equal firmness, although I know in my heart how our resolution will work out: well, Pat Mangan and Matt Sullivan are somebodies, and Willie has a brother farming in Moorstown . . . and so on.

The farm where the auction is to be held belongs to an Irish-American who returned to this his native place three years ago full of enthusiasm and of go-getting ideas about how to run a farm profitably. We beat him: our life is too dull, our ways too slow, our ambitions too humble, so he is again uprooting himself and his hustle and returning to the United States.

The auctioneer stands on a wheelbarrow and reads out the conditions of sale. He first proceeds in a bored manner to set the land in grazing divisions. A thin man with a meagre beard flares out, "Let us go up to the new grass that you are setting. Only some of the chaps have seen it!" This recalls Breen, the auctioneer, to his sense of duty. "Come on!" he says shortly, and we all trudge soberly up the land and stand around him in serried ranks. Above us the wintry sun is like a raw egg in a glass of cold water.

Willie develops an interest in a certain parcel of land at a cross-roads: it comprises twelve acres of fairly good grazing, but with no water available. He thinks it might be useful to him when his lambs are bigger. He whispers his ideas to me, and while he is hesitating whether or not to open the bidding as high as £2 per acre, another man to his amazement starts it at £3, and the auction finishes at £3 : 17 : 6 an acre. "That fellow's ducks must be laying," is a bystander's comment.

On our return to the house front we find the dis-illusioned American hauling out kitchen utensils, arranging furniture, and helping the auctioneer's men to drag an incubator from a shed. When the sale is in full swing there is strong bidding for every lot and things go dear. I follow up haymaking implements to what seem to me dizzy heights without securing any of them. The corn-drill goes over our heads at the high price of £18 : 10s., much to Willie's distress.

Auctioneers' sallies are only a little less tedious than judges' jokes, but I had to smile at Breen's recommendation of a battered old plough, because it coincided with our recent talk on that problem: "Sure it would do for lending, anyway."

As is the common practice at badly organised auctions, a number of neighbours arrive with odd-ments to be added to the sale : these include a wire-less set, a brass bedstead, and a turkey cock. While chatting with John O'Connor of Upper Moorstown, he points out to us a poor devil of a fellow who had brought to the sale his home-made end-over-end churn. John, who had arrived a long time before the auction commenced, told us that this man had been standing for hours already by the side of his churn, speaking to anyone who would speak to him, enumerating the merits of his article, and lecturing all and sundry on the difficult art of butter-making. Willie and I approach him and size him up. He is a hungry-looking sort of wretch, excitable at all times, I should say, but now evidently worked up to fever pitch. We hear him several times enlarging on the beauties of his churn and surmising that it would fetch at least £10. Then he would demonstrate the ease with which his superlative article worked: "You see, you've only got to give it a few turns like this," giving the handle a couple of vigorous twists, then letting go and turning his back to it with a certain air of drama: "It goes of its own accord, you see, the Balance of Power makes it go."

A bystander, who knew more about the construction of churns than was convenient, asked him how the gases escaped. "Oh, all you've got to do," he said airily, "is to get an auger, bore a hole, and you'll get one of them little yokes for letting out the gas from the Shamrock Engineering Company for sixpence." Over and over again he demonstrated to the idle and mostly satirical onlookers how the lid was lifted: you unscrew here and unscrew there, brace yourself and tug. As a matter of fact, a cursory examination showed that the inside of the lid was much patched with bits of cork and that the frame had all the appearance of having been welded together by an ignorant blacksmith in a hurry. "What are they at now?" he would anxiously ask a passer-by, and when told that the sale had reached only the potato clamps, he would resume again on the merits of his churn.

John and Willie led the boastful craftsman into a long debate on churns in general and drew out, as a reward for their baiting, extraordinary evidence of his conceit. He waved his hand loftily in the direction of the crowd around the auctioneer and remarked to them confidentially, "Of course you and I understand these things, but not the Masses!"

At length the auctioneer returned from behind the hay-barn, with the crowd at his heels. The churn-seller approached him eagerly: "Will you put up mine, sir? I've been here all day." The auctioneer obliges indifferently: he is clearly tired and cold, anxious to finish his business, and thinking of other things. "Now I'm going to offer a churn," he sings out: the owner's face begins to work. "What shall I say for this churn, this end-over-end churn?" the auctioneer continues with his absent-minded air. The owner's underlip bulged up to meet his moustache. "Who'll make me an offer?" the auctioneer pursues wearily. After a long silence, someone at the back reluctantly offers a pound. A wild look comes into the owner's face; his eyes seem to shoot from his head. "Any advance on one pound, any advance?" Someone adds half a crown. "One pound and half a dollar, I'm bid. Why, you wouldn't get a new churn for four times that amount," cries Breen, dropping into one of his stock phrases. The owner bounds up like a madman to his churn and, for the hundredth time that day, heaves off the lid: "It *is* a new one, sir; it *is* a new one. I'll give a written guarantee. Ye don't know its value." The auctioneer is not impressed, nor even amused; he is only bored. He angles mechanically and indifferently for further bids, and slowly the price advances to thirty shillings and firmly stops there. He glances at the owner: "Will you sell, mister?" "D'y think me a fool?" answers the owner violently. The crowd has already lost interest and shifts away. The poor wretch seizes the child of his dreams, lifts it into his pony-cart, and tenderly stuffs hay around it, rage shaking him, tears almost blinding him, groaning as if in pain. He drives away mouthing insults and pronouncing maledictions on the "Masses" and on the whole lot of us as arrant imbeciles.

A savage north-west wind, every gust about as caressing as the slash of a handful of briars, does not add to the pleasure of the drive home in Willie's open two-seater. He is very downcast because of his failure to secure the corn-drill. He bites the slack at the back of his middle finger, as is his way when miserable. I had a suspicion that he is in a plight about sowing his corn, and this is shortly confirmed. He confides to me that this year he cannot beg or borrow a drill, because last year he broke a part of Blackledge's drill and for various reasons refused to replace it. The year before, he quarrelled with Lynch over the price he had been charged for its hire (£1 per acre—certainly Lynch is a Jewman), and vowed then that he would never again trouble him for his implement. This year, Carter has already refused him the loan of a drill, apparently because Blackledge had been telling tales.

When Willie lets me down at my gate he is in no mood to accept my invitation to a cup of tea, and I am not altogether sorry he refuses, because I have to inspect the work done in my absence. Throwing myself against the gusts of wind I reach Mick who is ploughing. He reports the land so sticky that the mares have to "go on their bellies" when pulling up the "horrid" hill. I return to the house in a cage of hailstones, little beggars no bigger than pills but with the devil's spite in every one that struck its mark. "There is only one sort of garb for this place," I say to myself, as I push through the hail and wind, "and that is galvanised iron."

Mrs. Meehan produces her version of muffins for tea. There is a gay fire in the grate, built up mostly of fragrant Weymouth pine logs. I am pretty nearly starved, and the pamphlet on Table Poultry Production, propped against the milk-jug, gets scant attention. There is borage in a bowl on my desk; it serves to soften my mood. I am satisfied with a few flowers, with plain food, warmth of body, and tobacco. So heaven help the country!

Hunger sated, pleasantly weary, with a sweet-drawing pipe and my feet roasting, I take down and re-read Austin Dobson's poems. He wrote delightful verse, in a sprightly, witty key! What jewels he turns up without littering the place with the debris of a frantic delving! There is a whole series of tripping poems with pitfall endings as unexpected as the concluding twist in O. Henry yarns. One does not wish to end the good fare. I find myself husbanding the pages to make them last. Three times in succession I read "The Ballade of Beau Brocade." To mark time I read "A Dead Letter" and "Tu Quoque" twice. I could not ask for pleasanter evening entertainment than that which Austin Dobson provides in such a gladsome, lightsome and humorous way.

A rap at the door puts an end to poetry reading. John dolefully reports himself as ailing. I bring him into the light of the hall and take a look at him. He does not seem to be very bad. "Kinda pains in my back and a sort of an old cold!" Without hesitation I press quinine upon him, because there was, I suspected, a whiskey-seeking look in the tail of his eye. In these hard times my rather foolish philanthropy had better stop short of whiskey as a free remedy for colds. It looks as though I shall have the ewes in my charge as well as the rest.

*　　*　　*

John having been absent from work for three days, I learn a lot about boiling, pig-feeding, cow-feeding, and milking. The steady work did me a lot of good. I was inclined to grow grand and tear about too much in a motor, or else potter about at small jobs. Time was when I did all the milking myself (though, I may as well own up, I kept only two cows then), fed all the pigs, and daily cleaned out all the yard-houses. Jimmy and I now do the yard work between us. First we clean out the byre and feed the cows; then he does the milking. He may be slow at this, but I am slower. While I feed the pigs, Jimmy proceeds to let out the hens and give them grain, and I bring in the milk and separate. Then Jimmy, back from the poultry runs, gives the young pigs their apportioned share of the separated milk, while I give the remainder to the calves.

After breakfast Jimmy gets the boiler fire going (the boiler having been filled up the day before with potatoes and pulped mangolds) before he goes off to scrape the dropping-boards. I keep the fire stoked up, between brushing out the pig-houses (one's face gets violently hot when sweeping fresh

140

pig dung). Next I give hay to the cows; then I go into the drawing-room to attend the chicks. Mrs. Meehan takes on the washing of the separator, a job usually mine. I improve on John's system of mixing the pig-feeds by hauling in a big wooden tub to the boiler-house. I tip into this the contents of the boiler, add the meals, and give the whole mess several turnings with a short-handled shovel. Apparently John's method is to tip the boiled stuff into an old bath and mix the meal separately in buckets; when feeding time approaches, he adds the boiled material to each bucket. The disadvantage of my system compared with his is that all the pigs—in-pig sows, sows with bonhams, bonhams, slips, and fattening pigs—get the same mixture (six parts pollard, two bran, two barley-meal, one meat-meal), which is of course highly unscientific. But the devil fly away with albuminoid ratios during the present labour crisis.

When I get time I move the ewes and their lambs, according as the latter are big enough for shifting. I brand them before moving. How poor Mrs. Meehan detests the sight of that pitch and tar bucket! I act as though I thought she loved tar, and dump the bucket on top of the range, ignoring the fact that she is either baking bread or roasting meat. When the branding mixture is melted, I catch the lambs, a task requiring guile and fleetness, press them against my knee and, with the tar brand, impress a large S.R. on their little flanks. It is amusing how in the course of time the little lamb grows big, while the big lettering becomes small in comparison. Long-eared, long-legged little

141

lambs, shaking their silly tails and wriggling from my grasp; they are difficult to manipulate, but that is as nothing compared with the trouble that ensues when we try to get the ewes and lambs into marching order after the branding. The ewes are demented: they ba-a-a ceaselessly; they rush hither and thither, their fleeces bobbing on their backs. They run to the place whence they were roused, smelling frantically for the lambs which at the time are practically under their noses; or they rush back to the site where they yeaned so many nights ago. They follow the lambs of other ewes and, on discovering their mistake, they give the innocent cause of their blunder a cruel poke in the tummy. Ewes with single lambs are bad enough, but ewes with twins are the very deuce. Laddie is worse than useless in the difficulty; discipline cannot be maintained; a pair of lambs stray into the herbaceous border; another slithers down the kitchen steps; there is a ewe lost among the rose-bushes. I grab a brace of stray lambs by their necks, squat on my haunches, and call "yeddy-yeddy," then do my feeble best to imitate a lamb's intonation of "ba-a," in an effort to attract the right ewe to the right lamb, but nine times out of ten the wrong ewe comes. Fortunately, the distance is short between the house lawn and Little Meadows where the ewes with lambs are running, and an ending quickly comes to the panic.

*   *   *

All is set for sowing oats tomorrow. Joe is putting down the very last of the apple-trees. In the big barn John is cutting potatoes into sets, preparatory to sowing, which ought to begin next week. I am painting the workshop door and windows a sea-green, the very colour I have always thirsted for. Jimmy is extra busy on a practically non-stop round with chick-mash, cracked wheat, and water to the chickens, all of which are now evicted from the drawing-room and in his care.

I interrupt my painting to walk to the orchard and see that Joe is tramping hard enough round the planted trees to suit my exacting ideas on this matter. On the way I hit on a hitherto undiscovered nest of wild violets under the ha-ha at the top of the new orchard. This spring there is an unusual abundance of wild violets, they have a lovely scent, like a blessing. I cannot suppress a beaming smile when I see Joe tramping round and round the last tree; it is an occasion for throwing one's hat in the air, but Joe takes a sober view of farm work and would probably frown on such folly. I fear I have too great a respect for the respect the men have for me. But if moral cowardice prevented me from making a demonstration, the sun had no such qualms: it burst out suddenly, flooding the whole orchard with light.

The day developed the amber quality of white wine. I motored to several places near by in an atmosphere like a clean sheet, the whole world transfused with gold. From the magic carpet of Peugeot I see expanses of vivid green, ruddy sweeps of ploughed land, shining hedgerows, blobs of furze, and a rim of deep indigo mountains to the south. In the pale spring sky are great glossy heaps of cumulus clouds. The object of my touring was an attempt to charge up the car battery; I had to mobilise the farm and get shoved before I got the engine running; once I got going I went to many a foolish place: to Murphy, the blacksmith, to enquire when he would have the stone roller frame finished; to Alec Carter's, seeking information on the whereabouts of his corn-drill; to Miss Hackett's for a parcel left there by the bus; to Joe Condon's to find out if he has any British Queen seed potatoes for sale; to Lawlor, the lorry-owner, with an order to bring me a ton of pollard from Dublin. All this while, I did not once let the engine stop, so if the battery is not in fine fettle tomorrow after this merry-go-round I shall howl like a dog.

Before it grows dark, I walk a boreen in Moorstown direction and cut down hazel suckers to serve as stakes for the dozen cordon apples which I have planted at the back of a flower-bed opposite the house. Spring comes less gingerly in Moorstown than in Cloonmore. The banks sparkle pilewort; chervil and sanicle shoot up their bright foliage; chestnut-trees fling out cream blobs of buds. Strolling home in the gathering darkness, happiness surging up in me, Orion lopsided in the sky, shrugging his shoulders, the tranquil panting of a canal boat reaches me from the Lowtown direction. Careering over my budding wood goes a young moon, seeking mayhap a suitable tree in which to build her nest, where she can bring out her young in health and security.

CHAPTER VII

DRIVING TO DUBLIN CATTLE MARKET ON the heels of the last stall-fed of the season, a dawn of deathly waxenness glimmers on my right as I approach the city.

The Cattle Market, that great concrete island of north-west Dublin, is growing lightsome as I arrive. It is a confused welter of roadways, alleys, loading-stages, exits and entrances, dotted with salesmasters' huts, and divided up by an intricacy of iron railings. This large open space is surrounded by embarrassed dwelling-houses and nondescript premises.

The market is situated on a height, and light seethes up to it from the south-east, behind the Wicklow mountains, back of the spiked city. The mountains take on sharp contours; spires and chimney-stacks stand out first darkly, and then roseate. Few have time to look: it is all a question of rumps and flanks and "Any rise on last week's price?" There may be other farmers besides myself extracting comfort from the sight of mountains hemming in the city, from the fact that the puffed-up, the smug city, is looked down upon by wild heights. Perhaps the sheep destined for shipment, or for immediate slaughter in the *abattoir* across the road, see the bulk of Wicklow mountains growing lightsome too, and bleat more pitiably remembering lost freedom.

The market's most impressive hour is before daybreak on a winter Thursday. High-swung arc lamps pour down their light on the ranks of tied cattle, the congested sheep-pens, the ever mobile and noisy pig-pens. When times are good the cattle-buyers work at fever pace in what is probably a freezing temperature. The pig-buyers vault the railings rather than waste time opening gates. The arc lamps go out, and that too is a spectacle: they wink off one by one and we are left in the grey gloom. In the half light, salesmen peer into little, grubby books, rapidly entering sales with a stumpy pencil. Midwinter lends an especial enticement to the City Arms Hotel, which stands sentinel over the markets. The long rectangles of orange light tempt one from the outside rain, and from slithering in wellingtons through dung and darkness. One ought not have breakfast until one has disposed of one's stock, but the lure of lighted windows and the prospect of hot tea and a big roasting fire is strong. The devil take cattle, sheep, and pigs! It was thus I weakened this morning and took my breakfast before my heifer was sold.

The hotel is a rambling, old-fashioned place, with highly ornate ceilings, large pieces of ugly mahogany, pretentious daubs in huge carved and gilded frames, long tables lined with set-out places, and interspersed with large and elaborate cruet-stands. A pale modern, typical specimen of present degeneracy, orders simply bacon and eggs, as an extra to tea and the small loaves peculiar to the establishment; but the real hardened breakfaster follows the tradition: he has chops; or bacon, eggs, and sausages; or fish followed by bacon and eggs; or a piece of steak; these are as nothing to him, constituting a mere preface to the great hungry day. For breakfast companions one has English buyers, Dublin butchers, big Meath graziers, large-scale stall-feeders, and small fry like myself. Here one learns about the market's progress, what So-and-so gave per hundredweight for a score of bullocks, what beef is making at Birkenhead. Newspapers are provided—the pro-bullock sorts—and one may be lucky enough after breakfast to find space before the fire for drawing up a chair and glancing at the news. Outside, there is an extensive view of serried cattle and pens of sheep, with flitting humans seeming remote and shadowy from this cosy vantage-point. Right below the windows, the turnstile to the hotel enclosure whirls unceasingly as men flow in to throng the bar downstairs. Beside the turnstile, the boot-cleaners and the wellington washers have their stand, but their trade is a dull one until the day is more advanced. It is snug up here amidst the breakfast debris and the gleaming electro-plate; companionship is easily found, for butting into conversations is quite in order. It is a wrench when the time comes to brave once more the elements and the slimy concrete.

My heifer unsold, I wander into the pig-market. A temporary lull in the cattle trade will often occur for a few hours until the smaller Dublin butchers roll up. The sheep trade goes on at an even pace, seldom very intensely. But business in the pig-market is over early, indeed it is practically finished with the coming of day. Excepting the pig-market,

147

the Dublin markets are man's domain. Even here, there is only a feminine sprinkle: a few farmers' or labourers' wives, who come up to see that their fat pig gets a square deal, and a dozen or more women who arrive in mid-morning to purchase slips or bonhams, which they fatten in Dublin back-yards, almost under the noses of the proud but unsuspicious citizens.

Spring comes to Prussia Street without a green streamer, the concrete sees to that. But the pollard chestnuts outside the City Arms Hotel break out in whitish green peaks, and the garden fronts of the houses of market-bounding roads are often gay.

Summer—and all Dublin lies like a magic city between the markets and the mountains. Suffused with sunny pink, its spires glittering, roofs gleam-ing. Now the lambs are in!—bawling, munching, blinking, butting, meditative. The cattle smell of grass. The cow-market is full of superlative cows at their best. Lambs in demand . . . the weather is hot, and roast beef is no longer relished. The lamb-buyers clang open and shut the pen-gates from the early hours until a clearance is made. They feel for hand-widths, test fatness by tail compass, lift the lambs bodily to judge their weight, and ask the price. On hearing it, they look to Heaven for signs of the Almighty's wrath, reluctantly make a low offer, and stalk away—a certain distance. "Well, is it any use to you?" Ignored by the in-dignant salesmaster, they retrace their steps a little. "Well, will you take it?" No answer is deigned. "I must be off. No use calling after me. Will you sell?" Some day surely the hour of vengeance will come, and the whole marketful of sheep, seeing the humour of this humbug bargaining, will ba-a so mirthfully as to split this concrete isle.

Poor little bewildered lambs, bawling out their hearts for a mother's comforting in wide fields. Once in a while, a troop of enterprising urchins wandering up from the slums appreciate the little creatures. I have seen big brothers dragging away little brothers from lamb-worshipping. "Come 'ome to yer dinner, or I'll mike yer." But we, the hard-boiled, are indifferent: to us a lamb is either "a good stamp of a lamb" or "a bad, thin sort."

Heifer still unsold, and the bell of Aungier Street church is announcing late Mass. The sky lifts, the drovers begin business, the buyers' men raddle the purchased sheep, salesmen and their staffs find time to get together for a confab. Almost every hour has its own characteristics in the markets. From the opening, when all is determined buying, to the latest hour when buying deteriorates into protracted coquetry between buyer and salesmaster; from the hour of lorries arriving, stock-laden to their utmost, to the time when the pair of little nuns arrive and beg alms for their poor. These are diminutive women: one young, shy, and silent; the other old, attractively ugly, and talkative. They seem extra small in contrast with the long-boned farmers and the burly buyers from England. Few refuse these mendicant nuns: conversations are broken off, hats lifted, there is a delving into trouser pockets and a check to the flow of obscenities and blasphemies, the careless coins of speech current between rough men at the peak of man's work. While the interchanges last there is a rippling of gracious smiles and "It's a lovely day, Sister," and "You're welcome indeed, Sister." The little old nun is the most popular frequenter of the markets.

There are other regular market characters besides the cheerful little nuns. The same fruit-sellers come there every Thursday, fine strapping girls in loose mesh black shawls, who horseplay, and smoke cigarettes with the young drovers. There is a mendicant blind man led about by his wife: an unattractive pair who do not inspire confidence in the worthy fate of one's penny. There is the caped policeman outside the pig-market, whose job it is to see that no pig enters the gates without an accompanying bit of script (do not ask me to explain why, why not, or wherefore). Many of the drovers also grow familiar, perhaps on account of the haphazardness of their clothing; most of them are oldish, some are half-witted, and many are wizened to the point of deformity; they are all hungry-looking, poor and miserable, for their occupation is a precarious one and badly paid, probably offering absolutely no opportunity for advancement. There is a trollop who makes a point of breaking into conversations with proffered boxes of matches, British-made to increase the annoyance. Many of the buyers are characters worth observing: Jewmen with their very own notions of that which constitutes a joke; Yorkshiremen with genial twinkling eyes and knobbly accents; and certain Dublin butchers reputed by the envious farmers to be stupendously wealthy.

I rest myself on the narrow bench in my salesmaster's office, hoping that something will turn up. The salesmen's offices descend in structural quality from solid blockhouses of concrete to flimsy wood shanties. All are provided with a counter and some semblance of a desk. Some have built-in stoves, but most of them are heated with portable oil stoves. On very harsh days, one is glad to shelter in the salesmaster's office. At least there is a short bench on which to sit, and a roof over one's head. But otherwise there are few comforts, for the place fills up continually with buyers paying in cheques, sellers receiving payment (carefully buttoning up their coats as they step out again), and drovers bursting in to obtain orders for moving the cattle or sheep that have been purchased. The stand-men come in from time to time with armfuls of rope halters, as the ranks of beasts begin to thin; they fling the halters on the floor, missing or not missing one's outstretched legs. There is much to learn if one listens to the news of the market; every man approaching the desk has some pronouncement to make to the clerk about the tone the market took. Jokes are exchanged, and one gets new and oft-times unexpected slants on the political and economic situation. This is the place to get one's finger on the farming pulse, if not of all Ireland, certainly of the whole province. Far too early in the year for comfortable sensations, one learns that the hay is made up in Nobber, or some such place, or that threshing is already in full swing in Kilkenny. One gets an inkling of prices at the last Mullingar Fair; or of what wool is now making in Newbridge; of how the tobacco stood up to the recent high winds in Athy; of the kind of potato crop grown by the Cooley men this year, and scores of other interesting snippets of farming news.

But nothing has been said about the Dublin Markets unless one investigates the fate of the stock: the prime beasts, the old cows and bulls, the milch cows, the wethers, hoggets, lambs, the old ewes and rams, the bacon pigs, the pork pigs, old sows and boars, slips and bonhams. The economy of the weekly market may influence the politics of the nation. There is, too, a sermon in this great hebdomadal gathering of animals: a story of long oppression and injustice, of evictions and emigration.

Fianna Fail's wheat-growing policy scarcely stirs a single beast's hair up here. Whatever else may be a good trade in the market, patriotism of the new order is always a drug.

*　　*　　*

Spring bounces lamb-like across the breadth of Ireland, insisting on notice. Now Graigue hedgerows are vernal with that accursed snow-berry and the scarcely less accursed privet. The trees are holding themselves back for a "bring-down-the-house" yell of green. Nosegay-sized foliage is grabbing sunshine like babies grasping the air with their ridiculous little hands. The sky is as happy-faced as a First Communion child in her veil. Furze is reconnoitring with scented scouts; the half-open umbrella of the horse-chestnut recommends itself as an emblem for a Youth Movement.

Chestnuts and sycamores are decently clothed, but the beeches have not yet put on as much as a loin-cloth. The limes are pointed with brick-red, the ashes with inky bud jackets (their flowers are like purple-sprouting broccoli). The cadaverous oaks spoil the party, being in comparative nakedness. We have a perfect chestnut in Cloonmore which in full foliage looks like a green tea-cosy on a stalk; but when not fully clothed, it seems decorated with blobs of foliage, like a child's attempt at painting a tree. Sycamores, for all their gross vulgarity, are fine and green at this season.

Tommy Waters roars up the avenue in a new yellow-and-white sports car. Would I go with him to Marymount monastery to view the pleasure-grounds which his firm is laying out there? No, I won't. I have nine dozen eggs to wash, grade, and pack. Will he come in and have a glass of sherry? No, he won't: my sherry is always cooking sherry, and besides he has to be back in Dublin by five to see the Minister of Lands and Fisheries. "Oh, you needn't try to impress me," I scoff, "I know you're always conferring with ministers. I've got to finish painting the yard pump; I've got to sow vegetable seeds which ought to have been sown a fortnight ago, I've got to . . ." "Ah, what do you keep men for? Can't the boy do it? Come on and sit in! You'll like those gardens," he added persuasively, "and I do want you to try my car." "Well, anyway, I've got to shave. The boy can't do that for me . . ." Thus I weakened. Tommy agreed to wait just so long as I was shaving and no longer. From my bedroom window, as I lather up, I watch him draw sécateurs from his hip-pocket (it seems that doctors produce stethoscopes from their pockets, carpenters foot-rules, tailors tapes, and nurserymen produce sécateurs). Tommy advances in a business-like way to my cordons and industriously begins to snip. I rap furiously on the window-pane, but he does not hear me. Horror-stricken, I see him mutilate my James Grieve, but I calm myself with an effort: after all, a nurseryman must know his job.

Mrs. Meehan shows her usual remarkable good sense by handing me a package of cake and sand-wiches as I pass out. Tommy waxes eloquent on the merits of his new car: it is a twenty-horse-power six-cylinder, all "lines" and speed characters, no top, no running-board, no nothing, except an iron grip to seize when the speed attains the hectic eighties. As we whiz down the avenue like a swallow's flash I try in vain to stem the flow of Tommy's laudatory comments by pointing out the beauties of the new concrete-post fence. At ostrich speed as far as Moorstown Cross and then like light-ning along the Milltown Road. "I wish I had a hat-pin," I yell in the ears of the intrepid driver. "The brakes are wonderful," is his reply. Clutching my seat, my eyes watering, we reach Milltown in what seems seconds. There is a pig-fair in progress and the town is all cluttered up with traffic, but Tommy is unconcerned. We whirl through the streets at fifty miles an hour, making a series of vindictive rushes at defenceless creels of pigs ("The brakes are good, aren't they?" he howls), then in a mad career across the bridge and into the square, a dead-set at lorries, a premeditated charge on cyclists and 'sdeath to all pedestrians! As we emerge from the stunned town, Tommy half turns round in his seat once more to extol the brakes, when an ass-cart shoots out from a laneway. Tommy jerks back, describes an S hook, the figure 8, and we are once again in comparative safety. That jerk sobered him and he slackened speed.

On we go through mountain roads, with wide-spreading views, gorges and boulders, forming a rare sight for the sore eyes of a midland farmer. We pass through the zenith of Irish landscape beauty. At first the green hedges, their buds closed, the blinds still down, but wait a few weeks and see what a Mammoth White Sale will here commence. Then high hills, blue-shadowed on olive ground, heathered and brackened; fields fluttering their young grass flags; tender-leaved birches, hazels, and oaks. The road seemed to go dancing before us, up and down, looking back to laugh at us. At first it was a grey road, then red, and finally yellow, the hues graduating with the declivity. The clouds above us were swelling and shrinking, curved and creviced, blue-stained, umber-stained, and grey. The merry water of a far-away lake was dimpling. Hill-slopes were gaudy with blazing furze in a scented spate. Glory be to God, what furze! A cavalry charge of it down a whole range of hills. We drive on the rim of a paradise peopled with furze, and I make a prosy enough comment to that effect to Tommy. He answers drily, "*Spartium junceum* makes a better show." "Oh, does it indeed?

2s. 6d. to 5s. 6d., I suppose. Well, let me tell you that *Taraxacum Dens-Leonis* makes an even better show. Strike in pans or shallow boxes," I continue in his own jargon, "and when large enough to handle, prick out; a graceful and free-flowering plant, flowers rich yellow, and a very striking novelty."

Tommy swallows the bait, ruminates for half a mile or so, and then asks:

"What is *Tara*—what do you call it anyway? Is it in our catalogue?"

"Well, no, I don't think so, but I've seen it in your place dozens of times."

"What is it? Or is it a fake name?"

"No, sir, *Taraxacum Dens-Leonis* is just the Latin name for dandelion."

Tommy damped, I return to my own thoughts. When I am dead, send a wreath of furze. Plant it over me; let it rip wantonly on my grave; let the artillery of its seed-popping be my last post, and its scent my incense. May I marry a girl with furze-coloured hair! Give me bouquets of it, sheaves and posies; stick it on wands for me; nail it to my mast; and hang it out of your windows should I come riding home in triumph.

Within sight of Marymount, we draw up and eat: a one-man package of sandwiches for two, and nothing to drink. Ordinary agricultural land lies about us now. In an adjacent field, a man in navy-blue dungarees shoves before him a bleached blue seed-barrow, the thin trickles of grass seeds spilling as he goes, like the milk-stream from a flush cow; the broad field, which is already the mother of a million oat blades, looks rosy brown (how seldom soil is really a colourman's brown), happy at the prospect of more child-bearing.

Tommy did not exaggerate the charm of Marymount nor the good taste with which his firm laid out the pleasure gardens. His only error was an under-estimate of the monks' hospitality. Though neither of us have great appetites, we are forced to eat and drink when we return from viewing the gardens with the Superior. Down a long path sheltered by a hedge of *Cupressus macrocarpa*, we were conducted to a shrine flanked by a medley of flowering shrubs, brooms now breaking into waspish blossom, almonds still clinging to pink petals, and standard *Viburnun carlisii* making fragrant the surrounding air. At the back of the shrine (a statue of Our Lady, soft-smiling and womanly as Raphael would have her) is a bank of azalea and rhododendrons, and, according to the Superior, these gave offence when in flower by colour clashing. Perhaps I belong to a newer school of thought than the priest's, but I revel in a good and violent clash of colours. The matching of floral hues into harmonious blends is surely only a nasty nineteenth-century conceit.

Tommy having made divers entries in his notebook, we recite our little farewell speeches and set off again down the furze-blazing hills. Half-way to Milltown we are hailed by a man seeking a lift. We squeeze him in beside us on the front seat. He is not long in telling us that he is an ex-soldier, a Boer War veteran, and hero of many a martial exploit. Having regaled us with several specimen

157

stories of his soldiering experience, he told us impressively that the whole secret of success in life and the preservation of good health is to keep the guts warm at night. I expressed some surprise at the simplicity of the formula, but he was very insistent and emphatic: "What you need is a naggin of rum and a woollen body belt; whatever you do, keep the guts snug."

Restored to Cloonmore, I go back to the monotonous grind of packing eggs in the workshop, resuming the task where I had left off. Then when I finish this dull duty, I go outdoors for a little pleasant dalliance with the virgin spring. I lie on the grass (yes, long weeks before I have any right to do so), gazing at the nodding daffodils around me, and whistling bars of Grieg to the birds. Those who planted daffodil bulbs in Cloonmore long years ago certainly spared no pains in securing original varieties: one specimen has a face like the village idiot; another is like a bantam's egg just dropped on the pan; a third rises from the underworld with a mask across its face, like a Chicago gun-man. Beside me is the long flower-bed with the cordon apples at its rear, and bush rose-trees in front. I long for the time of roses. Give me roses and such and let the other fellows write the ballads and run the country. Behind me, the peas are overground, looking like little green chicks squatting in a patient row. Everything is growing and coming to life in April's womb.

Pregnancy is perhaps the most exalted state of life. When I die, could I not shed seeds profusely in my regretted wake? I wish that I could burgeon out in crinkled leaves, shoot forth gold-veined foliage from my shoulders, sprigs from my knees, and tasselled catkins from my ears. Alas, this vegetative insanity overcomes me because I have ventured to lie on the grass after sunset. It is certain that queer things happen to people who do this. You'll always find that folk who are a little wanting, who fancy faces in flowers, who go off the deep end about scenery, sing unofficially, or persist in whistling answers to blackbirds, have at some time or other lain on the grass and brought upon themselves the earth madness.

*　　*　　*

This being Holy Saturday, I shadow Father Hayes from 7 until 9.30 A.M. He cannot shake me off during the performance of the Paschal rites. When he strikes the fire in the porch, and when he blesses the five grains of incense to be placed in the Paschal candle, I am just behind him. As he reads the Twelve Prophecies I pant after him in the Missal (he upon the altar and I in the pew); usually we are neck-to-neck, but as I read in English and he has to speak the Latin, I beat him in the end. When he is robed in a purple cope and departs to the baptismal font, I too leave my place in the church and see him divide the waters and throw some to the four quarters of the earth.

When the priest returns to the sacristy there is a wild and enthusiastic dash for the newly blessed water. A representative of every house in Cloonmore, Graigue, Firlands, Ballinamona, and Moorstown makes an onset on the font to obtain a supply of holy water for house use and for the blessing of crops. There is a clink of bottles which would do credit to the back premises of any pub, accompanied by every sort of noise water is capable of making. Although I strive to maintain a liturgical dignity and aloofness, I cannot help seeing Mrs. Hackett colliding violently with Mrs. O'Connell, each of the dames being burdened with a five-noggin bottle of holy water, and the three small Lawlor children convulsed with mirth, doubtless considering this the best fun that Holy Saturday offered.

The ceremonies concluded, the church woman shows both speed and efficiency. In a twinkling she has the altar decorated with daffodils and pots of gardenias and cinerarias; the candles are lighted and the Mass begins. One is positive that the world is a better place since the candles and flowers have been restored to the altar (the penitential season of forty days being over), more joy and more hope have surely entered the world since the dawn of this day.

If I had charge of the sanctuary bell, Lord, but I'd wallop it. Paddy Maher's gossoon hasn't got the idea. Christ has risen! Lent is over. Make it ring, boy, hit it again. Alleluia, alleluia, alleluia! Strike it hard, boy. *Gloria in excelsis*—that's the ticket. In the perfect parish after this Mass, the congregation should shake hands all round.

Mangold sowing is the job for us today. Already forty-five drills are open. As I cycle home, Mick and Joe pass me on the avenue, each leading

160

a dray of reamy dung. After my breakfast, for which I am ravenous, I join John and Jimmy with a four-grained fork in hand for work on dung spreading. This drying weather takes all the good out of spread dung if it is left too long exposed, so that we shall try to get all the opened drills dunged, spread, and closed before night. Our task is to shake out and bed down the dung in the wake of the carters. The work is just sufficiently strenuous to make John peel off his coat. It is evident from his back view that his woman is a careful soul who does not waste flour-bags; he is inscribed with a large legend in a patch across the back of his waistcoat, *Erin's Pride, Seven Gold Medals*. It is my hope that Jimmy won't notice this, or his working pace will be badly hampered by a fit of "the stitches." Although Kit Healy was hired specially to turn the dung-heap, the stuff that is now thrown down to our teasing forks is often firmly matted; otherwise ours is an easy, sociable sort of job, permitting a certain amount of chatter, and occasional glances in directions other than the tillage field in which we work.

Just now, the oats-crop is covering the adjacent field with a wispy veil, delicate and sort of dreamy. There is something pathetic about the first stage of growing oats. Trusting as an infant, it shoves through the rough soil, seeking the "rational milk" which in its case is light and warmth. The blades are so tiny and yet so strong and confident; snub-nosed and very fragile and translucent, they yet advance with the force of tidal waves or forest fires, sundering the earth's skin to fulfil their mission:

161

which is to wax wavy, green, fruitful and golden, and to fill granaries.

On the lawn the ewes and lambs are spread out widely. The ewes often assume a kneeling posture when nibbling the short grass. "There is great growth these days," volunteers Jimmy. "How do you know?" I say crushingly; young lads tending poultry cannot know much about the growth of grass. "Because the lambs aren't bawling for the ewes' milk any more. They are stuffing down the grass instead. Besides, there is a corn-crake behind No. 5, and corn-crakes don't come until there is enough grass to cover them." I am fully answered anyway.

For a wonder, I am left undisturbed the whole morning at dung spreading. Such four-hour spells of peace are rare enough; most days I am summoned to the house on some petty errand, such as selling a setting of hatching eggs, or refusing to buy fat ducks, or assenting to the loan of an implement, or giving pence to a poor man. The daily round of a farm is not what outsiders might suppose: a matter of beeves and fatlings, and transactions concerning hundreds of barrels of corn, or tons of potatoes.

When the day's work is finished I draw a deck-chair out on the steps and unfold the newspaper; Laddie tucks up to my boots. A mere eyebrow of a moon strays over the yew (which, since the snow-storm, looks much the worse for wear). Jimmy's corn-crake, the musical version of growing grass, makes himself audible; a blackbird is dragging sun-set motes on his outstretched wings as he flies from tree to tree. I am indolently scanning the headlines, when I drop the paper in sudden excitement and hearken attentively: there is no mistake, it is the Cuckoo!

My, but he has grown hoarse since he made his last public utterance! I would hardly recognise his voice; he screeches like an old gate that has been left shut all the winter. "I rejoice with you," say I, stretching out a hand to Laddie, "the Cuckoo is back." But Laddie only blinks at me; it is nothing at all to him. Like on New Year's Eve, there should be kissing all round on the day when Cuckoo first acclaims himself, but I have only Laddie—and Mrs. Meehan. Well, let it pass for this year.

More like a croaking raven than a blithe bird, but how welcome is his voice in Cloonmore. He speaks way off, unctuously, like an itinerant preacher, yet in sardonic tones for all that. The year has found its voice: little green tongues of leaves, myriads of grass blades, oat-crops bristling, trees unfurling, all dumb until Cuckoo played poet. He sets piebald April to music: wry music, often tomfool music. Sanctimonious in April, ironic in May, disillusioned in June, but always mocking, ever a Jacques, detached from action, contemplative, bantering, secretive and deep.

The feast is spread, not under the trees alone, but over the trees too. The sequence from snow-drops to furze (when white has come, can yellow be far behind?) is consummated. There is a blush of mazard blossom, sky-dust has settled on the myosotis, and so to the bleached lilac of the cuckoo-flower, blotching the dry ditches and spreading over pastures, cuckoo's special flower arriving on his heels.

The prologue is Master Cuckoo's part. The curtain of primrose and dandelion brocade, with lamb-tail tassels, may now ring up. The stage is ready: from a great expanse of tender grass blades to wilted stalks, from shy blossom buds to great hearty apples, from swards to endless skies, from midges to mountains. Cuckoo permits: summer by the Grace of God!

CHAPTER VIII

AT MANGAN AND MYSELF CO-OPERATE IN most of our big sheep drives, and so we planned to combine our flocks for washing purposes. Together we inspected the Coolalug sheep-hole. It is situated about a mile up a winding boreen. Pat shortens the walk by regaling me with information on the ownership of adjacent land, and with lore concerning the owners. When we reach the deep hole, which is about ten yards wide, Pat declares it greatly flooded compared with last year. I am quite taken aback on sight of it, so indescribably evil does it seem: a dirty, fathomless place to commit my valuable sheep; an eerie pool such as might have suited Hetty Sorrel for the drowning of her love-child; a haunted spot, perhaps meet for the obscene rites of witches, but not water for cleansing sheep. Then, in the fading light, we discern a rotting sheep carcass on the far side of the pond. "That's enough for me," I declare; "I'll wash my sheep in the canal and risk the chance of being caught by the authorities and heavily fined."

Yet all the same, such is Pat's cajolery, I take my sheep to Coolalug. I know it is a halving of labour to work in with the Mangans. So behold Pat and Peter Mangan, Mick, Joe, and myself, all marching behind our combined flocks. They make the grand total of ninety sheep (lambs of course being left behind). Mick leads the procession with the mare and dray containing creels for pen-making, ropes, and a drag for life-saving purposes, while the rest of us drive the sheep.

"What do you call this place?" I ask Pat, indicating the beginning of the boreen to the Coolalug sheep-hole.

"It has no name I ever heard of except the Coolalug sheep-hole road," answers Pat.

It is a delicious day, an azure sky (just the colour of that variety of notepaper), the hedges are greening, the blackthorn is still in blossom, dull blossom like grubby foam.

Lack of a place-name does not detract from that scented lane leading to the sheep-washing pond. It is as long, as warm, as crammed with flowers as the early summer day is long and warm and flowerful. Slowly we drive on the lagging sheep, furze to the right of us, furze to the left, dangling larks and a heat haze overhead, between high walls of privet and blackthorn and hawthorn, the road surface consisting simply of large stones padded into soft clay.

The boreen twists, dodges here and there, and arrives at nowhere in particular. Chesterton's theory that the winding roads of England were traced out by drunken men on their homeward way, is capped by Pat who holds that the Irish roads were laid down by old-womanish fellows, who always kept their backs to the wind when they were working. "Well, the wind must have been blowing for a long spell in the one direction when they laid the road between Cloonlara and

Firlands," comments Joe; in truth the said road is as straight and undeviating as a pike. Pat goes on to suggest that there must have been dozens of homesteads abutting on this roadway long ago, but that they were broken up in eviction times and the lands joined for the formation of ranches.

Larks hang from the sky, singing as though their very lives were sustained by song. The banks are crowded with primroses and violets in full bloom, a proud orchid stands solitary on a knoll, and the little white eyes of stitchwort peep at us from the cool roots of the privet. The sheep nibble wisps of grass, hedge leaves, and even furze flowers as they progress along at a leisurely pace.

The brunt of the business is taken on by Mick and Joe, Mick throwing the ewes into the pond, while Joe with a rake steers them to the landing-place. Peter, who seems destined for the hard jobs in life, catches the sheep in the improvised pen we had made; and I (who contrive to get the soft jobs) keep the washed sheep together in a corner a little way down the boreen. All the time the men are working they keep up a perpetual patter, the greater part of it addressed to the sheep, telling them duck themselves well, or swim out a bit there. The ewes bleat fretfully and nervously before immersion, and shake themselves violently when they emerge, wetting all the ground around them. Mick has an amazing faculty for distinguishing sheep. He tells Peter to "ketch that small brown butty one over there," and another he describes as "that bald old long-tail." His descriptions are slightly disconcerting to the

167

moderately proud owners of two good and standardised flocks of Wicklow-Cheviots.

In my job of penning together the washed sheep, I find opportunity to pick flowering heads of creeping bugle and water avens and bring them close to my face (unseen, I trust, by my fellow sheep-washers), delighting in the whorls of blue and in the wondrously tinted bracts of the bugle, while all the colours of sunset seem to be held in the five petals of the avens.

A moorhen chatters at us from across the pond. Silver-grey catkins dangle overhead. From every ditch of dirty water, marsh marigolds mock the goldsmith's ideal. A freckled sky above, the violent yellow of furze contrasting with the intense green of new grass. Yes, and I fling it in the teeth of the whole "Celtic Twilight" school—that's Ireland in mid-May.

But for all the bliss of May flowers, brilliant sunshine, and other romantic features of this early summer day, the halt at Mrs. Hackett's on our way home through Graigue was also to our liking. Glad to be out of the glare, we quaffed brimming glasses to relieve our consuming thirst, each of us taking a turn in minding the sheep outside the shop.

Furze, for all the laudatory bastings it receives from me, is a nasty, spiny thing to pick, awkward too in its conveyance from bush to flower-vase. However, I successfully snapped off a branch in Coolalug, flung it into the dray amidst the creels, and, having taken its vengeance of pricks, I fix it up in a vase on the dining-room table. Up comes

Mrs. Meehan with the soup, stands and stares at it, then breaks into a cackle: "What did you bring in the old weed for, sir?" We topple in each other's estimation. I am the *omadaun* unable to distinguish a weed from a flower, and Mrs. Meehan is an old fathead unable to distinguish furze from a flower.

A Wyandotte hen, weary of her thirty days' sitting on a dozen duck eggs, loses patience and stalks off when the eleventh duckling emerges from its shell. Fortunately, I find the twelfth egg still warm and, happily inspired, I take it to the kitchen, wrap it in felt and place it in the oven with the door left ajar. Half an hour later I go back to look, and find a little grassy creature with beady eyes. "Well, your name is Jackie as sure as a canary's is Dickie," I tell him, as I take him out to his brethren.

*　　*　　*

I take tea with the O'Connors of Upper Moorstown. John and his brother, Mattie, are ageing bachelors who live alone on their large and isolated farm, with no company save that of an ancient housekeeper. They are taking their declining years easily, having long since made their money. Their five hundred Irish acres are all gone back to grass, although at one time at least half of it was under the plough. For the supervision of the whole farm, including the care of one hundred and fifty ewes and their progeny, the herding of about ninety two- and three-year-old bullocks, the O'Connors employ only two men. The decline of Upper Moorstown does not end with a descent from tillage to bullocks: once there was a family of fourteen in the farm-house, now there are only two bachelors and one of them a little "delicate" (which, in plain English, means mentally deficient); for the O'Connors the spacious, crowded days are gone for ever.

Thus, all the glory of the farm lies in its past—its remote nineteenth-century past; for neither the prosperity accompanying the first decade of the present century, nor the War boom, seriously quickened the declining pulse of this establishment. Half of John O'Connor's remarks when showing me over the place were prefaced with such explanations as: "My poor father (God forgive him) divided up this field . . ." or "It was he put down that belt of larches below. . . ."

John leads me up to the fields to inspect grazing bullocks. We talk market prices and economic conditions. John O'Connor's comments on De Valera's scrap with J. H. Thomas may not, alas, be reported here, as they would render this innocent farming account unfit for virtuous readers. O'Connor's fields are big—a strong type of land and very sound (though he tells me that it is a frequent occurrence for cattle to die of black-quarter in neighbouring farms). No doubt Moorstown's immunity from disease can be attributed to the efficient land draining carried out by O'Connor senior in the 'sixties. There is good shelter too and a fairly good water supply; it is a farmer's farm: no park features whatever, such as solitary trees or fancy plantations. Most of the fields bear evidence of ancient ploughing. We reach the bullocks and creep up to them, pacify them by scratching their rumps, and feel for indications of fatness in all the parts of their anatomy known to professionals like ourselves. John relates meanwhile how he fared at last week's market and how he all but struck the little brat of an English buyer, who dared to tell him that his bullocks were both too fat and too big! Did I ever hear anything like that? In his day, there was none of that nonsense: either a beast was a fully-grown fat beast, or else he was only a thin store. Baby-beef my eye!

This clears the way for telling me the usual stories of that golden period when beef was ninety shillings per hundredweight. We go back to the house through the kitchen garden, a small patch nicely fenced by a mixture of beech and holly. Behind my host's back, I surreptitiously shake hands with myself, for every single vegetable growing here is better and more advanced over in Cloonmore, and yet I thought I had the wintriest farm in the midlands. I pause for a second to stare at a patch of cabbage plants gone into flower: my host might wonder at my interest, but to me cabbages in flower dash up in sparks like a Roman candle, a gladsome sight for those with eyes to see it. At the garden gate there is a dandy young copper beech: in its first flush of foliage, the copper beech assumes a tint like café-au-lait.

Four cats with bushy tails (the sole surviving links with the dead sisters, I am told) come from the kitchen door as we advance, and groom themselves on John's shins to his great pleasure. In-doors, Mattie has harnessed himself to the wireless, and the little parlour is waist-high in billowy music. I wade through it to an armchair. Mattie scarcely rises on our entry, but continues to twirl the dials. He succeeds in increasing the volume of sound, and then grins broadly at us. I sit with a look of studied contentment on my face. Everywhere there are what-nots groaning under plush-framed photographs, sea-shells, and china ornaments for the delectation of our eyes.

We take tea in the dining-room. John is a charming host, and the very pattern of courtesy. The gaunt housekeeper puts in her head, offering the addition of cold goose to the fare, but I decline: I sort of feel she might carve a drum-stick off herself!

For an hour or more after tea we submit to wire-less. I smoke continually and am, to all appearances, satisfied with life, but John O'Connor is a host in a hundred. He fetches his photograph album and passes it to me. I try to make intelligent comments on snapshots taken by John, the sub-jects being variations of red setters posed in front of dreary laurustinus and acuba, or the housekeeper and Mattie and red setters, standing in the porch. There are lots of old men like John who think that, by adding unto their weight of years such modern gadgets as a radio set, or by dabbling in photography, they become as young as the best.

When John starts to reminisce, I begin to see that the wireless has its uses; at least it roars down the noisy silence of a house that was at one time so peopled. He speaks quietly, his kindly face serene except when humorously creviced, but sometimes a film of sadness clouds his eyes. Though John is seventy or a little over, his age is not great, but he can claim a lot "back of that." When his personal recollections are exhausted, he has a rich mine of tradition and hearsay upon which to fall back. Once when he was speaking of the price of wheat during the "Bony" wars (£3 a barrel), I was deceived for a moment into imagining he himself was then alive.

When he was a boy they used to have thirty men and women employed for the harvest; these workers received sevenpence or eightpence a day, and were fed on oaten bread and buttermilk, with the addition of bacon on Thursdays and Sundays. Some of them could not eat meat (by which is meant bacon, of course), never having tasted it in their lives. It was the practice to add pea-flour to the rough wheaten bread made for these workers, so that it would be more sustaining, as whole-wheat bread was considered too light. They slept in out-houses or out-of-doors. They worked from 5 A.M. until "it was so dark that they couldn't find their coats, and they did not want them either in those days, when the summers really were summers. There might be one wet day in a fortnight, but that would be all; there were no showers, and no grey days such as we have now." The harvesters came from west Cork; they used to walk all the way to the midlands and back. They had their own travel routes, taking the shortest and most direct lines from place to place, these tracks being doubtless the traditional highways of ancient Ireland. They had a habit of collecting bits and scraps of their rations and saving them for journey fare, and they never touched a penny of their wages until they were home again. They worked all day, and could dance most of the night.

Men's bodily needs were easily satisfied in those days. One man whom they employed on piece-work, and who earned an average of eightpence a day, broke his fast only once in the twenty-four hours, when he ate a bowl of maize porridge at eleven o'clock in the morning.

Corn always stood in those days: it was all cut with hooks, and threshed with flays. John O'Connor's parents used to journey to Dublin by the express fly canal-boat. There were scenes of great animation when the boat arrived at the hotel in Lowtown. Cattle were mostly driven by road to Dublin, though there were occasional consign-ments by canal. Farm labourers living in used to get half a crown a week. Eggs were never eaten on the farm; they fetched fivepence and sixpence a dozen in the markets, and were considered an important source of revenue.

John, when a "chap," used to attend the big annual fair in Kilbride. Deviously known as the ewe fair, the rush fair, or the onion fair, this event took place early in October. They used to fill up the well of the side-car with onions and then stack rushes on the top. He described to us how rush-lights were made. He remembered the first paraffin oil lamp to make its appearance in a Low-town shop window: he joined with the neighbours and went off to view the wonder. The first lamp on his own farm was lighted by his uncle, who turned up the wick too quickly, thus cracking the globe, and the lamp was there and then condemned as a highly dangerous machine not fit for everyday use.

Is it surprising that I feel as though I had walked through pages of "Knocknagow" in Upper Moorstown this summer evening? John O'Connor's house and farm being still so little unspoilt (even Mattie could not succeed in dialling us out of its atmosphere), the stories ring extraordinarily real. I am unappeased when the evening comes to an end. An orphan hearing about its parents for the first time could hardly be more moved than I was on hearing tales of Mother Ireland as she was fifty years ago, nay seventy and ninety years ago, for John combines his father's and even his grandfather's memories with his own.

But the vision that smote upon my heart with most painful poignancy was not conveyed by my host in words, though it was conjured up very vividly in his conversation. It was a picture of this now silent and depopulated rural countryside as it formerly was, in the time of John O'Connor's grandfather. Teeming with life and industry and full of happy homesteads, the land worked by large families, a people who lived in conditions of most primitive simplicity, a race of splendid physique, independent-minded, long-enduring, and, above all, so extraordinarily happy and care-free. The people had far more heart in them those days. They were always laughing and always in good spirits. In this parish of now scarcely broken green and so sparsely populated, there were in the early nineteenth century nine schools, each

175

of them crowded out with pupils, where now there are but three schools and these but poorly attended. It is thus we have "progressed" from cornlands to pasture, and from the hedge schools packed with voluntary and eager scholars, to the falling and ever-falling averages of our compulsory National Schools; from large and happy families to a declining marriage rate, which has now dropped to a point that renders us ludicrous among the nations; to empty homes where desiccated old maids and elderly warped bachelors end out their days of unfulfilment. Genial and generous John O'Connor hardly guessed that he sent me from his hospitable home with a knife in my heart. Can we *ever* recover? I asked myself. Can we *ever* recover?

There is a jolly moon these nights: it is like a fairy's carriage, or again it is like a hunter's horn, or a silver slipper, or a canoe, or even a smiling mouth, or a straying eyebrow, yet, God's truth, like a crescent moon for all that!

*   *   *

As my young cousin Jim is here on a week-end holiday, and Sunday aided and abetted us, I took a whole day off from farming cares. We made an expedition across the Wicklow mountains, Jim to whip rivers with a fishing-rod, I to loaf in the intervals of driving, and perhaps indulge in a little mild painting.

Jim is rather a trial. I don't know which is the more irritating: his never-ending torrent of questions, or his very green advice on how to make farming easier and more profitable. A sample of the latter is the shocking proposal that scientists ought endeavour to breed a male animal that would be capable of siring all domesticated female animals! Certainly it would be a boon, for we are always and ever sending a man two miles with a sow to the boar, or one mile with a cow to Hartnett's bull, not to speak of my own quests for rams, cocks, and drakes. Jim, however, is not always so precocious as this fantastic notion might lead one to believe. For the most part, he behaves like a most exasperating small boy (his age is sixteen), with his sudden darts up trees, and his enquiries—oily and unnerving—into the inner mechanism of the separator. He keeps up a perpetual monologue on the subject of Laddie, the mares, and other "Little-Tommy-visits-the-country" topics. Since Duggie Sparrow left us (and after all he was an Englishman), Laddie has not received so much notice. However, Jim reads Irish well and speaks it fluently, which I cannot do, and last night he beat me twice running at chess, so perhaps at the age of thirty I am already experiencing the resentment of the old against the young.

Optimism, I suppose, being an attribute of youth, I really should not have howled with laughter when I heard Jim asking Mrs. Meehan to put a frying-pan for frying the fish among the picnic equipment which she loaded into the car for us. To me, the possibility of Jim landing any trout is an exceedingly remote one. My rod, which he is to have for the day, has not been used for six years. I find I can muster only two flies, and these had to be removed from an old cap. Finally, the cast is in a hopeless tangle. But Jim, for all my scoffing, will have his emblem of hope with him in the shape of a frying-pan.

When we set out, the heavens were emulating the Great Powers: increased output of armaments was their bellicose cry. Almost every cloud was a munition factory, and we sampled all their wares: the white bullets of their hail; the bayonets of their rain; the explosives of squally winds. However, towards midday, a truce was proclaimed and the sun struck out.

Hollywood, which is simply a cluster of guile-less houses, unaware of any ordering which might by street formation elevate them from a hamlet into a village, is the starting-point of the mountain route to Glendalough. We pulled up at the church and made a swift call, which gave us the feeling of being pilgrims about to undertake a journey to a shrine. Then we began the ascent of the mountain road. While the car showed, by her screeching vibrations, resentment at the severe gradient, we cast cautious glances behind and saw a large wedge of the midland plain spread out below us. It was very fair indeed when seen from a height: sylvan, cultivated, populous, and far-flung, but actually we know it to be flat, waterless, under-populated, and possessed of hardly any scenic features.

After the King's River is crossed, the road surface grows looser, it is reddish-gold in colour, showing a glitter of mica fragments; the wire fences and the quicks bordering the road give place to banks and boulders; houses grow infrequent, and farms less clearly defined on the mountain skirts, rivers brawl louder, furze grows more riotously, and the trees become first stunted and then altogether absent. Finally the last house is passed and the last field merged into the boundless area of heather and bracken which makes the mountain wilderness.

We halt at a bridge over the King's River. It suits us, "angler" and "artist." Jim bounds out, goes along the river-bank at the double, and throws out his line. Æsthetically I have a weakness for bridges, and live in perpetual hope that some day I will capture the quivering orange light that flits under their arches. Not today, though. "As dead as mutton," I mutter presently, in rueful contemplation of my daub.

We jog on to another bridge that spans a tributary of the King's River. Again Jim makes his reel sing as he wanders upstream, while I squat on a boulder by the sonorous water, painting the gorgeous mountains and humming to myself. For a wonder, the mountains behave and wispy clouds come out on paper looking rather like wispy clouds. Jim gives a sudden shout. "Surely not a fish?" I yell. "No, bluebells!" he howls back. I follow him around a bend and there right enough are bluebells, a great expanse of them spreading wide along the water's edge, following the course of the river, encroaching on cultivated land, and generally making themselves—in the Wicklow farmer's opinion—a nuisance. (It would be possible for one Wicklow husbandman to anathematise another in the words, "The curse of bluebells on you!") Behind the bluebell array and set a little distance back on rising ground, as though the better to admire, there are large companies of yellow heartsease (variety *Viola lutea*), rare in these parts, but familiar to me, most of my botanical knowledge having been gleaned in west Clare, where it grows profusely. And along this charmed river-bank there is a multitude of the floral bourgeoisie: milkwort, lousewort, buttercups, marsh violets, cuckoo flower, daisies, the tuberous pea, and bird's-foot trefoil.

Jim sees to a fire, and he makes such a blaze and a roar with his furze-stumps and dried heather, that the kettle is boiling before I finish a sketch of the girdling mountains. There is no sound except the sigh of running water and the breeze in action on wilted heather, while we sip the smoky tea. Afterwards Jim has no stomach for further fishing; he lies in the heather in dreamy indolence. I try out new methods in water-colouring; the most drastic experiment is immersing the sheet of paper I intended to work on in the stream. Then I tried introducing unseen colour into mass clouds; I even imitated (chuckling to myself) Steer's unaccountable and inexplicable streak of vermilion in horizon clouds. I find that I can do nothing to improve my reproduction of the hairy clouds—they just won't come. I even tried flipping with a handkerchief when the driest brush imaginable failed to make bald rents in the blue sky. My paper is not sufficiently "toothy" for this bold technique.

We continue our journey: the air in the heart of the mountains is feather-light; there are dizzy precipices on each side of the road; the sheep in the gorges are like dots, and above us tower the ruddy hulks of peaks grizzled with boulders of granite rock. We get a glimpse of a mountain-locked lake, olive and shadowy, sombre and merciless in this raging solitude, this land of rocks and emptiness. But there is nothing to paint: too much darned scenery for my taste. Wicklow mountains are too gross for reproduction; they are all rump.

On the top of the four-mile descent to Glendalough, I pull up to see what I can do with a boggy stretch at the foot of a mountain protruding its bony ribs of granite. An oldish travelling-man walking smartly up the hill pauses to chat with us. His comment on Glendalough was that one can get plenty of good stout and whiskey there. Synge might have relished this conversation, but I wanted to get on with my sketch. The wind was playing the devil with my clouds (yes, clouds are all mine when I want to paint them). I fear we were short with the friendly man.

A farmer living up a quarter-mile avenue on a hundred-acre farm, which is seven miles from the nearest town, remote from railways, telegraphs, shops, hotels, doctors, civic guards, and all such trappings of civilisation, may seriously declare, on returning from an excursion into Wicklow, that after all it would be pleasant to live in the country.

* * *

No doubt the practice of ringing apple-trees is ancient, but to me at any rate it is new and amusing. All one has to do is cut inch-wide half-circles on opposite sides of the bole, one half-circle being four inches above the other, after which one daubs the incisions with white paint. As I thus operated on the Blenheim Oranges, I felt as scientific as those fellows in the arboricultural bulletin photographs, though I lacked the immaculate white coat so essential to all scientific farming operations. While engaged on the job, I grew zealous about it, and I moved on to the old decayed pippins in the Little Meadows (how many old men around here have confessed to me that they stole apples from these trees when boys), and treated them to the same rejuvenating operation, and in my enthusiasm I even tried a little surgery on the wrists of lilac, laburnum, and holly arms! No result will show from the ringing for eighteen months. Where apples are concerned, my tongue seems to be always lolling out for results. Shall I ever be able to wait?

The pink secrets of the apple-trees of some days ago end in the show-white publicity of scattered petals. One cannot walk through the garden without catching a little of this confetti on one's clothes. Thus I reach Joe's side in the new orchard with all the appearance of a bridegroom. He is hoeing the strawberry drills with a Paxton hoe (a recent acquisition and a delightful tool), cutting through the detestable thistles and uprooting the insolent weed seedlings. The barley straw lies stacked on the headland in readiness for strawing down the plants, which will be the next operation.

Then I set out for the bog, where John Kelly is

182

clearing banks for the turf-cutting which is to take place next month. On my way I pass through the ranks of young apple-trees, childish and tiny of stature, yet many of them profusely adorned with blossom. I cross my neighbour's land: first a field of lush grass which Doyle is holding up for meadows; then rushy fields, the property of Murray; under Flynn's hawthorns, and over a stream to my bog. Having greeted John and assured him that all was well "above" (for he is released from yard work during the bog-bank clearing operations), I discuss banks and drains and other bog matters with him, glossing over as well as I can my really abysmal ignorance of the whole subject. I return home by the same route: there is an intoxicating smell from the hawthorns—sort of appetising like a whiff from a bakery, and a warm breath exhales from underfoot; the solitude of this green hinterland is immense. How the month of May tests a man—lunacy if one loves it too much, idiocy if one simpers about it too much. Some men may find the horrors of a rough winter in the remote country the greatest trial of their vocation, but for me the beauty of May is almost overpowering; it tempts me sorely to give up all work and lie about like a lazy coon just loving things.

I go on to inspect Mick breaking potato clods. This journey takes me through the wheat, a crop for which I had been trembling. It is now knee-deep; and the new grass coming up through it is as thick as the hair on my head. I verily believe that the big snow is accountable for the good results.

Clod-crushing is a jolly operation to watch. The horse plods onwards, the man stands on a heavy plank which is yoked behind the horse, and he glides along like a fairy queen making her arrival in the pantomime, or like Elsa's Lohengrin approaching in a boat drawn by a white swan. One would think it was a glorious joy-ride for the man on the plank, but in fact the clouds of dust raised by sweeping over clods engender a lime-kiln thirst for the rider. Mick wears a cheerful grin, however, and does not complain of discomforts; he never does.

Laddie's furious barking brings me out quickly after dinner. I find the collie patrolling the top of the front steps, snarling wickedly and showing his fangs, while old Kit Maher stands quite unperturbed at the bottom. I must confess to feeling delightfully flattered when told his errand, because it is the first time in my life that someone made use of my knowledge of herbs. The enquirer produces a slip of paper given to him by a Dublin herbalist whom he had consulted. Two plant names are scribbled on the paper: the first is wood avens; it happens to grow profusely within forty paces of where we stand. I lead him to the wood and we pull up the plant from the roots. The second herb is described as agrimony, and is probably *Agrimonia Eupatoria*, which has some value for kidney and liver derangements; but it does not grow on my farm. I describe the plant to the sick man and recommend him to try the canal banks. Both these herbs are really of very doubtful worth; at best they are harmless simples; the pharmacopœia which I possess does not recognise their existence. Kit Maher is a very sick man since I last saw him: his face has gone grey and his one-time tall and muscular frame is now stooped and flaccid. Feeling sorry for him, I drive him home; it is a short distance, for he lives in the "town" of Graigue. He carries the avens heaped up in his lap. He is very vocal in expressions of gratitude.

On just such a day as this in late May I first came to Cloonmore. Returning from leaving Kit Maher in Graigue, I endeavour to re-act the part of taking over the farm, and as I slowly turn in the gate, it gives me whimsical pleasure to recall my emotions on that far-away day.

When I first entered the gates of Cloonmore farm, they were like the gates of a dead man's property: dragging from the piers, hoarse for want of grease, parched for want of paint, the spud-stones clogged, several bars wrenched from their right position. The avenue within was furrowed with time-honoured ruts and overgrown with grass.

If late May covers a multitude of agricultural sins, it cannot conceal unfilled pot-holes in the avenue, and the complete absence of fencing; so I was in no mood then to be appeased by that which delights me now—the crispness of the bordering lime-trees, the fields glazed by buttercups, and the hawthorn's apparel of frothy blossom.

Cloonmore House, piebald, pink and dirty, gradually came into view between beech-tree boughs. Standing four-square on high ground, unpretentious and unclad, Georgian in style, it is a farm-house with aspirations rather than a gentleman's residence. It was then plaster-peeled, weather-bitten, a little dreary and down-at-heel. Difficult to imagine then that it had ever been an elegant dwelling, with poise, an athletic and confident air, such as it must indeed have worn in the hey-day of landlordism. The encroachment of surrounding vegetation had crushed out of it all that had once been Georgian and Beau Brummel in its character. In what seemed a surge of matted grasses, Irish bush pressed closely round an Irish blockhouse; choking weeds had begun a march across the gravel front from the tousled lawn. Man's masonry was on the defensive against plants and on the losing side, plants were fighting plants for their lives, and grass was advancing over the bodies of lichen; creeping clovers were strangling mosses where once the ground had been paved or heavily gravelled. Further back from the house the menace of snow-berry was added to a silent drive of brambles, nettles, and docks towards the dignified threshold. The process of hemming-in the house seemed to have gone on without the protest of a single hoe. Pearlwort and chickweed flourished in the interstices of the parapet extending along the front of the house; the broad limestone steps were almost heaved out of position by hart's-tongue, while dandelions impudently usurped the space where the wire foot-scraper ought to have stood. Cloonmore House flung down the gauntlet of its weeds to the new-comer. Then I pulled out the bunch of keys given to me by the Ballynash solicitor, and let myself in.

I was the owner of this bare, dirty, and dismantled dwelling through which I walked alone. What solace was there to stand in a big square hall, dominated by the Devon arms and crest, coloured in pigments still brilliant, and decorated in Wedgwood stucco, although I told myself it was a fine example of eighteenth-century craftsmanship. I felt solitary and miserable and scared in this barracks of a house, which if it were not haunted by the shades of disgruntled Devons, was such a place as one could by no stretch of imagination think of as home.

But let us get out into the day, the hot day of present summer, and forget that tight feeling around my heart. See the improvements made by the young man who took over old Devon's place. The tall house has since been cleaned by a wash of dove-grey distemper, the gravel front is more or less weed-free, and flower-beds gladden the eye where once were clumps of nettles. Sheep are lying about under distant trees and darting swallows slice the ceiling of the blue; the sycamores are heavy and drooping with scented honey, and the bees murmur gluttonously in the flowers. The cuckoo persists with resonant clarity, repeating his ironical comment, laughing like a god in the woods, or fate in feathers, always hidden, frivolous, and yet sober at heart. Glimpses of laburnum, lilac, hawthorn, and beeches make the earth delicious.

Do I regret having bought Cloonmore? It is always around my neck; it is a load on my heart; it eats money. Do I regret it? There he is at it again, *Cuckoo!*

*   *   *

Well, surely it has almost arrived, that glorious hour of summer when I may leave off my clouts. When that day comes, I intend to dash from my bedroom with my pants in hand and rend them into shreds outside. (Others may call these garments "drawers," but I hate the word, because the nursery-maids of my early childhood—spent in England—always went into raucous shrieks when grocer's boys referred to such articles of attire.) I shall do this, not altogether as a rite signifying the death of ugly winter and the advent of lovely summer, but because the said pants are in horrid tatters and only held together by Mrs. Meehan's determination. I have not finally decided what to do with the precious remnants, though on a farm where woollen rags have a value, there is a wide choice: I shall probably use part of them as a wind-screen polisher for my car; part as a gun cloth; part for applying oil to the backs of pigs; part for wiping my hands when I am painting doors; and perhaps odd scraps might be used for tacking roses to walls. Anyway, to the devil with pants, I would be Pan!

CHAPTER IX

UP AND OUT AT 5.30 A.M. FOG ENGULFS the world and dewy cold creeps on all-fours about the house. To my pyjama-clad person I add trousers and dressing-gown. I take the gun from its corner and fill my pockets with cartridges, intent on potting rabbits. Hordes of them are battening on the oats and cropping down the meadows.

The sweet-briar hedge is giving out strong fragrance under the husbandry of the morning dew. Flower-heads are closed in sleep. Tree-tops are just jutting out like rocks over surf. I draw a blank in the garden: nothing there but crafty blackbirds chattering in alarm at the unwonted spectacle of a jaeger-plumed biped. Then I take to the fields. Tracks across them tell where the cows zigzagged when grazing. In a field barred off from another by a palisade of stout beeches, I see from between these trees rabbits scurrying away. I crouch down and wait. A rabbit poised like a kangaroo surveys me cautiously from a plaguy safe distance. My slippers are soon drenched in the dew, my trouser-ends likewise, and I feel chilly about the shoulders. Nothing to look at except four antique apple-trees in a demoralised row, and clumps of snow-berry befogged. Every vein in every grass-blade is sending forth scent; dew seems to have that power. There is a mere pittance of sunlight. Played out by tarrying, I cross a crumbling fence and steal along a grass-grown roadway, my neighbour's property. May bushes stand up white as death, looking in this wan light more like illustrations to Christmas stories than bushes in the prime of life. There may be a presage of a hot day in this blanket of fog, but my feet are becoming intolerably cold. I walk along a tree-dotted ditch; the nettles are bearded by the dew: a rabbit cocks his head up, his ears stretched, his cheeks mobile. I aim, fire, see the head duck into the nettles—and miss. Sport spoiled for the morning hereabouts, the whole tribe of rabbits having doubtless scurried to their burrows when the shot rang out. I uncock the gun and go back dolefully over the loose fence on to my own land. There is not a living thing to be seen, but the clanking of buckets from the yard indicate that milking is about to begin. The tails of my dressing-gown are drenched and my slippers are like soaked cardboard. And as a marksman I have no existence.

In the yard I find John chaining in the cows which have just been driven in from the Night Park. I go to the loose-box where the Foxy cow is lodged, remembering that she is within a day or so of her calving time. I glance in over the half-door, and metaphorically speaking, swoon away. Am I seeing double on an empty stomach? Two white-faced calves are standing one on either side of Foxy, and all three gaze mildly up at me. Excitedly I yell the news to John. "That will bring great luck to the place," is his immediate comment. He comes to look. Twin bulls, the parturition all un-

aided: go up to the top of the class, Foxy! I get a
bucket of bran, add a pinch of salt, and to scald it
commandeer the first kettle of boiling water produced in the kitchen, and which was probably
intended for Mrs. Meehan's reviving cup of tea.
The rare event of twins is especially welcomed just
now, as there is more milk coming in than we well
know how to handle.

A red-letter day this, for it is the date of the
first Turf Festival. After breakfast I cross the fields
to the main-road boundary fence, scramble up a
tree, and hang out the Tricolour. On my way back
I disturb a bunch of ewes and lambs. When a man
appears with a dog at heel, the ewes leave their
browsing and dash to the crèche (sheep always
arrange such a convenience in every field) and
there ensues much bleating and tail-wagging, the
infants being more concerned with the chance of
a suck than the need of protection.

Joe does not turn up for work. He had already
notified me that he is competing in the Bog Competition, acting as a wheeler to his father. As I half
expected, Mick requests time off to go to the
Festival; John follows him up in a short while
with the same request. I am soft about consenting:
after all, the occasion is unique: a turning of the
tables, the Feast Day of the Papist Bogtrotters.
When Jimmy, slightly cap-twisting and embarrassed, asks if I "would think bad of him" if he
absented himself for the same event, I again consent, though now feeling slightly shocked. I go
into the house fully prepared to put my foot down
at last if Mrs. Meehan should show any desire to

disport herself on boglands, but she does not: she probably considers bogs, like furze, rather low and disgusting.

The carnival on the bog takes place under a sky of innocent blue. At first there were clouds like caterpillars overhead, and then a purple bank of cloud formed, and we had a heavy but brief shower. (Mick's weather forecast is proved correct: "There may be odd squibs of showers, but it will be fine all the same.") The landscape is made up of illimitable drowsy browns. The Number One Army band is like a tiny drop of perfume in a lake of water, so feeble does its music sound in that spacious silence. The bog-larks think us cracked. A barge all festooned across her middle rides up the canal, laden with men to danger-point, a band playing merrily on the prow: we cheer them from the bridge; they wave flags at us and echo our cheers. Thousands and thousands of pedestrians are trekking the bog road. Every cottage by the wayside is in festive garb: recently whitewashed and freshly curtained, the flower-beds edged with white stones, flags waving from larch poles.

Everybody is saying gleefully to everybody else: "Did you ever think you'd live to see such a sight of people on a bog?" No, never. Bogs were never in fashion, never, never. They were always considered horrid benighted places unfit for Christians, let alone gentry.

Con Tuohy, the motor mechanic from Cloonlara, first fastens on me, and as he has been already on the bog for over an hour, he feels he is entitled to do the honours. He tells me at length how De

Valera's arrival created such a storm of enthusiasm, the like of which he (Con) had never heard. Then he is about to lead me around, but I want to see everything terribly slowly. However, he does manage to draw me to the banqueting tent where the Big Fellows are now feeding. It was not a very nice thing to do, but we spied through the slits, saw De Valera just about surviving the suffocating heat, and heard a minister's speech. They had lovely things to eat. "Who pays for that now?" asks the nasty-minded Con. "I suppose we do, hah?" he answers himself.

Observing a parley of the Sullivans and Hogans, I excuse myself from Con's society and join my friends. Matt is apparently criticising De Valera for his reluctance to adopt the monetary reform of Social Credit, while Willie, who is a De Valerian maniac, parries by dubbing Social Credit sheer Communism and pronouncing De Valera as the Apostle of Democracy. Willie's mother is tearfully bewailing in Mrs. Sullivan's ear the absence of her late husband: "Oh, if only he were here this blessed day to see such a sight of city people coming to our bogs to watch men cutting turf!"

We move on together in a bunch and stand at the touch-line gazing down on the scene. I have stood on many other touch-lines—often indeed more as a duty than a pleasure—and cheered myself hoarse in the poor cause of a local hurling match. The touch-line here is the top of the turf bank, crowded three-deep; on every face intense, almost carved interest, combined with a sort of national enthusiasm hard to describe.

The arena of labour is a stupendous scene: five or six feet below the level of our feet, scores of men are hewing out turf with flashing sleans, their bared arms standing out vividly white against the brown background as they throw the turf with a rhythmic swing to the catchers. The arms of the catchers move in harmony, their barrows growing higher. The wheelers, their shirts puffed-out, spurt away with their barrows and tip the contents on the spreading-ground with nice thought for the limits assigned to them, and conscious of the thousands of critical eyes arrayed on the bank above them. There is a colourful assortment of barrows gathered for the work, orange-red, blue, and just turf-coloured, new for the occasion, or scarred from the battle of winning turf through many seasons. Mostly the onlookers are silent, but occasionally friends of the competitors urge those below to greater energy, and jokes are exchanged between the upturned and the downturned faces.

Here, where the wing-slean competitors operate, there is to be seen a great variety in the methods of cutting, catching, wheeling, and tossing out: some labourers catch the sods in their hands and others catch with short forks. The western men both cut and carry with long sharp boards. There is endless variety even in the implements—sleans and shovels. The former at least has not yet been touched by art-destroying mass production, being nearly always made by blacksmiths.

But for elegance and seclusion, the breast-slean division of the competition area is to be commended to those desiring peace. Here comes the connois-

seur in the fine art of turf-cutting. The workers'
motion is comparatively slow. The barrow-loads
are upturned in a dainty pile, more like some
edible removed from an oven than a crude fuel
taken from the brute carcase of bog-bank. Here
each man cuts out for himself a little cubicle in the
bank, working horizontally and not delving at his
feet like the vulgar herd wielding wing-sleans; he
scarcely bends his back at the work, and he is
always neat and calculating. He reduces his
division of the turf-bank to a thin partition a few
inches in breadth, so slender that it shakes at a
touch, yet still serves to divide him off from his
neighbour in competition.

President De Valera emerges from the marquee
as we return from the breast-slean division. He is
immediately mobbed. How radiant he is on occa-
sions! Tall and benign in these surroundings,
amidst the sallow-complexioned turf cutters and
under the great bog-lark filled sky, he is altogether
different from what he is in Dublin. (Why in
God's name is alien Dublin made the capital of
new Ireland?) Here he is one of us. There he goes
now shaking hands with a rotund farmer; perhaps
they were in gaol together over in England. He is
now among the people who idolise him instead
of being surrounded by civil servants, or mingling
with reactionists of the British régime, or wily city
personages, who in their hearts despise the idealism
that is the very breath of his being.

Personality. . . . Dev is all personality; there is
no-one quite like him on earth, unless it be Gandhi.
It is a pity his roseate vision of a Gaelic-speaking

state blinds him to the domination of an antique economic system which frustrates the natural development of our people. But there he goes anyhow, chatting in easy Irish with the Conall schoolmaster, all of us standing around them gaping. Almost gay he looks just now (the Irish language seems to be the medium *par excellence* in which to crack jokes), and full of an athletic vigour. At Dublin functions and banquets, twopenny-ha'penny affairs seldom worthy of his presence, he can look as cadaverous and as forbidding as a Calvinist's caricature of a Jesuit. From the schoolmaster he passes on to greet none other than Matt Sullivan —they fought the Clare elections together—and warmly shakes him by the hand. Matt, I imagine, makes an effort to speak boldly on his pet subject of monetary reform, but can find no words. There is a magnetism and a charm about Dev which take the words out of a fellow's mouth.

Members of the Bog Festival Committee now come forward and gently urge the President into a tour. When Dev goes bog-trotting, half Ireland follows him. Next year we may confidently count on the presence of the foreign consuls, who are the darlings of Dublin society. And if this festival be made an annual event, we may count also on the attendance of legions of civil servants, so that in the end the bogman will be in danger of being squeezed off the bog, just as the cow has been squeezed out of the Ballsbridge Spring Show.

Once again I do the round of the competitors. My companions are the Purcells, left-wing, or ultra, Republicans from Rathmines, who are here just to show the milksop Republicans, headed by De Valera, that such as they have no monopoly of Irish bogs. We stand together on the edge of the arena of labour: the competitors are now racing against time, perspiring profusely, for soon a bandsman will sound a bugle to signal the end of the competitions.

Bog air seems to have the quality of muffling the sound of Irish melodies from the bands; but the lark may still hold an audience at the extremities of the large competition area. Seagulls swoop over the concourse of people: puzzled by this invasion of their silent solitudes, they think it is the Last Day.

What a bagginess is here! There is not a pair of trousers which has not concertina-ed, nor a shirt that does not bulge out around the waist, nor a pair of braces doing a full-time job, nor a sleeve button on speaking terms with its button-hole. Here are hats that have seen prosperity and adversity, gone from black or brown to green and pinkish hues, lapsed from hat-block shapes to an utter unshapeliness. But there are fine faces under them: shrewd, keen, honest, hardworking, and innocent faces. The competitors include tousled old men and young men with their hair oiled; midlanders in city cast-offs or in shoddy ready-mades; westerners wearing bawneens, and southern men in homespuns.

The Purcells are wreathed in smiles, and Mrs. Purcell, habituée of a dozen British and Irish gaols, is the family spokesman. "Here is the real

Ireland, not the Ireland of the politicians, nor the Ireland of niggardly British concessions (Home Rule and Free States!), nor the Ireland of backsliding leaders!" Here her voice, usually soft and pleasing, rises in a malicious crescendo as she sees approaching the President's conducted tour. "That's right," I acidly retort, "nor the Ireland of militarism, chauvinism, and Irish-language cramming," and with that dig, I lose myself in the crowd which adores Dev from a respectful distance.

I find myself on the fringe of a group of Dublin literary men, most of them known to me by appearance, and I overhear with amusement the ironic playfulness of a tubby poet who is holding forth to the others: 'We knew this would happen! We told you! No sooner were our forces of law and order removed than you started to fight with each other. And in a short twelve years you revert completely, you go bog-trotting once more. You even glory in it. Your so-called President and his gunmen go bog-trotting; your superstitious priests join the peasantry and bog-trot. All the lessons which we strove to teach you, our civilisation, our culture and our moral code, are now as if they had never been. You wipe out your redemption with a barbarian implement called a slean!" This conclusion is inspired by a precious sight seen some moments ago, when the President picked up a slean and in Irish questioned the owner about its origin.

The old dispersed and dispossessed Ireland finds herself on a bog. For one day at least, there is a truce to the faction fight of party politics, and the bog-trotter comes into his own.

* * *

A domestic disaster second in awfulness only to the bursting of the kitchen boiler occurred today. While Jimmy was churning the makings of about twenty pounds of butter, the lid of the churn flew off. When I arrived on the scene, cream hung in blobs from the dairy ceiling, windows, walls, and door; the floor was one slimy sheet, while Jimmy and Mrs. Meehan were on all-fours with cups and saucers vainly trying to make good some of the loss; about two pints instead of six or seven gallons of valuable cream remained in the churn. We spent several hours mopping and swiping and swilling and stemming rivulets of dirty cream with kitchen rubbers. There must be a high place awaiting me in heaven, for I lent my large screw-top, superlative, and almost new churn to my neighbour, Mrs. Carter. Owing to a milk strike, she has to churn the produce of twenty-five cows and, sympathising with her in her difficulty, I agreed to take her small, battered, spring-clip and ten-year old churn in temporary exchange for mine. However, I'll forgo that celestial place, for at the very earliest opportunity I mean to take her back her whizzie old churn and retrieve my own good article. The net loss from this deplorable accident is only about 25s., but the chagrin caused to customers by the unexpected cutting of their weekly supply will be a greater worry.

We are making shiploads of butter these days. The cows are in full flush of milk, and in spite of the twins recently born and four older calves, we cannot use anything like one-tenth of our supply for stock feeding. Even cheese-making does not seem to help in diminishing the milk that floods in on us relentlessly. The cheeses we make are of the simplest description (to be precise, the British Ministry's Pressed Cheese No. 2). As we have no market for cheeses, and no regulation cheese-making equipment, we are satisfied to use for the process the largest vessel we have, which is a five-gallon bucket; but five gallons are very little out of a daily twenty gallons.

The dairy work is now distributed between three of us: Mrs. Meehan washes everything after use, Jimmy does the separating and churning, while I do the making up and the weighing of the butter. Whole afternoons are spent working as a dairymaid (a dirty resentful drudge detesting the task). Last day I slapped up twenty-four pounds; regular orders amount to only twelve pounds, the surplus must be shunted on to a shop at any price they choose to offer, or else salted, and already we have twenty pounds salted and potted; twenty pounds too much, I should say, for no matter by what process butter is potted, I cannot eat it afterwards, and I do not want to ask others to eat what I do not think good enough for myself. A bare six weeks ago we were so short of butter that we had to buy a pound of it occasionally from Mrs. Hogan. Truly, the ups and downs of butter-making are most exasperating.

Smelling like sour milk slops, I borrow Mick's

bicycle, put painting materials in my pocket, whistle up Laddie, and take flight for the canal. There is a melting heat and a cloying heaviness abroad, the trees are drowsy and vegetation has gone limp. It was pleasant to take that wild plunge into the clear, still water, pleasant the blowing and the puffing, and the cool embrace. There is the song of mad larks overhead, and snipe go tearing round in aerial arcs like demented motor-cyclists. I stay in the clear, caressing water for half a minute only, then I grasp the tussocks of rushes and clamber back on the bank. Laddie is amazed at my naked state and scarcely recognises me; I catch him and force him over the mint-edged brink. A sheep-dog, he is no lover of water. When he paddles to land, I race up and down the tow-path with him, still without a thread of clothes on, not a solitary human within sight to report me to Church or State. I plunge in once again. The water is a glorious dug-out from the bombardment of the sun. After a short swim, I haul my clothes further up the bank, spread out the legs of my trousers and sit on them, light a cigarette and puff luxuriously. How gloriously free I am from any vestige of serious thoughts, only dimly conscious of the medley of lark song, a remote cuckoo, the fierce blue shadow cast by the far-away canal bridge, and the scarcely perceptible swaying of a meadow across the reflection-filled water. Only a mile behind there is farm and work and all that, but I am immorally light-hearted. Laddie gallops in idiotic circles all round me. Am I a mixed farmer with responsibilities, or the Barefooted Boy? Anyway, having combed my hair and inspected the result in a pocket mirror, I put on my trousers and sit on the towel. Later, I make another move, to a place where the canal bridge throws its clearest reflection in the water. I block out a rapid outline in my sketch-book, and use up large quantities of cobalt, indigo, neutral tint, and Chinese white, but without much success. The scene is too sharp and too dazzling. I am about to bid farewell to the water sedges in the foreground and the cuckoo music in the background, when a canal barge comes slowly swishing along. Barges progress at a snail's pace, and yet almost too quickly for pursuing pencils, but I accept the challenge and make a rapid pencil sketch which turned out well: "A wow!" I cry to my half-naked self.

I pedal homewards in a leisurely manner, along roads festooned with chervil that looks like Limerick lace in the hedgerows, and bridal veils when spread under trees. How it waves and smiles as I go cycling by, as though I were a sort of national hero and the chervil the populace trooping across the fields on hearing of my coming, lining the banks, with lace handkerchiefs a-flutter, with laughing happy faces, and salvos of cheers.

At Moorstown Cross I change my homing course to make a surprise visit to the turf-cutters. Just now the world is almost too beautiful; in its young loveliness there is a pang that catches me at the throat. The mazards growing around Walsh's farm are all in muslin party frocks (heaven may forgive the departed Devons of Cloonmore their avarice, their tyranny, and their lechery, but neither Heaven nor I can ever forgive them their sin of not planting mazard-trees); the oaks are out in flower like gold lace; the beeches are dropping their bud scales (when the beeches rain tiny scales, I am in gravest danger of falling in love); roan cattle move in sheets of buttercups; the fields are framed by the riotous blossoming of may bushes. The summer festival extends even to the perfidious nettle; for where these congregate near may bushes, they become flecked with white petals. Vicious and misanthropic plants, even they for a space assume the air of wedding guests, champagne-giddy and spotted with confetti. Show me chervil under sprays of young beech leaves, or show me lilacs rising like steeples in the hedge-row, and I crumple up like the devil does when sprinkled with holy water.

Salutations exchanged with turf-cutters are of a serious kind. No nod from the men indicates that my arrival on the scene of operations has been noticed until I open with the unvarying formula: "God bless the work." Then the answer comes with cheerful readiness, "You are welcome, sir." I sit down above their heads and fill a pipe. While I am thus engaged, they come on a great "stick" of bog-oak, which they probe out and fling up on the sunny bank; it is the mummified corpse of some ancient specimen of forest tree.

We are having an eight-day turf-cutting campaign this year (other years the average time spent at the work was five days). If I fail to introduce turf and abolish coal from the kitchen range—and I am likely to fail, for Mrs. Meehan, despite her staunch ruralism, will probably have none of that "dirty ashy stuff"—I haven't an idea what I shall do with the surplus.

Before returning home I pick bog cotton and rhododendrons (growing profusely here as the result of the old landlord's enterprise). Curlews fret above my head, probably their nests are near by. I capture without effort a butterfly (answering to the ugly name of *Greasy Frittilary*, as I discover when I get back to books). A wren is in dire distress because of the threat of a hovering hawk: with his little tail furiously erect, he "tinks" away, jerking from twig to twig until he exhausts his small store of indignation.

*   *   *

While filling in a few odd moments by languidly tugging up weeds from the cobbled parts of the yard, I find a strange plant. "I don't know you," I mutter, while quizzing at it, "but I feel you are hare's-ear." Plant in hand, I stalk into the house and consult Messrs. Bentham and Hooker on my find. Hare's-ear as I live! I am staggered by my own cleverness. I have never before seen the plant; I never expected to see it; I have never searched for it, nor given it a moment's thought, and yet there must have been a nook for it somewhere in my memory all these years. *Erysimum orientale* occurs in a few eastern shires of England and is just about known in Ireland as a casual, but is nowhere established.

It is the bane of my existence (I speak ironically)

that I am never discovered by city visitors engaged on romantic tasks. Instead of being found milking a cow, or shearing a sheep, or gracefully mowing with a scythe, I am usually discovered feeding pigs, or doing something even more trivial but quite necessary, such as shaking insect powder on hens or bringing in potatoes for the dinner. When Father Donovan and his brother Tony, accompanied by a fox-terrier, made an unexpected call, I was busy on nothing more glorious than collecting old tins in a basket; at least I began with a basket, but I ended up with a wheel-barrow.

Old tins accumulate like magic. There are old baking-tins, old pots, buckets, baths, water-cans, oil-cans, paint pots, sheep-dip drums, scraps of iron and tin, and every imaginable sort of disused receptacle. Then there are bottles too, but because of the visitors I never got to them.

Showing people round the place—Lord, how sick I am of this diversion! A visit from country people is sometimes a pleasant pastime, but from city people it is not so: one has to talk down to them, gloss over the facts about stock-breeding, and laugh at their joke about adding water to milk. First, we politely sit around in the study and I wait until an opportune lull occurs in the conversation. (The tree-tops are sun-lashed, the net curtains float out the open window.) At last my cue comes, "Would you like to take a stroll outside?"

Summer sky, summer breeze as gentle as a touch on the cheek with a full-blown rose, summer feeling. The spell of it holds us for a moment; then we descend the front steps. I affect hesitation, but in

205

reality I feel none: my heart hungers for a sight of the apple-trees as the diviner's hazel for water. We saunter down the rough avenue towards the new orchard, shade of trees to our right, the frolic of calves to our left.

Three hundred and thirty-nine bush apples, a row of half-standard plums, a couple of pears, black-currants beyond counting and not worth it anyhow, and shelter belts of forest trees never reckoned in number; strawberries ripening in drills; a dance of beech-tree leaves behind and above us; the sun playing on it all. I gaze complacently and recite the old piece: "Put down only last year, extended this year. Why do I use straw for strawberries? Well—many reasons. . . . Yes, there will be a lot of waiting before these trees are in full bearing. All or nearly all are dessert varieties, any fool can produce cookers. No, the birds don't do as much damage as you might think."

(It is wonderful how the Laxtons' blossoms set: I shall have to thin drastically. I must see at once about getting those gross spear thistles rooted out of the headlands, else seven years' weeding. Judging by these people's comments, it is not worth telling them about Type IX. Not indeed that I myself see the benefit of Type IX; I wonder did they cost me more than the ordinary Type II stock.)

"Let's go as far as the potato drills. I mean to plant more apples here next year if I have the cash." These drills are one hundred and fifty yards long, glossy, robust, and uniform. I never had such clean crops, and I never had such order here

206

before. The summer before last, this place was rich pasture-land supporting a few cattle. We go back along the headland as we came, beside the rows of little sparkling trees.

Returning towards the house, the shade of the beeches revives us. The cuckoo still favours us with his caustic remark. I make a detour to show the secret passage into the house. Nothing is said to prepare the guests for this thrill. We tread on the carpet of dainty herb-robert (so pungent when it is bruised) spread through the wood, walking in a dim green light. Then we slither down the slope to the passage entrance, on leaf-humus ankle-deep. The guests are slightly unnerved now and have to be reassured; no need to bend their heads. "I do not know why the passage was built; you can see it is beautifully constructed, mostly of brick and vaulted. Yes, we should have brought a flash-lamp along with us. The passage leads directly into the house, two hundred yards as straight as a die, through a door into the basement. It was constructed well over one hundred years ago at least, and perhaps five hundred, I don't know. Someone said it was built for the purpose of bringing turf into the house. Yes, ridiculous, even the most disgusting grandees would hardly have built such a long and expensive tunnel for the sole purpose of making a passage-way for turf carts."

It is pleasant to emerge once more into the daylight. There is a sort of prismatic glow on the heaps of old withered leaves. Hogweed rises over the apologetic-looking herb-robert, both of them mean successors to the lovely carpet of pilewort now faded and bleached. The whole wood has gone dark and jungle-like since the spring, and is now meet only for bats and hogweed and armies of nettles.

"Would you care to see the poultry?" "No, Nippy might go for them." (Well, that is a mercy anyhow.) "Oh, there is nothing very interesting to see at this season. Would you like to walk up on the mound?" ("Wonder where the hell Jimmy is going with that bucket?") "Yes, it is nice, but I'm afraid the weeds have got the better of it just now. This is supposed to be a burial mound, of the neolithic age, or two thousand years before Christ." (Moses, what patter!) "Oh, a king or at least a great chieftain. He is buried sitting upright." I illustrate the squatting position, privately hoping that my bags won't burst.

(Those Shirley poppies certainly begin to look jolly, somehow like Santa Claus, or ballet girls, or lovely crinkled tissue paper. And the *Linaria* is ablow; I would most confidently recommend *Linaria*, otherwise Toadflax, to gardeners, for the ease with which it can be grown, its magnificent range of colours, and its suitability for cut flowers. All the charm of a wild orchid, such as the bee orchid, is recalled in each flower-stalk, a sort of congregating of vivid, never-never insects, perhaps caddis-flies or lace-wings as they might be in heaven. Mix a bunch of linaria with catmint and quaking grass and then say if I exaggerate. I see that my first Madame Butterfly rose is out. It is surely the superlative degree in rosaceous declension; perhaps as the rose is the most perfect of flowers, Madame Butterfly is the peak of all floral creation.)

"Well, if there is treasure buried below this mound, it can stay there. I'm not going to root up the dead; I live too uncomfortably close to the zone of haunting. Yes, you must come up this spiral way, there are no short cuts allowed. That brick construction on top has really nothing to do with anything; it is only a bit of the ex-landlord's vandalism; the Devons were guilty of erecting a tea-house on the mound, and I simply made a seat on its ruins. Yes, it gives one a commanding view of the yard."

(What sort of a mess has the farm got into by this time? I only know that the butter is sitting in pale white water in the dairy awaiting making up, that the chickens in No. 6 are without water, that Joe is left to his own resources in the orchard, that one of the sows has broken out, and that there is nobody within sight to tell.)

"Would you like to see over the farm-yard?"

(How the hell am I to get those letters posted?)

"There is not much to be seen in the yard during the summer months; you must only take my word for it that it is a hive of industry in the winter. I keep oats and wheat in that loft. I don't suppose you want to see pigs? That's straw, not hay—I wish it was! Oh, it's all right, a common mistake."

The pile of fleeces in the barn are awaiting the lorryman's arrival; the woolpack hangs from a rafter ready for filling. I suppose wool in fleece might be described as beige colour, which is to me a very mysterious hue, though much favoured in advertisements of women's clothing in recent years. The largest and heaviest fleece came off the old ram, the belsire of some hundred and fifty lambs.

I give my visitors an abbreviated version of Pat Mangan's latest agricultural grumble. At the wool sale the other day he sold eighty fleeces, and then decided to treat himself to a new suit of clothes with the money. But he found that he had to add thirty shillings in cash to the cheque he got for the fleeces before he could muster the price of the suit. "And," as Pat adds with pathos, "I'm not such a big man either."

"Would it be too far for you to walk to the tillage field?" (I could kill two birds if they agree, one of the birds being to see how the barley is standing up to the weather.) "I am sorry this place is so mucky. If you step across here, it won't be so bad. This is all new meadow." (I suppose they think it is as old as the world, but they have not the courage to question my statement.) "That crop to the left is wheat, the next is barley, and the last is oats: isn't there a nice difference in the greens? Oh, wheat pays its way, but it is no substitute for cattle all the same."

(This meadow is doing well. Shall I have to take on extra men for the hay-saving, I wonder.) The visitors' fox-terrier, Nippy, scents rabbits in the wheat and goes plunging through the crop, leaping up out of it every now and then, like a porpoise playing in the sea.

"Yes, that is my land there too; mine extends as far as those aspens on the ditch. I am sorry the grass is so high; I know it is the very deuce to walk through it."

"Would you like to see . . ." Lord, how often have I said all this before!

*   *   *

This morning I was up before the most rakish cock, and I drove to Dublin, singing all the thirty miles at the top of my truly hideous voice. As usual, really healthy humiliation was lying in wait for me in the vegetable and fruit market. Every time I go there, I return home a graver man. This time, before attending the sale of lambs at the cattle market, I put in some useful time in the scurrying throng that was moving between mountains of scallions. As a result of Joe's campaign for more and better vegetables, I am all eyes and ears for what I can learn in this labyrinth of assorted green-stuff. Outside the glass-covered enclosure—which needs only the hiss of steam and a few whistles to turn it into a railway terminus—the "rakes" of cabbage-loads are drawn up. For artistic loading and for bulk, the cabbages lead. There must have been well over one hundred horse-loads this morning besides scores of pony and donkey loads, all beautifully arranged in pyramids. (One is reminded of Oscar Wilde's Lord Arthur, who wandered past Covent Garden in the dawn and saw carters with "masses of green jade against the pink petals of some marvellous rose.") Inside the market I witness the arrival of an important cargo of vegetables from Rush, carried in on a super-lorry manned by a veritable crew of strapping young fellows. Its arrival was the signal for great commotion, and there was a display of energy, fascinating to watch, as the potato baskets and salad crates were hauled out to the various salesmen. Cauliflowers were badly treated, just pitched anyhow on to the ground; yet if I am not mistaken (for there is a conspiracy of silence which I am too timid to break) they fetch about four shillings per dozen. A world of lettuce comes also from Rush: some of the bundles burst and spill about, but nobody cares much. This vegetable is invariably spoken of as salad. I watched one of the handsome young men from Rush idly squeezing a head of it into a ball between his hands, as he stood on top of his vegetable kingdom waiting for help to complete the unloading. This plentiful commodity makes fourpence a dozen.

There is a little stir when a salesman calls out that he is going to open the auction (first of the season) of new potatoes. A score of people gather immediately around his "bank." Having made a brief statement about the potatoes, this, the leading salesman, obtains a single bid from a tall well-dressed man, probably the buyer for a company of chain-shops, who offers three shillings a stone. The salesman pauses only for a second before he assents, and then he informs all and sundry in an undertone: "Three shillings is the price today, no more and no less." I make sad calculations on whether I should have some potatoes for sale next week, and how far the price would fall between now and then.

Compared with the vendors of potatoes and vegetables, the flower traders are quiet and genteel.

I judge that despite the tariffs imposed, a great deal of their stuff is foreign. There is not much variety in their wares: irises, pyrethrums, carnations, and other lasting blooms, welcomed by the modern labour-saving housewife. Responding to a raucous holler of *Violets, Violets, Violets*, VIOLETS (the acoustics are remarkably good here), a group of girls and women cluster around a salesman. These women have hard eyes, determined jaws, and set faces; shrewdly and noisily, each one purchases her quota of little bunches. It is hard to associate those buyers in their bold and independent seeming with the plaintive girls with pleading voices who will later in the day peddle those same wares along Grafton Street and in St. Stephen's Green.

The disrespectful familiarity with which flowers and vegetables are treated here is amusing. Men lean comfortably on stacks of scallions; they simply walk on rhubarb; while bunches of flowers are flung from one vendor to another. Later in the year, when Irish apples are in, every pair of jaws in the market will be seen simultaneously in wry contortion. It would take a brave man indeed to tell off the apple-munchers. I live in hopes that some day I may be lucky enough to hear some old buffer of the Ascendancy cry out in savage protest to one of the offenders, "Stop eating my apples, sir!"

Just now there are tomatoes and plums from the Canaries, and apples from Australia. These, together with crates of oranges and the small consignments of strawberries (I saw only about a dozen punnets of Irish strawberries), are sold in a languid and polite way; there is none of the heaving and flinging about that characterises the sale of potatoes, scallions, and rhubarb.

But I am convinced that vegetable-growing for money is a farce, and I feel I shall never get back to Cloonmore quickly enough to hand on my conclusion to Joe. It seems to me that anyone who bids any sum of money can secure anything he wants in the market. And the unfortunate producer who brings in his stuff for sale will, when presented with his pay slip, stare in savage amazement at the amount of commissions and tolls exacted from him. Later on, it was balm to my wounded spirit to attend the sale of my lambs in the great open spaces of the cattle market.

When I get home to Cloonmore from the city, from the hard pavements, the strident insistence of advertisements, the traffic, the noise, the dust, and the heavy air, I take to walking through the fields as a restorative to soul and soles. How exquisite these big fields under a blue and gold sky—any patch of which would make the background of Fra Angelico's "Coronation." Encompassing peace of Cloonmore! Sheep in loose array throughout the pasture-land and creamy lambs moving in scattered groups. The coats of grazing cattle are taking a brighter gleam with the growth of grass. Grey wood-pigeons live out their shady lives in the attic storeys of trees, flitting from justice and cooing in concealment. How the swallows curve white bellies to the tall flowered grasses. . . . Space is our sandbag against the shock of the world.

In the flower-beds opposite the house, steely delphiniums stand sentinel, and the blue eyes of campanulas follow the gambols of the sun. Oriental poppies like votary lamps are glowing from the edges of the shrubbery. The corncrakes clapper from the meadows. The birds are calling like side-show men at a fair, a thousand scents are brewing from the earth, chafers striking against the poultry-run netting, moths flitting. The silence of the whole earth sponges up these little sounds. The sky above me is as soft as silk bales. Now the departing sun is beginning to spot-light the scene and fairy lanterns hang above the trees.

CHAPTER X

MEADOW AUCTIONS BEING UPON US again, I attend Breen's auction of Walsh's and Blackledge's meadows. It is a hot day, the ground pulls, one drags weary legs, and plucks an infinite number of grasses to suck their fleshy ends and find juicy insipidity. One also slaps the back of one's hand, putting a gory horse-fly out of action. One tries if one's hat would be any more comfortable placed crosswise. One attempts to clear a clogged pipe-stem with a stalk of grass, and the stalk breaks in the stem of the pipe. There are twenty or thirty of us following the auctioneer. I keep step with Pat Mangan, an uneven step to suit his feeble stride, bending down occasionally to catch his almost whispered comments. "Here are the Cloonlara boys!" he whispers excitedly at the sight of an advancing group of men. "We've no chance now. They have the whole thing planned. Oh Lord save us, do you see Patsy Tracey standing at Breen's hip so as he won't miss anything?"

Breen, the auctioneer (also a victim of the grass-sucking disease), waggles on his heels, juggles rather cleverly with his pencil, and mechanically asks, "What shall I say for this meadow? Who'll make me a bid?" His eyes are roving far afield, his thoughts have fled from meadows. Then he jerks himself back to the present: "A good old meadow growing on good land. What shall I say? Now, look-it here, I'm not so fond of me own voice as to be . . ." "Three pounds," from a Cloonlara man, who having fired his shot, turns right away from the circle to contemplate the Hill of Allen. "Didn't I tell you?" mutters Pat. The Cloonlara farmers continue to push up the price, and Walsh, the owner of the meadows, ought to be a happy man, whatever the feelings of the Graigue and Cloonmore farmers, who find convenient land filched from under their noses by outsiders.

Walsh has arranged his affairs well. Besides contriving to secure a little puffing from a friend, he has inserted a clause in the conditions of sale to the effect that 5s. will be deducted per acre for all those who mow their purchased portion before July 20th. This rebate suits Walsh, as he will have the benefit of the after-grass; also it has the effect of giving a fillip to the bidding. I give my ears a chuck on hearing concluding bids of £4 : 10s. for old meadow. At present this is an excessive price; "farming" ought to pay Walsh this year. We move off to Blackledge's. The blistering sun, the hot, dry, knee-high grass, horse-flies crawling on the fellow's back in front (refraining from giving him a crack between the shoulders is anguish), horse-flies on one's trouser-legs, and one's hands sticky with horse-fly guts. This dreary trudge brings us to the threadbare meadows of poor broken-down Blackledge.

In a cloud of flies, these hacked meadows now in their seventh year of cropping are put up, fetching a top price of 65s. and a bottom price of 30s. The contrast with Walsh's auction is very marked. Breen is even more spiritless; there is no-one to puff, or to crack those jokes which tend slightly to intoxicate the buyers. Blackledge is a spent farmer, a Protestant, and an outsider. "Did you ever notice," whispers Pat Mangan, "that in these parts, when a man is down, they are all down on him?" Pat is too hard on his own locality, the sin of neglecting the downfallen is universal. I take three acres of light stuff at £2; not much of a "fleece" on it (to use Pat's word), but free from gross weeds. Pat takes about two acres adjoining mine at the same price, his not quite so good, because it has a big sprinkling of yellow rattle (he calls this weed "rattle-bones"). He commented kindly enough that the two of us would be company for each other when the time came to save the crop.

*   *   *

Swallows swooping, claps of thunder, the smug coo of pigeons; the rose-bed now gleaming in yellow, scarlet, and white; elder bushes dishing up their platters of creamy smell; meadows ripening apace; the three-legged cat purring over her umpteenth litter in the boiler-house; hot sweltering nights, the air in lumps like bales of shoddy, or cotton in the raw. We hear no more the cool commentary of the cuckoo.

Without the compensation of gathering indulgences, I twice a day perform the pilgrimage of the seven strawberry drills on my knees. I have barely a rood of the foul things, but I am alone and unaided at the work; Jimmy is hard-pressed with the increasing needs of voracious fattening cockerels; Mrs. Meehan's spinal column is too stiff for such work, and farm men simply cannot be asked to pick berries. When one has come to the tail of a drill, one can commence again at the top of the same drill, so fast does the fruit ripen on such hot days as these. Each drill is laden too profusely with the scarlet berries. I have now neither punnets, nor chips, nor common or garden shoe-boxes left in which to collect the fruit. I am reduced to flower bowls as vessels and whatever else I can lay hands on anywhere, mostly dilapidated cardboard boxes which frequently burst under the pressure of the moist fruit. We have not yet established a selling system. If no-one responds to the advertisement running in the local paper, then I take out the car and try to persuade well-off neighbours to indulge themselves. If they refuse to nibble, then I take the fruit off to Ballynash, where I sell at any price, thus not letting down the flag at home, where strawberries are at all times a good stout price by our arranging—a one-man price ring, heaven forgive me.

But the knobs of my spine cry out; my knees are flattened. If the strawberry season lasts much longer, I'll begin to walk about on all-fours. For the unfortunate pickers of this delicious berry, I can vouch that the mere smell, after a time, will act as a perfect emetic.

After dusk, I lounge in a deck-chair on the front steps until the stars begin to prick the hazy

sky. Presently a ruddy moon with the mien of a
scullery maid travels up from the bronze-mauve
rings that lap the distant Wicklow mountains. I
hearken to the delicious monotony of the corn-
crakes and their mechanical counterpart—the
Lowtown barge. The whiff of night-scented stock
hovers around the kitchen steps. How amazingly
white is that Frau Karl Druschki! But the glory of
the night is dissipated for me by worrying and
mercenary calculation: how soon now shall the
sweat of haymaking be upon us; what are the
chances of a holiday, or of "doing" Croagh Patrick;
how much money should I rake in between pigs,
lambs, and poultry next Thursday; shall I manage
to pay all the wages at the end of the week out of
my Thursday's gathering, or shall I have to cash a
cheque?

*　　*　　*

Great saints, what days spent in the toil of saving hay! There is a brazen light, an evil-eyed sun,
heat enough to roast frogs, a black blueness in the
sky. I feel the scorching on my neck; I suffer from
burning feet and dazed eyes. Yet my attire consists
only of a shirt, an old pair of trousers (with a hole
in the seat censored by a safety-pin), tennis shoes, a
rubber belt, and a hat. On Tuesday, half Blackledge's meadow is knocked; on Wednesday it
sleeps, bleaching while it sleeps; on Thursday, the
remaining portion is knocked and the first half
teddered, Joe and Jimmy doing fork work, with
Mick on the swath-turner. When I get back from

the Dublin round, all puffed and rushed, I find these three shoving up cocks. I shed garments and join them. We work on after tea (which I fetch down from the house), and on until dusk falls and the boundaries of the meadow grow dim, putting up five cocks, each about five hundredweight, before we are ordered off the land by the dark.

Sweet-scented hay be hanged; perspiration is much more insistent than any perfume! On Friday we turn swaths. Heavens, the heat of this work! Round and round we go, not a word, not a murmur, a little crispy noise arising, a sense of the presence of scented dust, the trees around us stiff with the sun's fire. I am awkward with a fork, and I can only hope that the rasping I create is not noticed by the men: like eating toast, one probably bears the brunt of the din oneself.

Saturday, up at six in the morning and a white mist on the ground, so that one could not see fifty feet away. Soon the sun shook itself out of the clouds with a heated vengeance. Down at Weston with the boys before breakfast dressing cocks, tugging around them, raking here, patting there, and roping them down. When I return from breakfast, one man has tackled the handyman rake and presently the swaths are no longer recognisable, heap coming on heap into rough circles for the making of the cocks. Plunge the fork, then, into that tidal wave of new ripened hay, plunge it almost up to the hilt, brace yourself and hoist. Be careful that you don't let it in, or your cock will be top-heavy. Go again at the hillocks of hay, raise it over your head, never mind the flies on your nose, or the tickle of hayseed inside your shirt. Lift it, put it over—no, not over, but on, exactly so, or else that cock will be a stork, all towering and headachy, a cockshot for Pat Mangan's wit. Now careful, it's getting high, take smaller sops, raise them gingerly; if there were a breeze, you might have cause to complain in this delicate task of capping, but it is a flaming, still day. On to the next cock (ignore the pail of watered buttermilk under a pad of hay—your thirst can wait another while), round and round the butt, with a wad here and a wad there. Keep it out, keep it up, above all keep awake. Seventeen cocks up now.

If you feel terribly bad, the sweat blinding you, your arms like a yoke of wounds, then turn your hat about so that the sweat-wet part of the band is reversed. The sky may be like toast, the site like a model steam laundry, but keep it up. Let them see just this once that you too can work, that you can stick at it anyhow, even if you are not as work-hardened as they are. Damn it, sirs, it is my hay! That is a surprising thought: all this sweat and trouble and fuss is over my own hay. Look at the way John over there is labouring! Look at his flaming colour, and the drops of perspiration on his face—for the honour of another fellow's hay! Dry, slippery, short, silvery, put it all up. Never mind the rude, glaring sun, get it up. If his eye burns your eyes, don't pretend it. Take care when you are at the east side of a high cock and are putting up the capping forkful, for the wicked sun, like a gleam from the devil's shield, will flash furious rays into your face. Put it up: every stalk will make a wisp, every wisp a sop, every sop a forkful, every forkful a cock. Although hot, tired, limb-sick, go away sprightly and smiling, trying at least to look fresh and fit for twice as much labour. Twenty-nine cocks up now, safe and saved for the coming winter. Salve enough for all aches.

*　　*　　*

No matter how I pad out the events of this reposeful Sunday, I cannot casually introduce the feat of killing two young hawks with a single shot. The brag may as well out first as last. I approached the birds stealthily as they pranked on the hammock-like branches of an old larch-tree. At a distance of about twenty-five yards, I sighted and fired. When I saw one bird tumble to the ground and the other somersault on the branch where they had been gambolling, I was too amazed for words. I picked them up and, carrying a dead bird in each hand, crossed from the wood to the workshop, where Jimmy was oiling his bicycle.

"How many shots did you hear, Jimmy?"

Jimmy soberly eyes the hawks and confessed to having heard only a single report.

"Well, here is the result of one shot!"

Is Jimmy impressed? Not a bit of it! There's a man at the other side of Lowtown (Jimmy's native heath), who killed a rabbit and a crow with one shot. . . . Just like Jimmy, always topping stories with one better; the youth should go far.

Now I have three hawks (the third killed four days ago and now getting a trifle high) strung from the railing of the hall steps (a slightly Landseer effect, I convince myself). If somebody doesn't call today and admire my prowess, I'll scream—hawk-wise!

Summer has become like a woman of a certain age. There is just a little leakage in that bellows which was forcing everything to glow and flame. Buttercups have yielded place to hawkweed and the burgundy red of the sorrel inflorescence is less prominent in meadowscapes. The hawthorn has long since abdicated in favour of the elder; millfoil is making ready to close up the dying ranks of chervil. The birds are song-surfeited. Dragon-flies cut through the air, imitating the flight of swallows. Little dapper moths flutter up as one strides through the long grass. A hot odour arises from banks where Lady's Bedstraw grows. The limes are in flower, massy, bee-mad, and fragrant. The sycamores have a blueish bloom on their leaves and there is a scent of honey under the trees. Holly leaves are so tender that one could chew them. Details of the Hill of Allen stand out clearly, a certain local sign of bad weather's approach.

To the sheep that falls into a pit on the Sabbath, and gives its owner an excuse to break the day's observance, add a swarming of bees. Something must be done at once, or the swarm is lost. No place would suit my perverse bees to congregate but the precious bough of a young apple-tree. At first, I am of two minds whether to sacrifice a limb of a beloved apple-tree, or a swarm of bees which —as the verse has it—is not "worth a fly" this month: the bees win the debate. I deftly sever the bough with sécateurs while holding a butter-box under the cone-shaped swarm. The bulk of the massed bees flopped into the box all right, but I did not see the queen; I can only hope she is where she ought to have been.

Returning from a walk to Ballinamona bog with Willie Hogan (where his men have been footing turf on piecework, and where he makes pencil calculations on the inside of a cigarette carton), I emerge through the yard wicket-gate and see Cloonmore House moon-bathing. How quickly the Devon fortress has acquired for me the meaning of home! Now cool and solitary under the luminous night sky; tall, square, and clean-cut; honest and unpretentious: for a crazy moment I rank Cloonmore House with things of eternal beauty: Leighton's *Sluggard*, a naked man on a prominence, Gothic spires, Lombardy poplars.

*   *   *

In modern years, summer is flittered away by hay-making. Nowadays, one can comfortably open the hay-saving campaign in late June, and bring it to an unsuccessful ending in late September. Hay weather is, like hard winters, a thing of the past: there is about one good hay day in the week, and that day, perversely, is usually Sunday.

Today we waited until a slow, dreamy sort of shower was well over and then we repaired to the Slang and turned up quite harmless swaths. Only Joe among us foretold more rain, but we crushed him, for our expectations of getting up the rest of the hay were high. He proves maddeningly right in his weather predictions: just as the Angelus rings out from Graigue, the weather explodes and we retreat with heavy loss. We leave behind us several acres of disturbed swaths exposed to the ruinous downpour and only a paltry brace of cocks put up.

The men improvise umbrellas by holding forkfuls of hay over their heads as they trail to the gate. On the way up the avenue, Mick brings forth the whiskered yarn of the baffled farmer, but as we get this story every year, our smiles are somewhat forced. A certain old farmer was endeavouring to make hay one season in which it never stopped raining, and before the summer was ended, every wisp of his hay was spoiled. He swore at the heel of the worst day that, come what may, he wouldn't be beaten at any rate, so he took a bundle of mown grass under his arm, saying that he'd dry it before the kitchen fire and make at least that much hay. But when he was crossing a plank over a stream, didn't he fall in, hay and all, and that finished him!

Before the downpour, the sky was blue-black like a bruise, the swallows were all about our ears, and the flies were out for blood. In the inkiest part of the sky, thunder growled. We decided to concentrate on the upper end of the field, hoping to leave at least seven cocks up, while the lower half we hoped to leave in grass cocks, as it was not sufficiently "reared" for cocking.

Four of us went up and down the swaths with our busy forks, while further off Mick clattered up and down on the horse swath-turner. There was a dead, oppressive heat congenial to flies. Under the almost motionless aspens, and parallel to the water trench with its stuffy scent of mint and meadow-sweet, we threw up the rows of fragrant grass, hooked out the greenest bits and laid them on the crest. Silence and peace walled us in, as though time itself were falling into a slumber.

The bone-cracking round would be almost un-endurable if it were not for the pleasant chatter that accompanies it. The subject of local farmers' eccentricities brings us speedily through several rounds of the meadow. There is a certain John Byrne of whom we never tire; Kit Healy has first-hand gossip about him, as he is near neighbour to this butt of our jokes. Kit has a droll way of spinning his yarns, always in a mumbling voice, and with never the hint of a smile.

John Byrne is one of those old buffers who are for ever deploring the age, the effeminacy of modern men, and the vanishing of the grand old race of people in general. But at the same time, John himself demonstrates none of the fine farm-ing qualities of the older generation whose dis-appearance he deplores. It is alleged that he does not mow his meadows until October, and that he then lets the mown stuff lie out in grass cocks until near Christmas (or else our Kit tells tall ones). The ancient John Byrne likewise sows corn, but seldom bothers to reap it. His potatoes are left rotting in the ground until the plough evicts them for another sowing in the spring. Last winter, he stall-fed an old bull for so long a period that the dung rose up about five feet in the house, and the beast got so fat he could not get it out of the door when the time came for selling him, so that the roof . . . or does Kit surpass himself in the gentle art?

John Byrne's maxims are many, a typical one being, "If you wait long enough, a fine day will come!" Kit's rider is that John always waits for the next fine day after that again.

Our neighbours, the Walshs, also come in for a share of ridicule. Joe is never tired of telling against them how, when sent to borrow their turnip-sower, he was informed that it was lost; they had left it out twelve months ago after use, and the grass and weeds grew over it. After an hour's search around their farm, he tracked it down in a ditch. These farmers employ a certain labouring man, the mere mention of whom causes merriment. As I am ignorant of this man's exploits, the men regale me with stories. When he was being hired, he was (like Flynn's man) too bashful to admit that he could not plough, and all his furrows turned out as crooked as the Coolalug road. Joe supplemented that it would take the Council men's skill to re-move the corners. Walsh's labourer got over the difficulty of closing potato drills by the simple expedient of bending down and flinging into the ditch any potato seed that his meandering double-mould plough had failed to cover.

This same caubogue had been hired by another farmer some years ago, to whom he swore he was expert in making drills. While the farmer re-mained watching his work, the drills were reason-ably straight, but when the boss returned in the evening to view the field, most of the drills were wavy. "What's this?" demanded the furious farmer. "Oh, that'll be all right," answered the caubogue coolly, "sure the sun is after warping them and when it sets, they'll come back straight!"

The same genius was once knocked down by a bicycle when he was mounting the hump of a canal bridge. "Oh, be the Lord, and what do you mean?" he fumed, as he picked himself up more testy than hurt. "Holy God, if you only went the way you were looking, you wouldn't have hit me!" That story, racy enough to stand as typical of our best-loved ones, capped the collection and left us chuckling for half a row of bleached grass.

The clink of hayforks, the occasional and very glad rustle of cured grass bespeaking some progress: there is no other sound to be heard. It is ominous, however, that there is no purr of mowing machines from the fields around; evidently public opinion is not disposed to believe in a spell of fine weather. Mick having tossed up his portion of the meadow, dismounts from his machine and joins us at forking. Kit Healy, or anybody else for that matter, could never come within yards of Mick's yarns, so Mick thinks. Having heard the end of the impostor ploughman saga, he begins a series of stories about another local idiot, a serious competitor with Kit's hero. This fellow has been known to come out of his house at night in order to form some opinion of weather prospects for the morrow, and strike a match to look at the stars! When he was in the employment of a big farmer on the Ballinvally side, he was told to put out the cow-byre light, which happened to be an electric one, and he was discovered blowing vigorously and vainly on the bulb. However, this same man later on enlarged considerably his knowledge of electricity, for when he was blamed for not doing a certain job, he retorted by saying he wasn't an electric wire that he could be in two places at once! There follow some rather complicated stories of the hero's exploits, the main fact that emerges being the victim's ignorance of book learning. "You might as well hand him this fork as the newspaper," is Mick's round-about way of conveying that his hero is illiterate. He is cross-eyed, moreover, and the men explain that if you were to speak to him here in the Slang, you wouldn't know whether he was looking at you, or in the direction of Hanna's cottage. The compass by the way has only three points on this farm: Dublin, the Hill of Allen, and Hanna's cottage.

Haymaking is apt to go silver mid-way in the process. The cut grass not alone fades to silvery shavings like that stuff sold for scouring pans, but the aspen leaves on the near-by trees are silver-backed and the surroundings take on a silvery sheen. Blackberries shoot out their blossom heads silver-plated; thistles are shaggy brushes of silver, and even the birds show a streak of greyish silver in their flight. The moon and haymaking are akin, just as the sun and harvesting.

But for all the loveliness of an aluminium meadow with argent furnishings, and all the awe of barbed-wire thunder showers, more blue skies and less metal would suit us better.

The moral of modern summers ought to be obvious to me after this and last year's experience: be merry and take a holiday before the hay-making comes, because when it does come, the work may well be prolonged right on into winter.

And if a farmer does not think weather, curse weather, pray about the weather, and lie awake at night fretting over the weather, then he ought to give up farming and go into something easy like the haberdashery business, or insurance. Weather to the farmer is worse than twins to a mother: if the weather is wooing your corn to ripeness, then it is burning up your turnips, or breeding a plague of flies, or making thistles doll themselves up in flowers. Have I a means of livelihood? No, I am just weather's dependent.

CHAPTER XI

THE WHEAT IS RIPENING, THE BARLEY heads are bowed, though root crops are static and, in the garden, vegetable marrows pine. The trees are deathly still, ponds are reduced, the grass has gone burnt sienna, and the tillage-field headlands are heat-cracked. The droning of mowing machines has ceased, and the neighbours come less often to borrow haymaking implements. The swifts rehearse their departure by swinging on wires; magpies are educating their young in excited gibberish; the corncrakes have put away their fiddles. There is a trembling vapour over the bogs, a dreaminess about the distant mountains, and by-roads are sheeted in dust. As the wood betony sinks, the ragweed rises; the hogweed is shedding its seeds; nettles are ravaged by black caterpillars; butterflies bent on causing destruction hover over cabbages. The horse-flies bite less greedily, but crane-flies increase; moths fly in the open windows at night. The lodge garden is all ablow with mari-golds, plums ripen on the garden wall, and Mr. Gladstone apples are colouring. The creaking of the yard pump is almost continuous, as there is only a black stink at the bottom of the rain-barrels. One sits to meals clad only in shirt and trousers, afterwards the temptation to take a siesta is almost overpowering; the men show bare chests, and the postman arrives almost in *négligé*.

Sunsets are cerise; there is the least hint of a nip in the evening air; after dark, the hedgehogs go for ambles. Nights are hushed except for the noise coming from the road where the young people cry out to each other as they go home from dances. The stars are dim, and there is a lemon moon in a violet sky.

Like the detestable Summer Time Act, Bank holidays are ignored by country dwellers. I, for one, am glad to be liberated from the duty of resting when and so the bankers ordain. I prefer to consider holidays as holy days and to take my rest at the orders of the Church, when there is at least a saint to be rejoiced in. Monday Bank holidays are for jaded clerks and for city folk generally, who like to take breakfast in bed on that day and read the previous Sunday newspapers. But we rural people work on, content to wait for the feast of the Assumption, or for the more distant day of All Saints.

*   *   *

There is an idea current that farming is in a depressed condition: an embargo on cattle to England, high overhead charges, labour expensive and skilled labour almost impossible to secure. But such news as this does not stir a hair of the Weeds and Agricultural Seeds (Ireland) Act of 1909. Short of abandoning one's farm, as folk do so lightheartedly in the Middle West of America, one must cut one's thistles, or else face "summary conviction and a penalty not exceeding, for the first offence, five pounds, and for the second or any subsequent offence, ten pounds."

The creeping thistle chuckles satirically. Even if the cohorts of Thistle Inspectors were doubled or trebled, the thistle is not thereby doomed, for what farmer is in a position to follow the instructions so airily laid down by authority? "Cutting must be repeated from early spring until late summer," and again, "Cutting or pulling must be resorted to, and persisted in early and often." But repeated and annoying visits from the personage known locally as the "Thistle Man" cannot intimidate me into making more than a single cutting. And even this is strictly a cutting for show purposes: it consists of going over those parts of my farm which lie exposed to the road, and there making a slipshod hacking of all the larger thistles.

Thus stimulated by a seven-day notice from the itinerary inspector, I laboured at thistle destruction on the lawn for several hours today. I made use of two implements, a scythe and a thistle hook: the first is advantageous for groups, but unwieldy for solitary plants and small ones. Scythe work makes the unpractised arm ache, and long wielding of the thistle-hook results in a painful wrist. Besides the creeping thistle, there are occasional marsh thistles: these are worthy of my mettle: tall and stout, they need a mighty swipe before they "bite the dust" like a Red Indian brave of the penny dreadfuls. No matter how skilful one becomes, one often misses a thistle, returns to miss again; and missing three or four times, one begins to mutter, "Well, if I don't get you this time, I'll kneel down and bite you with my teeth."

One is rather exposed at this work, not merely to the elements, but to the unsympathetic gaze of pedestrians. If I relax for a moment, I find that someone has stopped to stare fixedly at me from the road, and seeing me thus momentarily idle, concludes that I am spending my time looking around me.

Properly speaking, if one were alive to one's own interest, a conscience is needed at this work: first in order to be diligent in seeing that even the tiniest thistles do not escape, and second, in order not to mow more grass than is strictly necessary. Yet how lightly I would order any man, even the most casual of casual labourers who came up looking for a day's work, to cut thistles for me, hardly taking thought of how he would do the job. This realisation comes to me with a certain shock. The longer I live, the more tasks I discover which a farmer should really do himself, so if I live much longer, life won't be worth living.

Ministries of Agriculture, Departments, Boards, State laboratories and such-like, may do splendid work, but to the best of my knowledge they have in no country done anything yet to provide an effective means of thistle extermination. I believe that the present practice in Ireland of cleaning conspicuous fields of the more showy thistles once or twice a year does more harm than good, because the creeping thistle gains in vigour in the catacombs below as a result of the mild persecution overground. I should be very glad to rid my pastures of thistles. Apart from the expensive labour of cutting, their presence means less grass and an impoverished land. So far as my experience goes, only meadowing in succession for a larger number of years than is reconcilable with good husbandry will materially reduce them. Entries in my farm diaries for several years back show that every year I have cut thistles in July on the same land. The only result seems to be that the pest is at least kept in check. When will science send a bug, or a poison, or a mechanical contraption, or a good fatal disease for the annihilation of thistles?

The wood-pigeon shooting campaign opened officially this evening with four misses. Our wheat is going to suffer badly from vermin: huge flocks of pests soar up from the crop when disturbed by a hand-clap; the crows are of course in evil league with the fat robbers. In an ideal state, I will go forth every morning before breakfast and shoot crows. At present, I go as far as making a good resolution to that effect on dropping off to sleep each night. A progressive farmer.

* * *

Don't talk to me about droughts, the stench of empty rain-barrels, or trousers with ventilation-holes in the seats. For now there are tons, barrels, bushels, acres, miles, and hogsheads of rain: the heavens avenge themselves in that we had grumbled about the drought. It is enough to make whole colleges of cardinals blaspheme. The corn is ruined ten times over, but one hopes even still that it has more lives than a cat. Wheat anyway is always full of pleasant surprises: one declares it dead almost from the time one watches the crows attacking the seeding, yet it nearly always threshes out trumps. But the oats are battered almost out of recognition by the cruel torrents, and begin to look like something the pup played with. The lawn is sodden and the Night Park, which is the sort of land that can usually take its liquor like a gentleman and show no sign of being fuddled, is now pocked with ponds. Judging by the lowering skies, there is more to come.

The weather is making such a bloody mess of everything that I am driven to dope. Being a fairly tough pipe-smoking and afternoon-tea-less farmer, dope in my case consists of smoking cigarettes, eating chocolate, and reading novels by modern woman writers. Having viewed the horrors of my battered and lodged oats, I am so demoralised that I come into the house and order Mrs. Meehan to make me tea. Since the tanks are full to the brim upstairs, I decide to take a bath—heaven only knows when I last had one. The bathroom tap is temperamental; first a trickle, then a snort, then a mad gallop of water, followed by a dead stop. A bath is a melancholy business too (or else the bad weather is getting on my nerves): the first water after rain is usually a sooty black, the bathroom furniture is sort of dismal, the view from the window just grass and trees, with further on grass and more trees. (When Mrs. Meehan first came to these parts, she spent a great deal of time gazing out of the windows on such fat, green landscape: "'Tis very different from Clare, surely," she would

mutter, leaving her hearers always a little doubtful
—was she bestowing a compliment?) While waiting for the inky water to cool, I stand on my head,
for no particular reason except to prove to myself
that I am neither really downhearted, nor decrepit.

*   *   *

Choosing the seeds of annuals from catalogues
is almost like a game of blind-man's-buff to me,
but I sometimes hit a bull's-eye. This year's lucky
strike is certainly Lavatera. It has the most graceful lines imaginable, together with a fine solid
colour. The plant cries out for pencil sketching: its
stems are like lyre strings, its leaves cordate, its
flowers tubular, and there is a lovely rhythm in its
stance. I never see it without feeling that I am
confronted by an amazing water-colour of Lavatera
hanging in the Dublin Modern Gallery, one of
a series of flower sketches by Ursula Tyrwhitt,
who seems to be a genius at poetic lineation.

I have autumn crocuses also for the first time,
but I do not like them: pallid, ghostly things, like
maidens in a "decline," their message is doleful
instead of merry like that of their kinsmen, fore-
runners of the spring. They are an unsolicited
repetition, or else the ghostly return of spring's
children; but then children ought not thus go
about in grave shrouds, scaring folk.

As harvest work is waiting for us just round the
corner, we are not prepared to make a start on the
hay-rick, a job that once commenced, must be
brought to a finish. But Mick, Kit and their respect-

ive drays are beginning to make an impression on the Weston House cocks. Each dray takes two cocks at a time and makes four trips in the day. Unfortunately, the journey is too long for the use of a bogie (which of course takes only one cock at a time), otherwise we could slither the cocks off in the yard according as they arrived in, and there they could await our convenience to be built into a rick. As it is, the hay is now forked into sheds, a dangerous practice; if the hay is not completely cured, it is sure to go mouldy. Our total barn or shed capacity is only about fifteen to twenty tons, so that Blackledge's hay will tax all our storage capacity.

Joe spends these days crawling on all fours through the turnip drills, thinning out the crop. In addition to doing the turnip-thinning he is told to do, he does a lot that he is not told to do, such as surreptitiously planting out Brussels sprouts: I consented to a single drill of these. I connived at a further half-drill, but now I note that that half-drill is adding yards to itself each evening when I go out to inspect the amount of turnips thinned —an hour when Joe has left off work for the day and so escapes my sarcasm.

John is finding the turnip thinnings a blessing as bulk for the pig tub. Boiling for the pigs gave place, months ago, to feeding them weeds (sow-thistle and hogweed chiefly—the fellows who named these plants had a knowledge of their uses); this is either fed as it is or put through the chaff-cutter set at its coarser grade.

By dint of hanging round the yard for a little

while and looking into the houses, John can be coaxed to the lawn for a bout of the endless thistle-cutting; when he realises that I realise that there really is not another tap of yard work to be done until pig-feeding and milking time comes round again, he gives way with good grace to the inevitable.

Jimmy is engaged in creosoting hen-houses and hen-run gates. He has taken to pipe-smoking. I gave him some fatherly advice about not going in for strong tobaccos which would make him vomit, but when he tells me that he has already consumed two ounces of plug, I bow before my superior. Next thing will be a request for a rise in wages, I suppose, or else he will flit to greater heights, for Jimmy, like his predecessors, is turning himself into a man with uncomfortable rapidity. Of all things fleeting, there is nothing so transitory as a farm boy.

Blackcurrant-picking goes on every day, even in the teeth of savage weather. Among the pickers, Mick's two little girls are constants, Mrs. Meehan is an irregular, and I am a casual. The children are paid a halfpenny per pound. The Goliaths are in great abundance. On the whole, however, our small fruit production is very unimportant. It is a pretty sight to see a little girl in a print dress pop out of a currant bush scarcely taller than herself, with a billy-can swinging from her arm. Only on one day this season did I spend anything like part of a working-day picking the fruit, and when I was dropping off to sleep that night, visions of currant clusters set in their foliage sprang up on the black screens of my eyelids. Sometimes the vision seemed to hold for an appreciable time, and I tried to puzzle out in a drowsy way whether my hallucination was of a typical cluster of currants, or of some particular cluster.

John, Jimmy, and I spent three hours last night in the company of a farrowing sow. It rained a good deal; the farrowing shed has a corrugated-iron roof, a type of roof which lets those beneath it know all about the intensity of the showers. We sat companionably on the farrowing rail in the dim light of a yard lamp. John was present because sows are his job; Jimmy was there because he had nothing particular to do and because he enjoys yarning with John; and I was there because I had been lazy all day. Having been made uncomfortable by pricks of farming conscience, I was acquitting myself in my own way.

We smoked a lot and talked mainly of harvest prospects, and ways and means of wintering and housing stock in the coming months. Next door to the house we occupied were two gilts that snored heavily in their sleep. "You'd swear it was a Christian," Jimmy remarked. Except for the spatters of rain above us, there was a big yawning silence outside. The sow was slow: the first pink and glistening bonham popped out at ten o'clock; a second wiggled about in the slime a few minutes later; and after that there was an idle interval of twenty minutes. John cuts the navel-strings with his pen-knife, blows into the bonhams' mouths (of very fanciful benefit, I imagine), and hands them to Jimmy for a rough drying in a piece of sacking. Until the litter is almost up to full

241

strength, I have no job; then I do policeman work, preventing assault and battery and generally keeping the peace in the family. Providentially, a sow's feet soften before farrowing, and she is thus kept from unwittingly causing injury to her offspring.

All the while the sow is in a high fever; she quivers and grunts without any respite. As a matter of good swine husbandry, we should not congregate in a farrowing pen, because the presence of humans and their fussy ways excite the patient more than is necessary. Before John came here, when Mick and I did most of the stock between us, I was always content to keep watch from outside the farrowing house if the event came off during the day, or if at night, to sit quietly inside on an upturned bucket, merely rescuing the bonhams from being overlain, giving a sloppy drink, and hanging up a lamp before I left. However, the rain partly excuses us for congregating in the wrong place, and also we stand excused because this is the sow's fourth litter, so that she is becoming an experienced old hand.

Jimmy, despite his advanced taste in tobacco, has still very childish ways. He is delighted with the infant antics of the bonhams just born, their nuzzling of each other, and the way they wrinkle up their snouts when sampling the maternal milk (almost as though they were gourmets, appraising the bouquet of a choice wine). In the course of conversation, Jimmy's innocence is rather shown up when he remarks enthusiastically that a certain farm on the Kilbride road is the best mushroom-growing land in this district. John quizzes the boy for a while, suppressing the least suggestion of a smile, and drily retorts: "That must be a paying place, surely!" Jimmy looks crestfallen, realising his *gaffe*.

On come the bonhams, wiggling, sneezing, and steaming, until fourteen in all have accumulated, being two more than the number of the sow's teats. One of them, a "wee-shee" one as Jimmy calls it (it is only a matter of weeks before he will discard this term in his plunge after manliness), sets up such a miserable squealing and fends so badly for itself that I undo my waistcoat and button him up against my side. Mrs. Meehan is quite accustomed and more or less resigned to finding a bonham or two in the kitchen oven without warning, but she will be spared this time. The little creature makes a good recovery and, having been held up for a drink, joins his family without much protest.

After the last bonham has arrived, we await the coming of the cleanings and the pandemonium which will afterwards ensue, for a sow always stands up and reviews the situation when she has finished. In order to replace the now sodden bedding, I send Jimmy to pull straw from the rick and put it through the chaff-cutter. Nothing irritates a sow more than long straw in her bedding. She stoutly believes that her young will strangle themselves in it, and even if she is midway in the heat of farrowing, she will take immediate steps, if she observes long straws around her, to chew up all the lengths into suitable scraps. If it were a little later in the year, we could provide chaff, which is the ideal bedding, always of course with the exception of barley chaff, which is never used because of the beards in it.

By this time it is half an hour after midnight. I go to the house, where, with the aid of the bellows, I blow up the study fire into a glow and put on a kettle in order to make the sow's bran drink. I also procure a saucepan of milk to make cocoa for ourselves. By the time we have finished our beverage, the sow is ready to be settled down for the night, having had her stand up, her drink of slops, and having sunk down contentedly once more without crushing to death any of her family. The lamp is hung in safety on a wire suspended from a rafter, the litter is heaped into a nest within the security of the sow's sprawled-out legs, and a bag of hay is thrown outside the door to fend off cold draughts.

I feel it in my bones that John is going to ask me for those two surplus bonhams in the morning: I don't grudge them to him, but I do feel a spark of pity for his wife. She will have to feed them from a baby's bottle at least six times a day and four times a night for weeks on end, and after all her trouble, they may die on her at any moment, even when they are as old as ten or twelve weeks. If those little unwanted mites ever enter the Dublin market as fat pigs, it will be the result of a miracle of feminine patience and industry, which no money value can repay.

*   *   *

Harvest weather has come at last. A stained-glass sort of gold transmutes plain things into objects of beauty. A gauze-blue sky and insignificant clouds stand above a hazy and dreadfully still earth. The red-gold of ripe wheat contrasts with the silver-gold of almost ripe oats. There is not a sound around Cloonmore except noises of industry in our neighbours' cornfields, and birds singing very sweetly near the house.

I am all astir about planning the harvesting of the wheat. Giving up Joe Condon's machine as hopeless, because he has already promised to lend it to Pat Mangan and to at least two other farmers, I make two journeys this morning to Bill Liddy in an effort to borrow or hire his reaper-and-binder. On my second and successful call, Liddy agrees with alacrity, and presently I discover that his unexpected eagerness to let me have his machine is explained by his intent that I should lend him my horses for his own harvest. However, I am quite willing to do this. If Bill takes on the job of harvesting my oats as well as my wheat, making no charge but accepting in return the loan of my horses, all will be well indeed, or else I do not yet see the snags.

In my journeys between my farm and Bill Liddy's, I enjoy from the road views of Cloonmore and long-distance views of sleepy Wicklow Mountains away off beyond Ballynash. Though modern woman no longer grows dowdy as she grows older, the year has not changed its habits. A fearful dowdiness is apparent on all sides: the trees show it particularly, and rank growths such as nettles, hogweed, and thistles go grey and shabby. The earth has produced her myriads of children and is looking spent and tired. And yet sometimes she can be gay, baby-proud, and radiant.

A beautiful instance of symbiosis comes my way. Pullets that had wandered into the pig field from the yard had found a perch on the sows' heads; and while the pigs lay in the dusty soil, the fowl snapped up the flies that were bent on tormenting them.

I suffered a peculiar revulsion of feeling all of a sudden today against a circle of robust marigolds, and I proceeded to pull them up recklessly and fling them over the netting of a poultry run. No matter how highly prized in Chelsea and Rathmines, they are nasty, sticky, smelly, cabbage-like things, with gaudy flowers fit only for the garnishing of mutton broth. I gaze now with perfect serenity on the nice round bed with its asters and snapdragons, relieved from the companionship of low, cook-faced marigolds.

*   *   *

The sun pours down, every harvester's face is the face of a god. There is just breeze sufficient to waft thistledown languidly but harmfully across the farm. Liddy's reaper dominates the scene. There was a long delay before it was rigged up. I sat smoking (for there were plenty of knowledgable men helping Liddy's man) and eyeing the radiant picture of unshaven gods and dirty cupids (represented by Liddy's children) under a sky of Grecian blue. White butterflies performed marital rites in flight; the swallows darted squeaking almost a mile above us; the waiting horses were crunching stolen oat-heads; beyond the lake of ripe wheat was the cool aftergrass dotted with ochre haycocks. It was half-past twelve before the gross machine got properly under way and began to eat up wheat and spew out sheaves.

It is a tremendous sight, this harvesting by reaper-and-binder: behind three sinewy horses, the big animated thing goes careering around the rustling wheat, heaving out tousled sheaves with clockwork regularity, framed by still trees and under a cover of burning blue sky. This is a grander and a bigger thing than the best of my cherished roses; better far than the wistful face of Mrs. Sam McGredy is this shaggy bunch of wheat held together by an unromantic bit of twine manufactured in Canada. The crop is moderately clean this year, in spite of rain; there is not a solitary thistle in it, but plenty of yarrow and a few starry knapweeds (did not the Centaur cure his wounded foot, that wound inflicted on him by the bullying Hercules, with a timely application of knapweed?).

The horses are halted, for the machine fails; something has gone wrong again with those plaguy canvases. The driver jumps down from his seat, his lean brown face and intensely blue eyes peering about the sheets and rollers. The mares attempt to reach at heads of wheat while they wait. The machine is drab enough, not having seen a paint-pot since Liddy began to go downhill after the War, but there are still flecks of blue and souvenirs of white on it here and there. The man

247

working the machine is in a blue shirt, the sky is in another, and the colour contrasts vividly with the rectangle of gold wheat, the line of dark trees, glistening horses, and the dancing of pool-brown lights in the eyes of the boy standing at the horses' heads. There is a sparkle off the neighbouring second-crop grass, a distant glimpse of a harvester in shirt and trousers, bare-armed, with a battered hat pulled down to shield his forehead. There is sharp colour in outstanding masses, resembling more the work of some ultra-Cubist whose name I scorn to remember, than of Monet or George Clausen; a vivid, spangled scene, peopled by attenuated figures and mobile horses.

Here is Joe standing some fifty yards away, familiar (too damned familiar for words), but today there is a new glamour about him, today the twist of his braces, one side altogether off his shoulder, and the bagging of his patched shirt are accessories for any model of male perfection. He carries a long pole which he uses for guiding the cut corn into its proper course and, for a heavenly moment, he is for me that statue of a Hellenistic prince in the Roman museum, "standing after the heroic manner," with a spear-shaft rising two feet above his head.

Bill Liddy himself being here, with his man, in addition to my four men and a boy, there is not a lot for me to do (nor indeed for most of the others either, except that the old machine has a trick of needing things that require a messenger to be sent off to the workshop, the dairy, and even to the shops of Graigue). I come and go, attend to poultry jobs necessarily neglected by Jimmy, draw spring water for tomorrow's churning, pick French beans for the dinner (at which Liddy is to join me), and for a wonder generally make myself useful in Mrs. Meehan's eyes. I must have gone out to the harvesting at least twenty times, even if I did not take a hand at the actual stooking. On the roadway leading from the yard to the tillage field, there lives a single plant of nipplewort, which in the lacework of sunshine and shadow, nods to me as I come and go.

In the evening Jimmy and I carried down tea to the men in the corn. For a very short spell, they loll on sheaves, drink prodigious quantities of tea, and chew slabs of bread and jam. Mick talks of a certain part of the oats as in a "kneeling" state, a good description of a crop neither wholly standing nor altogether lodged. When the square of corn grows small, rabbit-hunting becomes more important to the men than harvesting the wheat. It is extraordinary how these tough fellows seem to enjoy hallooing and cap-waving across the stubble in pursuit of a small rabbit, but as the wage-payer, I am inclined to be grateful to the little hunted creatures for giving a fillip to the men when they are most tired.

We have done a good day's work: half the entire wheat crop is cut, stooked, and headed. The other half, the "kneeling" or (if the truth must be told) the lodged part, is going to be a blister, I fear, even if the weather should hold up.

Heaven take the future three days into its special consideration.

CHAPTER XII

THE LORD SENDS LIGHT THROUGH A yellow chrysanthemum. The autumn scene is so fragile, musk-smelling and rarefied that one is afraid one's breath might dispel it. Sunlight is paternal, mild, and gracious. Trees brood, birds tell chimney-corner tales; a honey-tinted film suffuses all plain things, making them as garish as theatrical props in the limelight. Everywhere there are vistas reminiscent of Watteau's "Departure for Cythera." Often a tree drops a handful of leaves, meditatively rather than sadly, but the game is by no means up. Summer but muses over her box of cosmetics, using none of them yet.

There is no end to these lovely clear days with their little wisps of clouds (like the drapery of painted nymphs) in a very airy sky. The apple is the reigning monarch of the era, and climbing apple-trees in an apple-hunt is kings' sport. Give me an empty head and let me pick apples, and I'll start whistling like a thrush.

The campaign opened as long ago as the last week of July, when Mr. Gladstone was stripped. Small and rosy, early to come and early to go, having little piquancy, the public are gulled by him because he is pink and neat, but actually he lacks flavour. Beauty of Bath should have followed next if my three representatives had consented to fruit; youngsters still, they showed some blossom, but thought better of fruiting when it came to the point. Next in order came old granddam Devonshire Quarrenden with her usual large family of tiny reds. It is almost impossible to gather them; one must either gaze up hopelessly, or share the windfalls with rodents. My tree bears freely and is thoroughly reliable; the flesh of the apple is blood-red almost right through. According to Mrs. Sullivan, who comes from the north, the correct name for this apple is Blood of the Boyne. She is wrong, of course, but northern dogmatism is hardly to be shaken by southern accuracy.

The Golden Spires, which are not all garnered yet, hang out an abundance of lemon-coloured and almost lemon-shaped fruit. It is a spongy apple, not very sweet, yet passes as a dessert among the undiscriminating: my considered opinion is that Golden Spires are not worth growing. A solitary Irish Peach on the front lawn dropped in production from four dozen specimens last year to under two dozen this year. It is also badly marred by canker, lusciousness is almost absent; this season I have a dull and diseased fruit instead of a delicate and juicy one. If I had to select one early dessert apple to give to friends, it would be an Irish Peach; but it is not an apple that stands much hawking about, or selling in the market; it should be eaten practically off the tree or not at all.

The six James Grieves (on cordons) consented to present less than a dozen apples—fine specimens, however. Grieve is such a juicy apple that if one does not take precautions in eating it, ungenteel streams will trickle down one's chin. Of course there is another way of eating apples, I understand, besides biting them, but he who peels and slices an Irish apple is not clean of heart.

I wish I had time to pick all the apples myself and do nothing else. It is lovely out in the orchard in the glow of yellow fruit, the birds giving out little melancholy songs. Apples hanging from trees like whole schools of philosophy, moralising, preaching sermons, filling the eye, and satisfying the mind like fully-grown sons. It is hilarious pleasure to me simply to go from tree to tree and size up the crops.

Jimmy and I picked seven and a half stone of Lord Derbys this morning, giants in Robin Hood green, but bad cookers, spongy and soapy. Already the Lord Derbys have brought in some revenue this year. The books say their season is November, but I prefer to get them off my hands before my bigger quantities of Lanes, Emperor Alexanders, and Bramleys come crowding in. Lord Derby is large, prosperous-looking, and short-stalked. It has the advantage of minding its own thinning affairs; one rarely finds more than a single apple to the spur, but that *is* an apple. I'd rather eat raw parsnips than venture on a raw Derby.

The sun blazes yellow. Van Gogh considered yellow a colour in which God delighted. When evening catches us in the orchard, we bathe in gold pools. The air is like a spirit. The view from the ladder is still, gentle, and heart-warming. I spend happy after-supper hours sorting windfalls into three grades: those for the pigs, for the house, and the best of them for sale. I love the almost metallic clink of clean, steely apples against one another.

How terrifically, dangerously, almost insanely happy I can be when I wander about the farm with a gun after supper. Banana sunlight, the beech-trees turning foxy, and the sycamores putting on khaki. Summer totters, its eyes deep in the future, sensing death; winter is defiant, confident of its coming sway. I rarely kill anything, and sometimes I do not even get a shot, but I live tensely. Thieves and villains bunch together—crows and wood-pigeons; they drink in large bands at the pond, the very openness of which protects them from gun-shot. Grouse, pheasants, and partridge are frequent enough in Cloonmore, but from giving the numbers which fall to my shot I beg to be excused. Stumbling on mushrooms, I bend for them and string them on a stalk of dog's-tail, thus hampering myself should the chance of a shot arise.

Such mushrooms as we have this year! The snow is accountable for that too, I expect. Returning from tea with the Hogans the other night, I picked at least two pounds of them by moonlight —a huge, honest moon moving amidst sheep-clouds. Incidentally, I have eaten the most villainous-looking mushrooms without ill effect. The variety is called Boletus and is bright Indian yellow, with a honeycombed under. I had not the courage to present my Boletus to Mrs. Meehan, as I know well how she would react, so I secretly cooked them myself in a cigarette tin on the study fire. They are not particularly strong-flavoured, nor so very different in most ways from ordinary mushrooms, except that they are much more fleshy. And I live on.

This evening, on a shooting round, the sky was in flames, the trees seemed to bunch themselves together for sleep, and the grass was heavy with dew. Daylight packed up suddenly and was gone in a twinkle over the western brim of the world. I lay in one of those little cup-like hollows south of the gravel-pit; soon stars crept out of their burrows, even if the rabbits sulked in theirs. Behind me was a great unwieldy larch, lichen-covered and long past its prime. Lazily I hold trial on its presence here: the verdict being that it should be cut down, even if we have no particular need for the timber; perhaps I might allay my silly conscience by planting a few more apple-trees on another part of the farm. Strolling homewards, wisps of grass-blades cling to my boots, Cygnus in a headlong dive out of the Milky Way on to Cloonmore House, I heard no certain noises abroad, but a whole medley of little voices from the earth. What a pity folk speak of being spellbound for slight causes! Else am I.

*　　*　　*

The word of a threshing-mill owner is proverbial. He will promise to come in a week; he may come in three weeks. He will solemnly declare that he will set up early next morning, and he may trail in by evening.

"You might as well try to lead a bull by his

254

tail," declares Tommy Farley when told on arriving too early that the mill has not yet appeared. Farley has been sent over by Hogan to help on our big day. There is nothing for him to do. He is a man of few words at any time, and now his dark face (as though carved out of elmwood) is sullen and depressed.

We assemble at the corn-ricks. All is in readiness, even to the basket of rather sour apples which is perhaps the pitiable heir of the former barrel of porter. If there were even slight preparations to be made, the wretchedness of the position would not stare us so stolidly in the face, but even the forks have been collected, the pot-holes in the roadway filled in with rubbish, a ladder brought out for mounting the ricks, the sacks of coal wheeled out in readiness for the engine, water drawn and left standing in barrels under the crab-apple; in short, no detail has been forgotten.

Farley and my own four men are lolling by the ricks, or supporting themselves against the mare and dray, which is optimistically ready for drawing in the threshed grain. Soon we are joined by two others from a neighbouring farm, Peter Mangan and his nephew, Seamus Murray. We face the distant road seeking vainly for a sight of the threshing-set procession, our eyes skimming between the low trees and resting hopefully on that stretch where the distant road hedge is low enough to permit a view.

There is a good high wind which would dissipate the clatter of the oncoming engine. We converse in ordinary speaking tones only because we are on the lee side of the ricks. A little way off, the wind may be seen bullying fallen leaves and driving the blades of aftergrass to the ground. Overhead, a clean blue sky with no depth. The trees all around are growing yellow. Near us is a bowed crab-tree weighted down with a stupendous crop of pale fruit.

Talk ranges through the whole gamut of farming affairs. Peter Mangan and Mick Kelly toss the ball to each other, while Joe and I play backers. Threshing-mills are uppermost in everyone's mind and the men review all the mills in the county: the type of engine that operates them, the men who own them, and the variety of drink these men most favour. The misery of waiting for the mill to arrive and the disappointment caused by the broken pledges of mill-owners are dolefully considered. Peter Mangan declares that farmers around are "worn out watching out for Daly's mill," which he describes as "the biggest mill upon the walk."

Kelly starts a long debate on draught horses; it is agreed that a horse worked in Dublin is no use afterwards to a farmer because of the short step it develops, a kind of "mixy action." Our own young mare is sworn to be the "handiest tool a man ever got hold of." Stallions are discussed: some of the "travelling horses" are all "full of old chemicals" and are not prolific; the favourite type of stallion being a "fine snappy horse with plenty of hair on his legs."

Local shops are then put through their paces: those in Ballynash and Ballinvally, as well as the shops in Graigue and Lowtown. Some shops have "purty snug standings," while others are in poor under-populated places. Some excel in a stock of spades, others keep good tea, or the best white bran. Some are owned by open-handed men, and others by cheese-parers. Seamus Murray has a tale apropos of the latter kind of shop, Duggan's of Ballinvally, known as the Quaker shop ("Quaker" having the same implication here as "Jew" has elsewhere). A farmer was getting a shore made in his yard, and he told the workman, who was a smart boy, to lay the shore straight as a pike. When the farmer came back in the evening to look at the work, he saw that the drain was anything but straight. "Come here! Sure that's not straight." "Isn't it, then? Well, it's straight to me." "I tell you it's not straight." "Well, it must be the fault of the string so." "Show that string here to me! Where did you get it?" "Sure I got it from Quaker Duggan, and he never sold a straight thing in his life." Seamus's story falls rather flat (though I myself am much amused): perhaps waiting for a threshing-mill is no time for jokes.

Crouching around the rick-butt, smoking pipes and sucking straws, peering across fields and fences for sight of the mill now three hours late, the men resume talk in a more serious vein: a neighbouring farmer in bad circumstances, an ailing old woman, fairs, crops, and again endlessly on tillage operations.

When my patience is almost played out, I send Kit Healy scouting on his bicycle in the path of the mill's approach. This squatting about is hideous waste of time when days are no longer long, and time has lost the elasticity of summer. Kit returns shortly with the good news that the mill is panting its way past Cloonmore cross-roads.

It is after twelve, and we have been keyed up about the business since before eight o'clock this morning. I go into the house for a hunk of bread and a glass of sherry. The train serpentines up the avenue at the pace of a snail in no hurry. First, the engine pants up with a deafening clatter, its funnel often losing itself in the branches of the trees, its great wheels churning up the road surface; next comes the mill, silent and meek in comparison with the engine; then comes a straw tyer, and last a Baby Austin, attached by a steel cable and solemnly steered by a burly man; a selection of sad and grimy men follow behind it in a procession, walking very slowly, each man keeping his thoughts to himself, their faces grave. The owner, as he alights, is voluble in excuses; a feeling of weariness overcomes me; I shrug off his apologies and make no protests.

The extra men required are engaged: "Five shillings for the job and no breakfasts." Final instructions are issued, and each man is allotted to his post. The engine pants around the ricks a few times and pokes the mill into position. The hatchways are removed, the mill wheels chocked, the riddles shaken out and shoved into the interior, the belts are produced and attached.

Meanwhile most of the men stand around with their chins resting on their fork-handles: they seem subdued and a little sad. There is a big block of work in front of us. Two men mount the oats-rick

258

and begin to strip it of its hay heading. A man clamps the sacks to the grain shoots. The sheaf-cutters and the feeder climb a ladder and take up their position on the mill's table. The sheaf-cutters sharpen their knives.

The engine-man puts up steam. Wheels begin to turn, at first slowly so that one can distinguish the spokes as they revolve, then faster and faster. Right, go ahead, boys!

The rickmen, among whom I have taken my place, begin to pitch down sheaves as fast as they can, the sheaf-cutters snip the bands, the feeder gathers the ungirdled corn and thrusts it into the maws of the mill. On the ground level, feverish activity is confined to one end of the mill, that end where the straw spews out. Masses of straw accumulate by the split second, kicked rapidly out by the dancing straw-shakers. Three men work ceaselessly carrying it away to the straw-rick. Here three more of the fork corps are working like niggers, spreading out the straw to make a butt for the great rick which is to rise up before the thresh-ing-mill waddles off again. The corn spouts out at a quieter rate from the other end, where one man attends constantly on the sacks, and two other men carry them off when filled and cart them away to the yard. As the work proceeds, it becomes neces-sary to borrow a man from straw carrying to attend to the accumulating cavings and chaff. The wet season is accountable for an increase in the bulk of these by-products.

From the comparative distance of the growing straw-rick, the noise of the threshing-mill is a steady zoom. But closer, it is an angry roar which varies with the rate of feeding: when an extra large morsel is fed into the great wooden beast, the answer is a leonine bellow. Underneath the straw-shakers, the noise resembles hoarse thunder. The even, rather metallic boom of the steam-engine at the other end of the belt is mild when compared with the heavy rumbling and ructations from the mill; it is the difference between steel and wood, between the placid reaction of an ironclad to a hurricane, compared with the tremors which beset a frigate groaning her passage through the same angry waters. An undercurrent of sound is formed by the thudding of the sheaves on the platform, the swishing of the unbound sheaves caught by the beater, the rustle of straw from the shakers, the occasional cries of the men, the heaving of full sacks on to the waiting dray.

A fairly stout wind blows from the west. The sheaf pitchers are aware of its exact intensity; even more so the chaff attendant, whose eyes and nose and mouth become filled with blown grime and fragments of husks. Sometimes the straw carriers waver a little as they emerge with their forkfuls of straw from the shelter of the still unthreshed rick.

When dinner-hour comes, seventeen ravenous men trudge into the kitchen for their meal. They are given corn-beef and potatoes, followed by tea and bread-and-butter, but feeding the threshers means a lot of preparation on the housekeeper's part. Mrs. Meehan as usual has been fussing over the event; she rounded up helpers this morning,

Mrs. Kelly and Nancy Tracey, who took a hand at collecting and preparing vegetables, setting the table, and improvising benches.

Dinner-hour today is cut down to the irreducible minimum. The engine speeds up again. All hands are at once in action like the mechanical figures that gyrate around those complicated mediæval clocks at the striking of the hour. The roar of the beaters and drum goes on, the grutch of over-feeding, followed by the angry grumbling and diabolical bellowing of the mechanical beast.

The rick-top soon becomes level with the mill platform and gradually sinks lower than it, so that the sheaves have now to be heaved up instead of being flung down, thus making our work harder. We try to keep the part of the rick nearest the platform as high as possible, and first strip the further parts down even to the mouse-nests in the straw foundations.

We who began our labours on a towering oats-rick are now working near the ground, and the three men on the mill platform stand out as silhouettes against the greenish evening sky. They work feverishly, trying to keep pace with the engine, seizing the sheaves which we fling up to them, feeling for the band, pulling their knives across it, and spreading out the loosened sheaves skirt-wise on the safety guard for the feeder's operation. The three men are all arms and heads and arched backs, like dancing bears.

Daylight begins to fail and still the grain pours out; the bright gold heaps of oaten straw and flakes of ribbed chaff increase.

The red-striped barrel sacks are lifted off the dray in the comparative peace of the yard. The two men handling sixteen stones of grain all day do not find threshing any less arduous than those who are full-time vassals of the mill. But we envy them the quietude of the yard, their opportunities to take a drink from the pump, and to rest their eyes on tranquil sights like calves and chickens. One man loads up the other from the vantage height of the dray; the man with the burden plods up the broad-stepped ladder to the loft, kow-tows to the floor, while letting the mouth of the sack open, and remains bent as the grain falls in a cascade from his shoulder. Soon the loft is knee-deep in oats.

It grows dark. There is too much risk to life and limb in going on with the work in uncertain light. The order is given to stop. The sheaf-throwers put a temporary covering of straw on their rick for the night. The sheaf-cutters loll back on the platform, too tired to descend at once. The straw-carriers cluster together, lighting cigarettes one from the other, their faces thrust out. The straw-rick makers, marooned on their high perch, shout impatiently for a ladder to be set for them so that they can come down. The chaff man is coughing and spitting and poking at his ears. The man in charge of the corn-spouts snaps down the traps and unhooks sacks in various stages of fulness. The mill-owner orders the guard boards of the platform to be placed over the drum's mouth and all is made safe for the night against the hazard of rain.

The procession for the house starts again. The

men speak very little: most of them are strangers to one another, the casual labourers who follow the mill are not from this district, and anyhow all the workers are dog-tired. The big kitchen is almost crowded out. Seventeen men sit down again to tea and bread-and-butter, together with sandwiches made up out of the meat left over from the dinner. They are as dry as lime-kilns, and five cups of tea is the usual quantity taken by each man. Towards the end of the meal their tongues loosen, but even then they do not wax very gay.

Early next morning the same cruel pace is resumed, only the mill gets a change of diet when we pass on to the barley. The barley sheaves are short and flat and contain an infinite amount of dirt, so that the chaff heap spreads out in hillocks and valleys almost as far as the bobbing crab-tree. The barley grain comes through damp and discoloured. The straws are mixed in the straw-rick, the limp barley straw being piled on top of the crackling oaten straw. It becomes necessary for a man to stand on a ladder and act as an intermediary between the bearers of straw and the makers of the rick. The grime from the chaff shoot is hellish. We are under-manned; there should be an additional man for the straw-rick and another for the fury of the chaff-clearing. The pace is terrific and unrelenting. But all the while one has the joy of seeing the unthreshed corn diminish steadily. When we began the work yesterday, the mill was walled in between the corn-ricks in a sort of twilight, but now it stands forth in crude light.

There are a few moments' welcome respite

between the change-over from threshing barley in the field to threshing wheat in the yard. The platform is swept clean with a yard brush and the riddles changed. The men on the ground make a dive for the apple-basket, shying up the fruit to their thirsty comrades on higher levels. The young sheaf-cutters extract their little screws of half-smoked cigarettes and enkindle them again. The weed-seeds are raked from under the mill, for now the wheels are buried in chaff and the pulleys are almost clogged with dirt. Then the set is shifted from the field into the yard.

In the confined space of the yard, the engine once again bullies the mill into position and the bulky rick of wheat is attacked; presently the yard is as busy a scene as was the open field. Again the continual and monotonous droning, the grime, the flying chaff and dirt.

The wheat-sheaves are long and bulky. There is an overpowering perfume of yarrow (one of the most plentiful forms of dirt in this year's crop); it is an odour pleasantly sweet at first when the wheat-threshing begins, but nauseating after a while when the whole yard is filled with it.

For a short spell I knock off and do some restful supervision. Standing near the loft ladder, listening to the tramp of the men ascending the steps under heavy loads, and the loud undercurrent hum of the engine, I can without effort fancy myself on board a steamship. There is that rather terrifying element of mingled engine noise and muffled human sounds common both to threshing and to steamers; one half expects an alarm to be raised and a cry of "Man overboard!" or "To the boats!" But nothing more dramatic happens than long-drawn-out feverish work and worry. Having kept pace with the men constantly all yesterday and this morning, my very bones cry out in protest: I cannot imagine what the regular men feel like who are engaged on threshing for nine or ten hours every day during several months on end.

In my job of overseer, I keep the rick-makers from piling straw so close to the barn gutters that the straw would be injured by overflows; I keep the sack-carriers from filling the sacks completely (for we shall endeavour to make of the wheat sixteen-stone units rather than twenty), and see that Jimmy, whose job it is to draw water to the engine, does not loaf in the intervals. I do very little, but I am tremendously active, passing from one business end of the threshing-mill to the other, then up to the loft, then mounting the straw-rick, and then down to the kitchen.

Sometimes I stand back and survey the scene: the black hulking brute gorged with corn, spewing out straw and spraying out the grain all in a wilderness of golden piles; around it dark men incessantly wielding forks. How would Pissano treat such a scene, or Millet, or George Russel? I wish that I had the talent myself to get an impression of it on to paper. I should not treat the scene conventionally: I would show the whirling cloud of chaff, the confusion of the straw masses, the little shapelessness of the men: colourless, clumsy humans in a lovely gold ocean. But I am not an artist, and my present job is to look worried, chew wheat grains, and be in five places at once.

The last sheaf is heaved up and a blessed ending has come. We of the farm are glad and smiling that the stress is over, but the casual workers do not perceptibly brighten. Each of them receives his five shillings and a word of thanks. The train is coupled up, the racket down the avenue begins again, and the "followers" trudge soberly away in its wake. They will attach themselves to the mill and work on for weeks and weeks to come in the same way as they did today. As for us, we will set ourselves to chaff burning, to heading the straw-rick, sweeping up the tailings and giving them to the poultry, and to a hundred other jobs pertaining to clearing up the mess.

It is a symptom of the times that a hungry wheat-buyer drove up the avenue immediately the mill had turned out through the gates. Being busy, I let him view the sacks for himself: he makes me a strong offer, but audaciously I let him depart without closing the deal.

* * *

Sheep-dipping being the order of the day, I was early abroad this morning. Still half asleep, I went off over the foggy fields with Laddie to gather in the flock. Later on, with Mick and John, I drove them a couple of miles to the dipping-tank at Graigue Park. Our sheep are brightly raddled: as we are culling many of the ewes, some of them have a red daub on the head, others have blue strokes down their backs, the last of the lambs have red bands across their loins, while the new ram bought at the recent Williamstown sale is dyed with yellow ochre. They are a curious pack to contemplate, docile poor devils straggling along the narrow road, a circus procession, clowns with painted noses and daubed cheek-bones.

The bath was full of stinking stuff used any number of times already; this we had to let off before refilling with the fresh water we laboriously drew from rain-barrels near the dilapidated house. Cloonmore House would be just as Graigue Park House is now, had not my timely arrival on the scene stemmed the decay which sweeps over the landlord era.

When the tank is filled with fresh water, we add the dissolved dip that looks like a bucket of patent custard powder. I am amused to see how many empty dip-cartons are strewn around the yard, and I smile to myself remembering how, when first I dipped my sheep, I went to great pains to start a fire in order to burn the cartons that had contained the deadly poison, as instructed on the wrapper. I don't worry about such details nowadays.

Mick and John catch the sheep, and I ram their silly old heads under water, using a well-worn yard brush for the purpose of sousing them. The sheep are thus rid (one trusts) of mites, ticks, kids, nostril fly, green-bottle fly, biting-louse, and suchlike pests. We ourselves emanate a horrible stench, but a good morning's work for that slight cost.

There is a large and fruity chestnut-tree over the tank, and chestnuts fall down with a wallop from time to time. I reach up between the pauses of the work and pluck a nut, strip off the green skin, and rejoice in the piebald mahogany and ivory sphere that lies revealed. What beauty in the womb of things. What miracles hang on every tree.

For the rest, I spent a grand old-fashioned sort of day, picking apples and helping Jimmy to fumigate No. 2. The best days of all are those in which I stay in my working clothes and never leave the farm. I love that: I love going about in pristine dirt, finding time to prowl around and make plans, even when my prowling reveals that fifty things have gone wrong. There are new smells and new bird songs and new views between moulting trees at this time of the year, which add thrills to my all too infrequent farm-roaming. If any single month had to last for always, my choice of month would be September.

The world holds nothing more pleasurable than apple-picking on such a charming day as this: in the pale, heatless sunshine, under a lovely deep blue sky. This afternoon, long hours on stretch were spent in pursuing Emperor Alexanders. Up the rickety step-ladder with a creaking bucket, reaching out and overhead, putting handfuls of apples gently into the bucket until it is filled. Then down the frail steps to good confidence-inspiring earth, solid ground which is appreciated on every descent from the dangerous ladder. The apples are sorted into boxes, the small, cankered, perforated, and ill-shaped specimens being rejected for market purposes, and the very small ones flung into heaps for pig-feeding. Up once more, head lost amidst leaves and apples and sharp twigs and spiders with long lacy legs. I fill bucket after bucket endlessly, all off one Emperor Alexander, crop-bent tree. I collect pale-green apples from the innermost centre of the tree, apples that have never seen the sun nor basked in it, and are wan and anæmic like slum children. But great, opulent aldermen specimens are perched on the top and outer spurs, rosy and mellow, soft from much sun-play, coming away at the slightest touch. Emperor Alexander is not a first-class apple, but it is hulking, durable, and a tremendous cropper.

On all sides of me as I work, I see evidence of the year's decline: rents in the sky and tears in the canvas of the trees. The western sky breaks through the wood; the effect will soon be as if someone drew up a blind in a darkened room. There is a silent sadness abroad, hard to define. Plants hold out their seeds to passers-by like the blear-eyed men who distribute handbills in towns. There is no more growth to be seen, nor hum from the harvesting industry of insects.

When the boxes are filled—they hold about one and a half stone each—they are carried to the turf-barrow, which can take eight boxes. By narrow garden-paths the barrow is pushed to the house, brushing against flopping Michaelmas daisies and bruising the sword-leaves of montbretia as it passes. From the barrow the boxes are brought downstairs to the apple store-room, where they are stacked on top of one another. Descending the stone steps, the senses are assailed with apple

269

perfume. The store-room is gloomy, but the scent is good. In years when farmers are marking time, God be thanked for the solace of apple aroma and for full store-rooms.

Already the Lanes, Bismarcks, Coxes, and Gascoignes are safe. Five barrels have been filled with Lanes and Bismarcks (the big ones on top, of course, and a collar of white paper inside the rim of the barrel for further effect, in order to attract those who are foolish enough to be so attracted). These barrels are to go to the Dublin market next week. Three potato-boxes are heaped with valuable Coxes. Fourteen others contain Gascoignes: these are to be placed in a sunny position with their green cheeks exposed and covered with a hot-bed glass, so that they may colour themselves.

A survey of the apple-crop still to be gathered gladdens my heart. There is a brace of Kerry Pippins on the front lawn which set up a record in production. It is a piquant variety, but rather small. Superior folk of today do not admit this pippin into the charmed circle of commercial desserts, but they are the losers. If I may not have a Cox or a Grieve or that little old nondescript that I have in the garden, then I should choose a Kerry Pippin, yes, before an Irish Peach, a Worcester, a Rival, a Laxton Superb, or a Beauty of Bath. This year the Gascoigne Scarlets are not such an abundant crop as usual, and the old orchard loses in beauty. There is a flush and an impudence about a Gascoigne that no other apple attains. At best it is a scarce cropper. Gascoignes can be sold as eaters to the moderately ignorant, as cookers to anyone, and, mixed with greener fruit, I find that they sell well to those who accept mixed fruit. Nevertheless, I do not consider that this variety is worth its place in the modern orchard.

Cox, which the whole world knows (or thinks it knows, for one can sell any little yellow rubbish as a Cox if one has a poker face), is a nervy producer here. It is certainly the dessert apple *par excellence*. I suppose we must be resigned to its drawbacks: it is timorous, finicky about soil, and has a touch-me-not attitude towards well-meaning sécateurs; but Cox's Orange Pippin is in a class apart, unless one begins to rank it with liqueur brandy, heather honey, or Burren oysters. Eat a Cox and die, having seen Naples and heard Beethoven's Fifth Symphony, but don't cultivate this apple on a large scale, or at least don't do so with your hopes high, even though it is certain that Coxes grew in the Garden of Hesperides, and despite the old gardener's advice to an enquiring novice: "What dozen varieties of tree should I plant?" "Well, first and foremost, you must have a Cox, of course; second . . . well, another Cox; third, Cox again; fourth, damme, but I'd have another one. . . ."

The King of the Pippins has this year also partly failed with me. It is a conical apple, running through a series of colour when stored, beginning with pale green and ending in such a bronze as any seaside-holidaying clerk might envy. Round about Christmas, after the Coxes have shrivelled, the King is still hearty, aromatic, and mellow.

One becomes accustomed in time to the idiocy of fruit variety names, but Peasgood Nonsuch still

271   s 2

tickles me. The fruit is rather absurd, too, being so immensely large and unwieldy. It is imperative to thin drastically, or else one pays the penalty in broken branches. On the whole, one does not know quite what to do with Peasgood Nonsuch; there are limits to the fun of exhibiting monster specimens to one's friends.

Of all cooking apples, Lanes Prince Albert does most to sell itself. Shiny, bright, perfectly clean, it is an apple that should appeal to collectors of brasses, or to housewives who take pride in glistening delph. It is a weak and pendulous grower, however; if one is entitled to call birches feminine and oaks masculine, then one can also call Lanes effeminate. It is tremendously fertile, never failing to produce quantities of alluring fruit; some years, despite drastic thinning, the branches sweep the ground with the weight of their load.

If a grower were allowed only one variety of apple-tree in his garden, I think his selection should surely be Bramley. It is an apple angelically free from faults: a certain cropper, attractive in appearance, an excellent keeper, and probably the best cooker, though I prefer a Blenheim. The trees are lusty, little given to disease, very responsive to spraying and manuring, not in the least temperamental, and returning honest value for money invested in them. This year my crop is only middling; last year it was a bumper one. We are not pitting any this year, as the whole crop can fit into the downstairs store. Somehow I feel resentful towards Bramleys: the secret is everybody's, and there is not a new plantation put down anywhere which does not include Bramleys—none, that is, except my own, for I rebelled against the convention. It is apparent that there will be over-planting of Bramleys; in ten years' time, there ought to be a ferocious glut. So I backed dessert apples: Worcesters, Laxtons, Allingtons, and Grieves.

If I were ever so foolish as to build high hopes on the economic future, I should build them on the universal application of Roosevelt reforms and Newton Wonders when these come into bearing. Actually, I have only twenty-two Newtons, but finding how they are shaping, how the apples keep, and how saleable they are, I am more than sanguine. Unless it be lustre ware, well-polished shoes, and the complexion of some old country folk, I know nothing so satisfying, so eye-filling as the Newton. It is a stout, hard, well-flavoured apple, and in my opinion much too good for cooking purposes. A Newton tree in fruit is a thing of unmatchable beauty, decorated with its round, bright yellow fruit striped with red.

Here my named varieties end. There are also in the garden some ancient pippins that no man is old enough to find a name for, and no man too old to enjoy. One of them is like apple-skin wrapped around honey and butter and toffee; but another is a pale and ghostly green with no more flavour in it than slightly sweetened water.

Apple-growing is a great mystery. Certainly one lifetime is not long enough in which to learn its elements. But it is huge fun and it gives me unspeakable satisfaction. And all my apples are the apple of my eye.

CHAPTER XIII

WELL, I HAVE DONE IT AT LAST, I HAVE climbed the Reek! The Pilgrimage has been consummated. Croagh Patrick has yielded to my bone and sinew, to my godly legs and my rustic stamina. I feel a giant amongst men. I am a climber of mountains. I am a picnicker in Heaven.

The feat has been performed and the Reek overcome. What matter now that every bone in my skeleton is askew, every muscle warped, garments rendered useless, an ache on the top of my head, a good pair of shoes ruined, whiskers growing from my jaws, my feet blistered, my best pair of trousers sopping and caked with turf-mould, my liver affected, my guts clogged with evil food, my eyeballs sore, my throat parched, or that I have been fleeced of all available cash? If God spares me, I'll go again, for the top of the Reek is surely an earnest of Paradise.

You shall hear how the train ambled its way through County Mayo, how this sick and reeling traveller sought for an inn in Westport, how the soft-speaking Irish were all gathered there, mustered from every county of Ireland. You shall hear how I conquered the Reek of Croagh Patrick in the rain and the torment of loose masses of stones. You shall hear (if your ears are attuned to the Song of Hiawatha—and if I can sustain its cadence) the crack of our ferrules against the cold rock, the gush of the descending waters, the crashing of stones down the hills.

In Broadstone Station of Dublin the train is drawn up. The people are surging, the seats are being stolen (for a cunning female robbed me of mine), the girls are shrieking, and the men are guffawing. Through Meath and Westmeath we go swiftly steaming, flocks of rent clouds fleeing beside us, the hills gathering together as we advance to the west. In Mullingar station, a wench sells us tea with the disdainful air of an empress.

We reach Athlone and pass over the smooth-flowing Shannon, across Roscommon of the stone walls, where the haycocks are built around poles, and the cottages are bluish.

Then into the patchwork quilt of Mayo, with its corners of oats, its little irregular shapes of meadow-land, its small rectangles of potatoes, and its tailor's snips of turnips.

When daylight is on its last legs we arrive in Westport. From the squalid station the travellers pour down the streets. The train journey has given me a megrim. I walk alone, intensely sorry for myself, fervently wishing I were at home, and cursing the enterprise which has thus landed me in a strange town, with a violent headache as my only comrade. I buy a cure from a chemist and then find an hotel: it is noisy, dirty, drink-smelling. I beg for tea and a bed—just a cup of tea, but they go to the trouble of producing the regulation tea-pot, and keep me in agony while they do so. Then I am shown upstairs to a small room crowded with three beds, all equally filthy, one of which is allotted to me. I spread my handkerchief over the soiled pillow and attempt to sleep off my headache. The walls of the room are like matchwood; downstairs a gramophone brays; next door there are a man and a woman seemingly going to bed. I can hear most of what they say. The man seems a nice sort of husband, sympathetic, interested, and a wonderful listener up to a point, until his assents begin to be marred by audible yawns.

I find I cannot sleep a wink, but the rest in the darkness cures my headache. I descend again to the drink-smelling ground floor. The hotel is in an uproar; the woman in charge is kindly, makes enquiries about my headache and suggests things that I could eat. I decide on ham and coffee, which latter turns out to be a spiritless drink. I leave the hotel and make my way towards a big building that has all its windows lighted up. A stranger in these parts I may be, but I have heard of Westport's new parish church. I enter, kneel down inside, and slowly the details of the interior impress themselves upon me.

Is this dream-stuff or solid architecture? Has the long-awaited Renaissance come about, or am I drunk? A smile springs into my face and hurts me, being so violent. Of a certainty I must be drunk. I have seen hundreds and hundreds of Irish parish churches and I know exactly what horrors to expect when I am entering a new one. I am surely drunk now, for I see brave beauty here, great space and clarity, luminous walls, and a mighty spread of Irish marble. I must be in a lovely dream, because there never was so fine an altar canopy as rises over this sanctuary, or such virile Stations of the Cross. There are lofty heights where anything might be taking place in this sombre hour: angels coquetting, or the shades of old parishioners grumbling at new-fangled church architecture. Not altogether asleep, for I drop a shilling into a box which asks help for the church building fund. Not altogether drunk, for I frown at a highly painted and spiced statue of Christ the King. Then, giving thanks to God, I follow on the apron-strings of my smile into the bustling street.

Westport throbs. Nearly every shop displays barrelfuls of walking-sticks; the Reek is not going to be an easy climb. The pavements are thronged, every shop is open, everyone is talkative, and just a few are drunk. There is an almost tangible feeling of excitement abroad. I go into a shop for biscuits. The little old woman behind the counter immediately launches into a discussion on past and present weather in relation to Reek-climbing. She is aided by another little old woman almost altogether concealed from me in the back shop. They are both indifferent to biscuit-selling, but not to the pilgrims. I am asked from whence I come. The answer "Near Ballynash" draws forth a very impressed "Lord save us!" We are here from the ends of the earth!

Returning to the hotel bedroom, I find that the other two beds are now occupied. Of the two men who shared my bedroom, only one of them spoke and he confined himself to two remarks: "I wonder are there bed bugs here?" and "This place would

277

go up in a blaze before you could wink." I would as lief he held his peace.

The way to drive a motor in a western town is to put your two feet on the horn-button and let steering and accelerating look after themselves. The noise was not to be endured. Buses and motors were obviously on their way to the Reek, a continuous honking and grinding of gears as the vehicles reached a hill just behind the hotel. I might have slept for an hour and a half, but not much longer. I dressed in the dark, not wishing to disturb the sleeping men. Downstairs, the din had scarcely abated; glasses were clinking in the bar; more or less drunken men were heaving in and out through the doors. It was raining furiously.

I braved a terrible torrent of rain, walked the length of three streets and found refuge in a bus. As the crowded vehicle nosed its way out of the town in inky black, one sensed dangers on every yard of the road; the darkness was perhaps merciful to one so motor-nervous as I am. The bus was crammed with young men and girls. They sang and shouted, behaving most unlike people bent on penance. A boy played on a tin-whistle. Between the songs there were shouts of "Up Castlebar," answered by "Up Ballyhaunis." The staid pilgrims were in a pathetic minority. A boy next me (so next indeed that he had his elbow wedged between my side and my arm), who was silent for a time, turned suddenly to me and said: "Do you know what it is? I have a splitting headache this minute." My formal expression of sympathy was scarcely finished when he interrupted by bursting into song: "Oh, oh, Antonio, my sweetheart. I'm all alone-io, All on my own-io. . . ."

The distance from Westport to Murrisk, the foot of the climb, is about seven miles. A flicker—the forerunner—of daylight appeared before the bus let us down. Rain fell unceasingly here as well, but not so harshly as in the town, perhaps because it sank into the ground instead of hopping back off the pavements. People were clustered about in silent knots, as though dreading the ordeal before them. With several other doughty but dim shades, I resolutely set out up the path for the foot of the Reek.

Light trembled, wrestling against the dark rain. The tracks ran streams of mountain waters. Ill-lighted and rain-sodden booths were ranged alongside, displaying uninviting minerals and ginger cakes. In a little while we felt a steepness creeping into our track. For the first half-mile a raging stream keeps us company: a great noisy limb of water almost without break or bend. My shadowy comrades are silent. We plod on, possessed by our unusual thoughts.

A statue of St. Patrick marks the first station; some of us hesitated, and a girl who had climbed the Reek before, turned to us and said, "Go around it three times and say three our Fathers and three Hail Marys." Mutely we obey. Looking back, one can see that light will soon vanquish darkness. Clew Bay is spread whitely beneath us, mapped by every variety of island, peninsula, isthmus, and headland, like a child's game drawn with spilt milk on a table.

Onwards and upwards we go. The track becomes rougher and consists of stones embedded in greasy mud. A Cork man in a shining oilskin turns round to me: "Have you ever been up before?" he lilts, Cork-wise. I answer "No." "Do you think we have gone up much of it?" he continues. I tell him I imagine we have made a good start. "Well, I don't think it's as bad as I thought it would be," he says, and on he goes, delighted with my encouragement, swaying his glistening posterior before me. Poor babies that we were! We knew nothing.

I overtake two girls, sixteen or seventeen, lissome, and climbing like deers; one was giving out the Rosary, and the other answering it.

The rain eased off for a time. "Oh, St. Patrick, St. Patrick, St. Patrick," wailed a woman behind, "what made you go up so high at all?" I passed out old men and poor stout women struggling valiantly along. A young girl going barefoot passed me out. At no time could one see far ahead, which limitation was a great mercy. When we had about a mile accomplished of the three and a half in the ascent, we began to see people coming down. Soon there were as many people coming down as going up. The mountain-side paths were thronged.

Up and up we toiled through the mist and drizzle, keeping to the merest token of a pathway, over rocks and stones, through ooze and mire, quaking bogs and landslides. Then a time came when we reached a level zone and my worn heart took courage; actually the track seemed to lead downwards. Oh, St. Patrick, are we really going downhill, or is it only a sweet illusion? More proximate than St. Patrick was a kindly-looking man in a raincoat; after the proper preamble I put my pressing question to him: "Are we nearly up?" My man is astonished and looks at me quickly. "Oh no, we don't start the climb until we get to the first station." Feel for my feelings! Very soon, however, we reach the point called by some the first station (though I prefer to think the benign statue which now seems miles below us, and as remote as a childhood prank, is the real first station). This second "first station," then, is a bed of stones marking the place where St. Patrick's companion was killed when he went ahead of his master to investigate conditions on the mountain-top. We walk around this station the regulation number of times and recite a given number of prayers, imploring at the end of each round that St. Patrick would shield Ireland from present enemies as he had vouchsafed to shield her in the past.

Then we start climbing the Reek in earnest, and truly all that we had hitherto done seemed a lovers' amble in comparison. I, who am hardy, young, and active, felt like thistledown in a cement-mixer when confronted with this terrible Reek. What a purgatory of a climb! Every stone is a rock on Croagh Patrick, and a whopping big rock! What sharp stones, flinty stones, slippery stones, greasy stones, yielding stones, angular stones, stones of every size and weight, stony-hearted and brutal stones, worse than flames, or floods, or plagues of stinging pests. The downcoming pilgrims tease us, telling us that we haven't far to go, when there are plainly infernal miles still before us; or assuring us that we have a great distance to go, when we are within sight, yes, but far from being within grasp of the prize. Sheets of drifting white mist obscure the tormented faces of the climbers; laughter and jests have long since died in us; prayers have dried up, except amongst the very devout; there is no joy, or comfort, or rest, or safety in our miserable lives. We cannot stay where we are, with danger of death at one side and a fierce acclivity on the other. But it is not cold, nor is it hot, nor is one hungry though fasting, nor suffering from thirst. In addition to myself, I am carrying up a sopping wet overcoat. I feel that I am dragging the weight of fifty houses, ships, steam-engines, and thousands of bricks and concrete blocks up a merciless precipice.

I am nearly spent. I take more and more time in resting. I am almost hopeless. Then wigwams appear; tiny shelters from which dark-skinned women glare over minerals and teacups; the smell of turf fires reaches my nostrils. Have we arrived? Surely we have! And I was game for another hundred yards at least!

Oh, God, I cannot explain or make anyone understand. God, who knowst every source, what was the beginning of my transformation? Do all men, do dirty men and ribald men, and self-centred men, undergo transfiguration on mountain-tops? Do new worlds spring out of every peak? Is it that angels are made of mists, that saints are boulders, that the stuff of Heaven is really mountain granite such as this? Is Christ veritably a Rock?

How else am I to account for my alteration? I was corrupt, and now my corruption is commuted into a spiritual elevation. It all came in a flash; I was aware of no transitional stage. Climbing the Reek, I was flesh; here I am bodiless; nay, far better, I am a released soul. Croagh Patrick takes the world out of a man of the world and leaves him recognising himself as a spirit.

For a moment I stand stock still, this miraculous novelty of possessing a new soul transfixing me to the ground. Then I force a passage through the dense crowds and join the pack of crushing humanity outside the chapel.

There is nothing, really nothing, on that mountain-top. Perhaps a half-acre of summit, and all this comparatively level area is covered with large loose stones. In the centre of it stands a tiny concrete chapel, which must have required herculean feats in its building. Around the whole mountain-top is a worn track. There are some stone "beds" representing stations, and several low walls very roughly built, used by the hucksters as foundations for their refreshment tents. There is nothing else whatever. All around is a sea of mist. There is no visible proof of height (we are 2510 feet above Clew Bay) except that at rare intervals clouds can be seen moving below us.

It was while waiting for Holy Communion outside the chapel that I became a prey to the cold. Frosty gossamer fringed everybody's clothes, their ears, their hair. We were a huge crowd, green-faced, jostling, and disorderly. Boy Scouts with their staffs attempted to keep us out of the chapel,

283

but their cordon was broken many times. All these people, some young and rowdy, were struggling, shoving, and squeezing. It was impossible to subdue the pressing throng of people; although Mass was being celebrated within ten yards of us, they continued to cry out, to laugh and chatter.

In one door of the chapel and out of the other; it hardly took an instant, but Christ leaves with me. I turn round then and face the altar end of the chapel, kneeling on the rocks with the others.

What is it that has me crazy for joy? Why am I as exhilarated as if I loved all the universe with a passionate love, as if I were born and bred in Heaven, as if the taste of Eternal Bliss were in my mouth? Am I not the same creature who lived below and came up just a few minutes ago, venal, weak, cowardly? Now I am a soldier, filled with countless graces and bursting to make a hundred vows.

Nor did this sense of glory pass from me. My happiness increased. I had only to look at the first person within eye-reach and I was sent reeling, dazed with the revelation of secrets I had found.

What did I find? God alone knows all. I only know that in every Irish face I found unutterable signs: of Christ and Mary, of the heroism of Patrick and the sanctity of Brigid.

Does God turn from us in disgust? Avert His face from our disorderly behaviour outside the chapel? Does it all perhaps fill Him with weariness? Maybe He turns His back on us, His gaze piercing the cloud-curtains, absorbing the spreading world below us, Clew Bay beneath the clouds begemmed with its hundred islets, the gaunt walls of Achill holding back the Atlantic, the waste tracts parting Mayo from the kingdom of Connemara.

Thanksgiving finished, I make swiftly for a tea-tent, the cold numbing my vitals. "You are famished," the woman greeted me. Tea? No, it was not so much tea as boiled turf-water allowed to get tepid. I asked for a slice of currant-cake, a home-made concoction. How much? Much, did you say? Not much, but the very most: a shilling for the cup of tea and threepence for the dry cake. "We couldn't do it for less, sure," she explained. Perhaps she couldn't; this isn't the world, after all, and prices are celestial.

I smoke a cigarette and watch the people. Old men are moving on their bared knees from one traditional mark to another, these being about twelve paces apart; there are boys and girls doing the same exercise. Piety will never die in Ireland; the lamp of devotion is passed on with hands that never falter.

The ancient Irish used to flock here too, attired in their striped cloaks, multi-coloured tunics, and mantles of frieze. These have now given place to this raucous-voiced generation in berets, equipped with thermos flasks, passing round cigarettes. The Irish people have been faithful to Croagh Patrick for nearly fifteen hundred years. The harassed, dispossessed, and persecuted Irish clung to the traditions of a symbolic mountain peak. Their rallying-ground was never in the Parliament House of "ould" College Green, and probably still less is it in the raw atmosphere of our new Dail; nor was their spiritual faith in the expressed catch-cries of *Liberty* and a *Republic*, but rather in Patrick's penance as carried out in this harsh theatre.

I watch a priest seated on wet stones, hearing confessions, a group standing behind him waiting for their turn. I have seen many moving things in my thirty years, but I have never seen anything so impressive as this scene two thousand six hundred feet above the sea. I sat down and gazed my fill at it. I drew a pencil and a damp sketch-book out of my pocket and vainly tried to reproduce the wonder: Christ in the person of a priest pardoning men and women on a mountain peak.

Around me, groups are taking refreshment: men throwing back their heads the better to swallow the contents of their Baby Powers; women growing visibly radiant as the food packages are unwrapped. Lord, are we nauseating to You? Or is this gathering perhaps a holiday from Your choir of angels, Your High Masses, Gregorian chants, Vatican Councils, and the exalted debating of Cambridge Study Circles? *Padre Eterno*, accept our mountain worship, commend it even, as You were supposed to have commended a similar naïve worship in Belloc's story. Are not all these folks good in spite of their frailties, their intemperance, their factions, their coarseness and selfishness, their superstition? The mists up here melt all these faults.

I ask a boy how I am to perform the station in which I see so many people engaged. He tells me that I am to go around the flat summit of the mountain fifteen times, while reciting the Rosary continuously. He advises me to keep tally of the rounds by dropping a stone at a certain point each time I arrive at it. I accept his counsel and put fifteen pebbles into my sodden hat. I must have done ten or eleven rounds of the Rosary before completing the walk around the summit, scanting, scandalously scanting, I fear. The stones underfoot were cruel. Will time or the traffic of men ever take the edge off those stones? And yet many were doing the rounds in their bare feet.

Thank God that I belong to these people. Nothing that I have done, or read, or held, could alienate me from them. They are mine and I am theirs. I am proud not only of the grand old people, but even of the youngest and most frivolous. Here are the "Oh, oh, Antonios" fraternising with young priests, girls smoking cigarettes, young men in ridiculous headgear and absurd trousers, old men with bared knees describing a circle that is a furlong in circumference. They are all of the right stuff, equally children of Patrick and fosterlings of Brigid. What dear faces they have; what soul is in the eyes of even the most flippant among them.

I can only be happy. I can only be thankful and give glory to God for that which we have saved from our magnificent past. It isn't in me to carp at superstitious practices. I cannot criticise this morning. If Heaven is no better than the top of the Reek, it would be worth our effort. The spirit finds rest here and the body is hushed (for mountain rain does not cause discomfort, nor does the belly clamour for food). There does not seem to be a dour person on the Reek. Maybe our Guardian

287

Angels have swopped places with us for a morning.

I had been told that it was harder to descend the Reek than to come up, but at the time I had only laughed, for such a thing seemed incredible. But it was *hard* to go down—hard is the word. There was no grip underfoot; the stones slipped from the grasp of my feet. I was forced to rest very frequently. In going down one seems to be driven by a flock of devil-possessed stones. I encouraged many of the climbers as we passed. Gradually below me the sun ploughed up the grey clouds. A king's ransom of territory was illuminated; a silver ocean expanded beneath, in which islands were hatched out by the score. A sight more worthy of a Moses or of a Patrick than of a mixed farmer like myself. Looking back, it seemed an impossible feat to have climbed that steep pyramid of stones now dotted over with human ants.

There was grim pleasure in overhearing an ascending girl ask her companion, "Are we half-way up yet?" Everyone within earshot burst out laughing. There was another girl, obviously a returned American, who struggled along shod in lovely white kid shoes. Poor innocent! I tried to picture her face when she reached that pyramid of stones.

I had hardly consulted my watch during the whole time I was on the mountain, for on Croagh Patrick it is not so much a question of what A.M. it is, as what A.D. it might be. Time does not enter into one's thoughts, which Lord knows are complicated enough without that. However, I reckoned that the descent took about two hours and a half.

I passed a pair of old women seated together, dressed in vivid red skirts and bright shawls. It was a privilege to gaze on their handsome, tranquil faces, for a time must come when there will be no more such faces. The new generations have not that calm nobility in their countenance.

I fell in with several people and talked to them on a variety of subjects, but I was too timid to approach any of them with the subject nearest my heart: why is it that I have discovered the beauty of God, of Ireland, of the Irish people, and the meaning of heavenly bliss all in one morning, and in consequence am not now stretched out dead?

Clew Bay had turned blue in the meantime, though its islands were rabid in their allegiance to green. Several hours after I took that boiled turf-water on the Reek, I ate my breakfast in Westport. Afterwards I attended last Mass at which the Archbishop preached. It is just possible that I slept through part of the sermon. The church still seemed exquisite though daylight had robbed it of its amber quality.

How banal is all the rest! Wandering aimlessly about the small town, reading the advance notices of a Stupendous and Mammoth Circus, taking a lonely tea in a little upstairs place where the flies had sticky feet, sitting on a damp bench in the deserted railway station awaiting the coming of an official with the key of the drawn-up carriages, and dozing in a cold compartment three and a half hours before the engine is hitched to the train.

Icarus, the Midland farmer, tumbles down (the mountain sun having melted the wax which fastened his wings) and crosses Ireland in a dispirited train which lopes dejectedly from dark station to dark station and pitches him out into a Dublin drizzle at midnight.

From the top of the Reek to Cloonmore it is all downhill. Sharp stones give place to hard tin-tacks, to common or garden or agricultural worries. From the exaltations of high mountains to flat plains and fat lands. From penitential peaks to green fields. From spiritual elations to a lecture from Mrs. Meehan on spoiling my best Sunday shoes. From hob-nobbing with the Blessed to receiving notice from Jimmy (may he make a big success of life).

I must brush the star-dust off my clothes and get back to work. Big schemes which keep me awake half-nights must be launched: cattle must be sold, and cattle must be purchased, orchard extensions planned, the tillage programme for next season must be settled. I must fret and worry. I must retrench and save and go about barking at all and sundry.

But, after all, only in the discontents of farming do I find content.

THE END

Printed in Great Britain by R. & R. Clark, Limited, Edinburgh